FRANK CAPRA

INTERVIEWS

CONVERSATIONS WITH FILMMAKERS SERIES
PETER BRUNETTE, GENERAL EDITOR

Photo credit: Photofest

FRANK
CAPRA

INTERVIEWS

EDITED BY LELAND POAGUE

UNIVERSITY PRESS OF MISSISSIPPI / JACKSON

www.upress.state.ms.us

The University Press of Mississippi is a member of the
Association of American University Presses.

12 11 10 09 08 07 06 05 04   4 3 2 1
♾

Library of Congress Cataloging-in-Publication Data

Capra, Frank, 1897–
   Frank Capra : interviews / edited by Leland Poague.
      p.   cm. — (Conversations with filmmakers series)
   Includes index.
   ISBN 1-57806-616-6 (alk. paper)—ISBN 1-57806-617-4 (pbk. : alk. paper)
   1. Capra, Frank, 1897– —Interviews.   2. Motion picture producers and
directors—United States—Interviews.   I. Poague, Leland A., 1948–   II.
Title.   III. Series.
PN1998.3.C36A3 2004
791.43'0233'092—dc22
[B]   2003055641

British Library Cataloging-in-Publication Data available

CONTENTS

INTRODUCTION

UPON HIS DISCHARGE from the U.S. Army in December of 1918, Frank Capra visited his older brother Ben in Sacramento, California. While there, he found work as an extra in an early John Ford western, *The Outcasts of Poker Flat*. More than fifty years and many Oscars later, Ford provided a ghost-written foreword for Capra's 1971 autobiography, *The Name Above the Title*. There Ford praises Capra as "A great man and a great American" whose life is "an inspiration to those who believe in the American Dream." From early on, writes Ford, Capra "was no stranger to the work, the worry, and the long hours that went with being a poor immigrant boy in a dog-eat-dog society." Moreover, while avowing that Capra's autobiography is "rich" in "heart-warming and sympathetic" anecdotes of the era in which Capra reigned supreme among Hollywood directors, he also forecasts Capra's efforts "to depict the agonizing responsibility and the constant struggle" required of those who do battle against "the concepts of Wall Street, Madison Avenue, and others who would intervene."[1]

I begin *Frank Capra: Interviews* with Ford's poor-boy-makes-good account of Capra's life and times because so many of the interviews reprinted here begin or conclude (sometimes both) by repeating capsule versions of it. Evidently, the story's appeal is part and parcel of the appeal exercised over some seven decades of American life by the films Capra directed during Hollywood's heydays, the 1930s and 1940s. Such films as *It Happened One Night, Mr. Deeds Goes to Town, Mr. Smith Goes to Washington, Meet John Doe,* and *It's a Wonderful Life* seem definitive of an era and a sensibility, though scholarly efforts over the years to describe that sensibility have hardly arrived at consensus, perhaps because Capra himself never arrived at consensus, was always of multiple minds and impulses. Was Capra an idealistic Boy Ranger offering "Capra-corn" populism to a nation desperately in need of self-delusion? Or did Capra's own desperations put him in touch with the times to such an extent that his impassioned efforts to pass beyond delusion earned credibility exactly by straining it—to something like the breaking point?

My own view is much closer to the latter than the former picture of Capra's accomplishment, though it is plain from the interviews here collected that the former view—of Capra as an endearing cinematic and cultural innocent with a predilection for fairytale fables and nick-of-time conversions—has been the majority opinion. Though early interviews with Capra tend to emphasize theories of film storytelling, in deference to Capra's education and by reference to his early 1930s successes at Columbia Pictures with *Lady for a Day* and *It Happened One Night,* it was not long before journalists began to remark (in the words of Paula Harrison) upon "the sunlit gaiety of the moods reflected in his pictures" and upon "those down-to-earth incidents which warm the hearts of people the world over." Frank Daugherty of the *Christian Science Monitor* describes the typical Capra story circa 1938 in similarly positive terms, as involving "a simple and direct sort of character with a set of persons and circumstances a good deal less direct." The Capra hero "triumphs by reason of his uncompromising forthrightness. And of these characters of Capra's, Mr. Deeds of *Mr. Deeds Goes to Town* is, of course, the archetype." Despite a forty-year gap, there is astonishingly little to choose between these contemporaneous 1930s descriptions of Capra's appeal and the following passage from a 1978 edition of *American Film:* "Capra's films are marked by zestful pacing and unfailing optimism. They unabashedly celebrate the simple virtues and strengths at the heart of American life."

In *Frank Capra: Interviews* this tradition of assumptions and interests is intriguingly alive and well. We see it in the frequency with which Capra is asked about his work with silent comedian Harry Langdon, often on the open assumption that Langdon's fabled innocence is premonitory of such subsequent Capra heroes as Longfellow Deeds and Jefferson Smith. Asked by James Childs whether his "innocent and childlike" heroes of the middle and late 1930s are "extensions of Harry Langdon's film characteristics," Capra replies affirmatively: "Yes. Most of these heroes have faith: faith in goodness and in the innate goodness of human beings."

Another way interviewers invoke Capra's reputation for all-American optimism is by quoting critical assessments of it, nearly always on the assumption that Capra will refute the accusation, though sometimes his answers are confirmatory. Thus Arthur Friedman pairs Richard Griffith's "fantasy of goodwill" formula with Alistair Cooke's anxious observation that with *Mr. Deeds Goes to Town* Capra was "starting to make movies about themes instead of people," and Capra replies by agreeing that the practice is dangerous, while avowing that, with a "good message" and sufficient "humor and warmth and comedy," it could be (and was) safely done. Similarly, Neil Hurley—discussing the prevalence of near suicides in Capra's films—evokes Parker Tyler's criticism of Capra's "false 'happy endings.'"[2] Capra addresses the narrative logic of Tyler's claim backhandedly, by observing how thoroughly John Doe (in *Meet John Doe*) and George Bailey (in *It's a Wonderful Life*) are made to suffer, but he counters that viewers "don't want to see Gary Cooper or Jimmy Stewart die." As if he'd been asked to choose between critic and audience, Capra opts to "trust the audience," which amounts to conceding Tyler's point.

A story he told obsessively in his later years speaks directly to Capra's conviction that the audience is the "third dimension" of film. I have in mind his "Burn the First Two Reels" account of the salvage job undertaken on the preview version of *Lost Horizon*. In *The Name Above the Title* Capra recounts the nightmare experience of hearing people laugh at the wrong moments and seeing patrons walk out during the film's Santa Barbara preview. (The story is repeated nearly word for word in the Silke and Henstell interview.) After two days walking "in a dark trance" of introspective solitude, Capra recalls, he rushed back to Columbia and ordered Gene Havlick to move the main titles to the film's third reel, after which Capra urged Columbia president Harry Cohn to schedule a second preview, which proved far more successful. "One small, seemingly insignificant change" had thus "turned an unreleasable, unshowable picture into the *Lost Horizon* that was welcomed by the world," and had proved, as well, that "The audience is always right" (*NAT* 200–01).

Despite the deferential tone of this latter pronouncement, however, the story is almost surely more legend than history. According to the research conducted by Joseph McBride in writing *Frank Capra: The Catastrophe of Success,* far more than the first two reels was involved in the process that created the general release print of *Lost Horizon* out of the raw material of its three-hour preview version, and Capra was hardly alone in accomplishing the task.

Disputes about the role of Father Perrault were ongoing between screenwriter Robert Riskin and Capra even after the Santa Barbara preview, for example, and Riskin convinced Capra and Cohn to recut the ending even after the film's premier.

It is McBride's more general claim that Capra's autobiographical account of his life and career in *The Name Above the Title* amounts to a systematic if deeply conflicted effort to exaggerate the degree of Capra's artistic autonomy, chiefly at the expense of his screenwriters, and simultaneously to underplay the political import of the films upon which his "fantasy of goodwill" reputation largely rests, especially to the extent that films like *Mr. Deeds Goes to Town* and *Mr. Smith Goes to Washington* are interpretable along leftist, New Deal lines. On McBride's account, indeed, Capra's writers—several of them literally members of the Communist Party, most of them, unlike Capra, strong supporters of Franklin Delano Roosevelt—just *were* his progressive social conscience, so that repudiating their work amounted to self-condemnation, all the more so to the extent that Capra claimed to have done the real work himself, leaving him little choice but to retroactively downplay the radical political implications of his films under the cover of "entertainment," especially during Hollywood's Red Scare period.

Of all the stories that he was fond of telling, perhaps none is more representative of Capra's nearly pathological bad faith, on McBride's account, than the story of his mid-1930s crisis of conscience, which culminated, so the story goes, with Capra rising from his sickbed to be told, by a nameless and faceless "little man," that in his refusal to work he was not only being "a coward" but "offending God," especially in a mass-media world where a Hitler could dominate via radio if his message of hate went unchallenged by those, like Capra, with the talent and the means to do so. In Capra's various tellings of the tale (see the Friedman and Hurley interviews), his apparently debilitating illness was self-induced, a defensive fear-of-failure response to his multi-Oscar success to date. On McBride's account, however, the illness was genuine—the long delayed aftermath of an appendix that had burst in 1919—and it happened before the 1935 Oscar ceremony in which *It Happened One Night* won five Academy Awards, which Capra did rise from his sickbed to attend. (As if the Oscar statuette itself were, in fact, the "little man" in question?)

Crucial to nearly every version of the story is the iink between Capra's feelings of guilt over the undeserved or accidental success of his career and his subsequent decision that his films had "to 'say' something," to have a "social-minded" message (*NAT* 182). McBride does not discount the prospect that Capra's "little man" story "was telling a kind of metaphorical truth" (*FC* 320). According to McBride, indeed, the metaphor likely derived from specific literary texts (chiefly Myles Connolly's novel *Mr. Blue* and Eric Knight's "The Flying Yorkshireman" story) that Capra was long familiar with when he first told the story as his own—to Arthur Friedman. But what the story most emphatically confirms was Capra's inability to express his deepest feelings without employing the words of others, which renders him all the guiltier when the borrowed words are used to deny the fact of borrowing, as McBride alleges: "By taking this [little man] apparition and combining it with the urgent social message written by Riskin for the farmer in *Mr. Deeds*, and then inserting them retroactively into his own life story, Capra not only could claim divine inspiration for his work but also could render his own life more Capraesque than it really was, thereby laying a spurious 'autobiographical' framework for his films which would diminish the contribution of his writers" (*FC* 323–24).

McBride's Capra is not the happy optimist of *The Name Above the Title*, however much Capra sought, in the words of the newspaper editor in Ford's *The Man Who Shot Liberty Valance*, to "print the legend" in his autobiography and in interviews. *Frank Capra: Interviews* thus amounts to a third installment in a legendary trilogy, though by now the Capra legend itself, thanks to McBride's examplary research, is a different kind of fact, openly so. The main contribution of *Frank Capra: Interviews* to the task of understanding Frank Capra and his place in American culture is to show the Capra legend in the making by providing in far more "raw" than "cooked" form much of the material upon which both *The Name Above the Title* and *Frank Capra: The Catastrophe of Success* were subsequently based.

Many of the interviews, for example, are considerably more accurate about Capra's early years than is the autobiography, in which Capra's first real experience with film is depicted as his collaboration with Walter Montague on *Fulta Fisher's Boarding House*. (The Daugherty interview mentions Capra's earlier experiences, though not by name, with CBC Pictures.) Similarly, the fact that Capra tended to tailor his stories to his interviewers—thus to change his story from time to time—is also repeatedly on view. The version of the Montague story that he recounts to Marcel Dalio differs considerably from the one he gives to Arthur Friedman. For that matter, the version of the "little man" story that Capra gives to Friedman differs significantly from the one in *The Name Above the Title.* Where the autobiography locates the "crisis" as occurring after *It Happened One Night,* in the Friedman interview it happened after *Mr. Deeds Goes to Town,* hence after the "say something" decision, as if *what* to say was itself (and still) the problem.

It is quite beyond the format of the Conversations with Filmmakers series to annotate or eliminate all such factual discrepancies. Per series policy, I have generally left the interviews as I found them. I have fixed obvious typos and regularized some usages (e.g., film titles are now entirely in italics). Where discretion has been exercised, especially in editing Capra's own remarks, intervention is marked by brackets or the occasional footnote. On the other hand, my chronology is by series standards extended and detailed, with the intention of including those particulars that seem most pertinent, in light of McBride's research, to the specific interviews reprinted.

It bears saying that McBride's picture of Capra as a guilt-ridden depressive is hardly news, nor was it when McBride was doing his research. For example, both John Mariani and Neil Hurley address the deceptive quality of Capra's official optimism. Hurley adduces Parker Tyler's criticism of *Meet John Doe*'s "false 'happy ending.' " Likewise, Mariani notes how easy it is to miss "the impeccable orchestration of [Capra's] comic tragedies in which a lovable hero is brought to ruin by the very forces that utilize that lovableness for sinister purposes" before going on to observe how "In *Meet John Doe* Capra suggested that folk heroes are manufactured, not born, and that they too should be suspect." For that matter, beneath "the Capra-corny comic anecdotes with invariable happy endings" of *The Name Above the Title,* as Ray Carney astutely observed in *American Vision: The Films of Frank Capra,* there obviously runs "a much darker subtext" of "Capra's recurrent fear of inadequacy, doubts about his accomplishments, and feelings of shame."[3] That McBride's biography of Capra was received by some as revealing (rather than merely confirming) these facts attests to the ongoing difficulty of coming to terms with Capra's extraordinary and strangely undervalued movies, despite the happy public reputation they have long enjoyed.

It is unlikely that the interviews here reprinted will change Capra's public reputation by themselves. Indeed, Carney has suggested that words alone are essentially incapable of capturing the manic energies that Capra's films aspire to embody. Though the social engagements attributed by McBride chiefly to Capra's collaborating screenwriters allow the films to be mined for cultural meanings, to be seen as allegorical enactments of civic ideals, doing so "cuts the heart out of his work" by leaving out of account "the sheer sensory gusto of the films," by which Carney means "the shapes of bodies, the timbres of voices, the movements of figures through space, the thrill of the timing and pacing" (xiii). In protesting the Norman Rockwell version of Capra that dominated the obituaries, Carney makes a similar point: "In the eulogists' description of the major characters—Robert Conway, Longfellow Deeds, Jefferson Smith, and George Bailey—Capra's desperate wild-eyed American dreamers were pacified. Their charged glances, stuttering gasps, and operatic urgencies of expression were robbed of intensity and power. Their imaginative extremity was tamed."[4] The pertinence of this last remark is overtly confirmed in the earliest of the interviews here reprinted, where Capra observes, in discussing the value of dialogue, how often on stage and screen alike "the most tense moments of the drama are moments of absolute silence" (Hall).

The crucial lesson to be derived from the foregoing remarks is that film meaning is rarely a matter of words alone, even when the words are wonderfully apt and well written. More to the point, there is no way for a transcribed interview to approximate those frantic all-or-nothing moments in Capra—like Gary Cooper's wounded, angry silence in *Mr. Deeds Goes to Town* or Jimmy Stewart's self-impaling bitterness when he nearly walks through the camera toward the end of *It's a Wonderful Life*—when words are entirely lacking or useless. If we wonder how these interviews extend or deepen our understanding of Capra's films, or vice versa, the closest useful on-screen analogues are those intimate, quasi-confessional conversation scenes when one character expresses an idealized perception in the presence of another character whose worldly circumstances, as the viewer well knows, cast a shadow of self-conscious cynicism across the proceedings—as when Jimmy Stewart waxes eloquent about prairie grasses and dancing streams while Jean Arthur, though obviously moved, is also obviously thinking about the Willet Creek land scam in *Mr. Smith;* or when Gary Cooper, in an airport coffee shop, expresses astonishment at his own hunger for John Doe idealism in the presence of Barbara Stanwyck, whose authorship of the John Doe character leaves her deeply and almost wordlessly depressed, aching for a way out of her predicament. Where readers might once have assumed that Capra should be taken as the Stewart/Cooper idealist in these scenarios, McBride's research effectively shifts Capra to the other side of the conversation, as the defensive and depressed (and female) secret-keeper whose yearning for deliverance is all the greater for having actively collaborated in the very process of her own oppression.[5] In that case, moreover, it is the interviewer in our scenario who stands for naive idealism, an idealism that Capra is clearly loath to discredit, however surely he knows a darker truth, as his films perpetually attest.

By way of confirming the degree to which the interviews here collected contain their own subtextual contradictions, at least when taken together, I want to address briefly two (obviously related) topics where Capra was frequently eager to tame his own idealism, to disclaim his own ambitions. One of these involves the question of visual style, which Capra repeatedly avowed should be invisible, and the other involves cinema's status as an art medium.

Cinema, for Capra, is "a people-to-people medium" (Hargrave) with actors as the director's "principal tools" (Drew). Few would deny Capra's wonderful ability to secure first rate performances; how he did so is under extended discussion in the interviews here reprinted—by giving each actor, no matter how minor the role, a sense of his or her character's life; by rehearsing mostly informally, so that the first take had the raw feel of life rather than the polished feel of theater, etc. But a corollary of this passion for eliciting animated performances was the conviction that (as he made the point to Hal Hall in 1931) "'directorial touches' and photographic splurges should be kept out of pictures. Excellence in direction is reached when the audience never thinks of the director's work." As he made the same point to Harry Hargrave in 1976, "You can only involve the audience in the lives of the actors and character that the actors are playing. You can't involve them in machinery."

Though frequently pressed on this point, Capra confesses to only a single instance of overt "stylization" in his career, which occurred in the production of *The Bitter Tea of General Yen*. Where Capra's other films adhere to the standard of realism ("things as they really are," as he summarized his credo to Hal Hall), *Bitter Tea* is "different from anything else" he ever made; because he wanted to win an Academy Award (as he told the story to *American Film*), *Bitter Tea* was "the only film in which I ever tried to become arty." The contradictions here are multiple. Capra's controversial insistence on his "one man, one film" philosophy of film authorship, for one, follows avowedly from the belief that art, by definition, is the expression of a unique individual—as opposed to a committee (see Childs and Harvey). In claiming personal authorship of his films, Capra thus assumes their status as art works, as being altogether "arty." (I will return to this point.)

But as a statement of fact, the claim that *The Bitter Tea of General Yen* is visually distinct from his other movies verges on willful blindness, even if we limit our notion of the "visual" to "camera tricks," to visually striking compositions that are somehow set apart from the shot/reverse-shot give and take by which the "people-to-people" scenes are crafted. Of course, much that makes *Bitter Tea* a wonderful film is how exceedingly well written and acted and edited its "people-to-people" scenes are. What most sets it apart from other Capra films is, as if literally, its Chinese setting—but then the China of Megan Davis (Barbara Stanwyck) is only slightly more exotic to her than New York City is to Mr. Deeds or Washington, D.C. to Jefferson Smith.

Bitter Tea also features an almost surrealist dream sequence in which Megan Davis pictures herself being rescued from sexual hazard by a tellingly westernized version of General Yen, though such "subjective" sequences likewise appear elsewhere in Capra, most spectacularly in *Meet John Doe* and *It's a Wonderful Life* (taking the "unborn" sequence as George's nightmare vision). What Capra most obviously has in mind in declaring *Bitter Tea* a heavily "stylized" film, however, is the use of soft-focus photography and/or diffusion lighting schemes to etherealize Megan's perceptions of herself and her world, and ours of both, seen most obviously when Megan and Yen discuss Chinese art on the balcony of her room, overlooking a Chinese garden, and in the film's penultimate sequence, when Megan prepares to give herself to Yen while Yen brews his suicidal bitter tea.

Capra to the contrary, such moments of transcendental "merger," almost always fueled by or associated with erotic potential, are found throughout the Capra canon. We get similar lighting and focus effects in the scene where Deeds and "Mary Dawson" take a walk through the fog outside her brownstone, as he prepares to read his proposal poem to her; and Jefferson Smith's impassioned defense of the spirit of liberty, delivered against the (painted) image of the capital dome seen through his office window, is another spectacular instance of film artifice, akin both functionally and visually to the balcony scene in *Bitter Tea*. The ordinary world in the films of Frank Capra is never, really, just "ordinary." But one always has the sense of another world, more extraordinary yet, abiding just beyond—out a window, off a balcony, over a ledge or a precipice—and that other world can break into this world at any time, though especially in moments when rain and desire wash the image in the reflected glow of moon or star light. Though Capra is right to say that such moments are rare, he sells himself uncharacteristically short in denying their implicit ever-presentness across the whole of his career.

Then again, Capra often sold himself and others short. To the extent that, in later years, Capra's reluctance to share credit with writers made it increasingly difficult for him to recruit first-rate collaborators, hence to make first-rate movies, as McBride suggests, this is obviously to be regretted. But the second selling short I have in mind involves Capra's anxiously skeptical assessment of the film medium in toto, understood institutionally as comprising the industry, its intellectual/critical apparatus, and the audience as well.

Capra's antagonism to the studio system is well documented in these pages. Early on, Capra tended to criticize the larger studios by emphasizing the virtue-of-necessity advantages he enjoyed as an employee of Columbia Pictures; in later interviews, and in Capra's own voluminous writings culminating in *The Name Above the Title,* his criticism of Hollywood is seen in his advocacy of directors over producers, endlessly thematized in his running-battle accounts of his relationship with Columbia's Harry Cohn. Capra's antagonism to the institutions of film criticism is also repeatedly on view, as in his remarks to James Childs about "Eastern seaboard" intellectuals for whom "sentiment is an almost *verboten* emotion," because "it's perhaps too common, too ordinary—it's not arcane enough for an intellectual." Capra's antagonism toward his audiences is far more muted, is often screened by cover stories, as in his preference for discussing the previews of *Lost Horizon* rather than the damage its production costs and slow profitability did to Columbia's bottom line, or in his falsely blaming the box-office weakness of *The Bitter Tea of General Yen* on the censorship offices of the British Empire— though in an early interview Philip Scheuer concludes, as if on Capra's behalf, that the "Not over-successful" fate of *Bitter Tea* "bore out Capra's declaration that the great mass of paying patrons are not intellectually inclined."

A note Capra sounds repeatedly in his interviews and his autobiography is that he "backed into films" as if by accident—when all the while his true calling, his true interest, was science or science education (*American Film,* Hurley). Though thinking of science as an alternative career may have made his early life as a filmmaker less anxious, it is also clear from Capra's last several interviews—after he had effectively *become* an educator via the university lecture circuit—that he never altogether escaped the elitist view that movie making was a second-rate endeavor. He acknowledges to William Drew that "people at Caltech were snobbish about films," a view he "shared . . . at that time," and he goes on in that interview to link the emergence of "the artist" in himself to the time, after *It Happened One Night,* when he felt compelled to "marry one or the other—science or film—and I married the harlot." Though Capra sought to make movies as intellectually respectable as science by "saying something," as the "little man" story was devised to confirm, his doubts about his art and his audience—seen in his back-and-forth opinions about whether film could or should be an art, could or should be intellectually challenging—were never entirely eliminated. Then again, neither was the amorously illicit but avowedly "sensual" pleasure Capra experienced during the process of filmmaking (see Glatzer, *American Film*); if cinema was a harlot, Capra was an enthusiastic if not star-crossed lover, and an ardently poetic one at that.

Though Capra's ambivalence about his art form and its audience might well seem to contradict his oft-avowed belief in "the innate goodness of human beings," I would suggest that, if anything, the converse is closer to the truth—that Capra's uncertainties inspired his faith, gave rise to it. It is less the fact of than the desire for certainty that animates Capra, a desire paradoxically activated by the yet deeper conviction that the world as it stands is astonishingly malleable, hence astonishingly vulnerable as well—as if certainty were only as deep as a thin strip of celluloid. Perhaps the endless desire to read Capra's films along political lines follows from the fact that his films almost always seem to put the whole world at risk, as if everything that mattered were on the verge of momentous change. Indeed, his films almost always begin with a seemingly chance event that renders the protagonist's world all but unrecognizable, often by removing him or her literally to another world. And that new world—precisely *because* of Capra's misplaced central characters—always seems on the verge of its own cataclysmic transformation.

Politics and religion are, not surprisingly, ready-to-hand popular metaphors of such cataclysmic change, but neither tells or is the whole Capra story. In *American Vision,* indeed, Carney suggests that Capra's "films are, in the great American Romantic tradition, about movements of mind and awareness, not about populist political movements. They are explorations of possibilities of transcendence of the very sorts of social categories they are usually said to serve" (6). In lieu of conclusion, then, let me call attention to Capra's repeated assertion that such transcendence is *exactly* his chief concern. In 1973, he told a film festival audience that "Every great work of art, every great classic play, every great novel has in it, somewhere, a transcendental love story—preferably, a sacrificial love story," and this was said in full awareness that listeners "can be cynical and laugh at the word 'love.'" But here is one place where Capra *never* changed his tune, can be taken, in my view, exactly at his word—at least to judge by his 1932 claim, in the pages of *Variety,* to the effect that "Good boxoffice pictures must project some great love—not necessarily of one human for another. The love may be for nature, a career, an art, a country, but it must be deep and true, humanized by everyday occurrences that translate its basic truth to the average fan."

Also deep and true is my gratitude for the many kindnesses I received in the process of compiling the present volume. I am again indebted to Seetha Srinivasan, director of the University Press of Mississippi, for entrusting me with the editorial task, and to my editor, Anne Stascavage, for steadfast encouragement and sage advice in the midst of considerable scholarly complexity. I offer personal thanks to all the interviewers and rightsholders in question, and also to many people who facilitated my permissions requests, especially Jim McCullaugh of *American Cinematographer,* Ali Smith of the Copyright Clearance Center, Kate McCarthy of the *Los Angeles Times,* Guin Harwood-Shaw of the *Christian Science Monitor*, Mary Marshall Clark and Jessica Widerhorn of the Columbia University Oral History Research Office, Caroline Sisneros of the American Film Institute's Louis B. Mayer Library, Sayre Maxfield at *Film Comment,* Carolyn Disney of Minto Developments, Daniel Greenberg, former *Take One* editors Peter Lebensold and Phyllis Platt, James Welch of *Literature/Film Quarterly,* Peter Cowie, John Mariani, John Tibbetts for *American Classic Screen,* and Christopher Chambers of the *New Orleans Review.* I asked for more permissions than I finally could use. In thanking Kristine Krueger of the Academy of Motion Picture Arts and Sciences' Margaret Herrick Library, I also thank the many editorial and curatorial professionals who handled these requests with courtesy and dispatch.

I am grateful to my dear friend Sylvia Rucker for translating the Marcel Dalio interview. Others also offered liberally of their time and expertise for the sake of advancing my research. Thanks are due to Robert Bernard and Oksana Hlyva for helping with foreign language materials. Interlibrary Loan wizard Wayne Pedersen of Iowa State University's Parks Library helped immensely, as did Setsuko Noguchi of the Asian Library of the University of Illinois at Urbana-Champaign. Rosemary Hanes of the Library of Congress and Stephen Leggett of the National Film Registry helped too. More occasional but much appreciated assistance or advice was provided by Diana Shonrock, Marshall Deutelbaum, Loring Silet, Robert Sklar, David Desser, and Aaron Gerow. Among my recent students, Joseph Irwin and Lucas Thompson stand out as two who have advanced my thinking about Capra. Melissa Poague and David Roberts were the first readers of my introduction; I am grateful to both for their insights and suggestions. Thanks to Susan and Amy Poague for helping with the chronology and the filmography. For its support of my research I am grateful to the Iowa State University Department of English (especially department chair Charles Kostelnick) and likewise to the university's Center for Excellence in the Arts and Humanities. Lastly, thanks are due, on behalf of all Capra fans and scholars, to Joseph McBride, whose painfully candid but splendidly researched biography of Frank Capra represents an immense advance in our historical understanding of Capra's creative circumstances.

Readers should know that my filmography, rather like McBride's, is "abbreviated"—in using catch-all production categories (rather than the precise wording of the actual screen credits) and in being limited to primary collaborators. As most readers are likeliest to be interested in the feature films Capra directed, I have privileged that category by placing it last, and have included there films for which Capra received writing as well as directing credit. Because of disputes among sources regarding the extent of Harry Cohn's control of Capra's Columbia films, I often let "Columbia Pictures" stand alone as the production agency. Readers wishing more complete credits should consult *Meet Frank Capra: A Catalog of His Work* (Palo Alto: The Stanford Theatre Foundation, 1990), compiled by the staff of the American Film Institute Catalog of Motion Pictures under the editorship of Patricia King Hanson and Alan Gevinson. *Meet Frank Capra* works hard to keep track of awards Capra and his films received over the years, and also of remakes. For brevity's sake, I have dropped most such information from my own chronology, with the exception of Academy Awards and those significant honors *not* mentioned in standard Capra sources.

Given the emphasis that Capra accorded to education and educators, it is fitting that I dedicate this volume to Professors Nils Peterson and William

Cadbury, both of whom encouraged the conviction that cinema was a subject worthy of lifelong scholarly attention—Nils by sending me off to San Jose State's Morris Dailey Auditorium one afternoon to see *Citizen Kane* for the first time, and Bill by agreeing to direct my 1973 University of Oregon doctoral dissertation on Frank Capra. As once to Frank, so now to Nils and Bill: Mille grazie!

Notes

1. Ford's Foreword to Capra's *The Name Above the Title: An Autobiography* (New York: Macmillan, 1971) was ghost-written by Katherine Cliffton, according to Joseph McBride's *Searching for John Ford: A Life* (New York: St. Martin's Press, 2001), though McBride's account also has Capra himself participating in the discussion of what Ford would "say" (see p. 512). In McBride's *Frank Capra: The Catastrophe of Success* (New York: Simon & Schuster, 1992; St. Martin's Griffen, 2000), moreover, Ford himself is given ghost-writing credit for the conclusion of *The Name Above the Title* (see p. 653). (But is not all authorship similarly haunted?) Subsequent references to *The Name Above the Title* (*NAT*) and *Frank Capra: The Catastrophe of Success* (*FC*) will be parenthetical, within the text, using the foregoing abbreviations. Ford's foreword comprises pp. ix–x of *NAT*. References to interviews will use the interviewer's name parenthetically where that is not otherwise clear.

2. Richard Griffith's famous assessment of Capra first appeared in his "The Film Since Then" supplement to the 1949 revision of Paul Rotha's *The Film Till Now*. I consulted the 1967 reprint (Middlesex: The Hamlyn Group); see pp. 449–54. Alistair Cooke's review of *Mr. Deeds Goes to Town* is found in his *Garbo and the Night Watchmen* (London: Jonathan Cape, 1937; Secker & Warburg, 1971), pp. 135–37. Parker Tyler's "John Doe; or, the False Ending" appears in his *The Hollywood Hallucination* (1944; New York: Simon & Schuster, 1970), pp. 168–89.

3. Ray Carney's *American Vision: The Films of Frank Capra* was first published in 1986 by Cambridge University Press; citations are to the 1996 edition, published by Wesleyan University/The University Press of New England (Hanover, N.H.); here, p. 37. Additional references will be parenthetical.

4. Ray Carney, "My Capra," *The Boston Phoenix* (September 20, 1991), Sec. 3, p. 8.

5. On the gender complexity of Capra, see my own *Another Frank Capra* (New York: Cambridge University Press, 1994) and "Capra/Gender/Race: The Matinee Idol," which appeared on the *2000 Film & History CD-ROM Annual* (2001), edited by Peter C. Rollins, John E. O'Connor, and Deborah Carmichael.

CHRONOLOGY

1897   Francesco Capra is born May 18, to Salvatore and Rosaria (Nicolosi) Capra, Bisacquino, Sicily.

1900   Capra's brother Benedetto sails for America in September; he eventually settles in Los Angeles and urges the family to join him.

1903   In May, the Capra parents and four of their seven children set sail from Palermo in the steerage hold of SS *Germania*. They arrive in Los Angeles, by train, on June 3. September 14, Frank starts first grade at the Castelar Street Elementary School.

1904   After the Capras buy their first house, Frank transfers to the 19th Avenue Elementary School. During his grade school years, "Francesco Rosario" becomes "Frank Russell" Capra.

1907   September 16, enters Griffin Avenue Elementary School; his teachers solicit the PTA to pay his parents the equivalent of Frank's school-time labor-value so that he can continue his education.

1911   February 6, enters Manual Arts High School, a member of the Winter '15 class. Studies stagecraft under art teacher, former Ziegfeld hand, eventual film director and journalist, Rob Wagner.

1915   January 27, graduates from Manual Arts High School. (Capra *might* have worked on a freelance basis as a gag-writer for Mack Sennett after graduation.) September 18, matriculates at Throop College of Technology (later California Institute of Technology—"Caltech"), though in his freshman year he commutes to Pasadena from Sierra Madre, where his father rents a citrus ranch.

1916   The best grades in his class earn Capra the Freshman Travel Scholarship Prize. Among other industrial and cultural sites visited during his trip is the Eastman Kodak Company in Rochester, New York. November 18, Salvatore Capra dies in an accident at the ranch. Capra's grades suffer.

1917   April 6, enlists as a private in the U.S. Army; is sent back to Throop to train through the ROTC program. (Capra discovers, upon enlistment, that he is not a U.S. citizen, and makes the necessary application.)

1918   Conducts research on an incendiary bomb at the behest of Caltech Professor Arthur A. Noyes. September 15, graduates with the Throop class of "War '18," receiving a "general" B.S. degree. October 18, is mustered into the U.S. Army; reports for active duty at the Enlisted Specialists' Preparatory School at the Presidio in San Francisco; is discharged on December 13.

1919   Visits his brother Ben in Sacramento; works as an extra in John Ford's Harry Carey western *The Outcasts of Poker Flat.* In Hollywood, works briefly at the Christie Film Company. Serves as a live-in tutor to Baldwin M. Baldwin and as an English instructor at the U.S. Army Balloon School. Becomes assistant to W. M. Plank at the Plank Scenario School; August, Plank and company arrive in Reno, Nevada, to establish the Tri-State Motion Picture Company, with Frank R. Capra as secretary and treasurer.

1920   April 25, *The Pulse of Life*—likely based on a Capra scenario and featuring "Frank Russell" among the cast—premiers at Reno's Grand Theater. March through August, works (perhaps as a director) on the *Screen Snapshots* series produced by CBC Film Sales Company, a precursor of Columbia Pictures. June 4, is naturalized as a U.S. citizen. August, moves to San Francisco; supports self by selling Hartsook photographs, Elbert Hubbard books, and "phony" mining stock town-to-town in central California. December, applies to Walter Montague, of Fireside Productions; is hired to direct *Fulta Fisher's Boarding House.*

1921   To judge by shooting scripts found in his papers, probably wrote and/ or directed other Fireside productions. Works in Waldon S. Ball's photographic laboratory, developing film, editing industrial and amateur movies, and writing titles. October, works as an assistant director for the Paul Gerson Pictures Corporation. November, directs a documentary commemorating the visit to San Francisco of the Italian naval cruiser *Libia;* the film premiered on December 3 at the People's Theater.

1922   April 2, *Fulta Fisher's Boarding House* opens at the Strand Theater in New York. Begins working—as "prop man, editor, gag man, and finally personal assistant" to series director Robert Eddy—on the Plum Center Comedies for producer (and Gerson associate) William A. Howell, whose niece, Helen Howell, features as the series ingenue.

1923   November 29, Capra and Helen Edith Howell are married.

1924   January, Frank and Helen move to Hollywood; he works as a gag writer for the *Our Gang* comedies at the Hal Roach Studios; his first complete script is for *Jubilo, Jr.,* starring Will Rogers; *High Society* is the last film he works on before losing his job in March. Works as an assistant director for Film Booking Offices of America, as a gag man for the Hollywood Photoplay Company, and then gets hired at the Mack Sennett Studios; receives his first Sennett screen credit as co-writer (with Arthur Ripley) of *The Reel Virginian.* That summer, is assigned to work with Harry Langdon.

1925   March 29, *Plain Clothes* is released, for which Capra receives his first Langdon-connected screen credit; Sennett promotes Capra to screenwriter, teamed with senior writer Arthur Ripley and director Harry Edwards. *His First Flame,* Capra's first feature-length screenplay to be produced in Hollywood, is filmed, though held back from release until 1927. September 15, Harry Langdon signs with First National Pictures, and takes Ripley, Capra, and Edwards with him after finishing two more shorts for Sennett.

1926   *Tramp, Tramp, Tramp,* Langdon's initial First National feature, opens on March 17; *The Strong Man,* directed by Capra after a falling out between Edwards and Langdon, opens September 5.

1927   *Long Pants* premiers on March 26, though Capra is fired on February 23. (Disputes surface in the trade press about the degree of Capra's participation in the writing and direction of the Langdon features.) April 12, Frank and Helen separate. After directing *For the Love of Mike* in New York, returns briefly to Sennett as a gag writer before going to work for Columbia Pictures in October.

1928   January 1, *That Certain Thing,* Capra's first Columbia picture, opens; it is photographed by Joseph Walker, who will shoot a total of twenty films for Capra. January, production chief Harry Cohn signs Capra to a multi-film Columbia contract, the first of many. Capra's fifth Columbia feature, *Say It with Sables* (released July 13), is the first to carry the credit "A Frank Capra Production." July 7, replaces Irvin Willat as director of *Submarine,* an A-budget disaster saga and, via recorded music and sound effects, Columbia's first sound film. August 13, Helen's divorce petition is granted, though it does not become final until August 16, 1929.

1929   March 4, *The Younger Generation* opens; though initially shot silent, it is augmented with dialogue scenes to become Columbia's first "talkie." During production of *Flight*—the middle film, with *Submarine* and *Dirigible,* of Capra's Ralph Graves/Jack Holt military trilogy— meets Lucille Warner Reyburn, who is visiting a college friend on location.

1930   *Ladies of Leisure* opens on April 2, Capra's first film (of five) with Barbara Stanwyck, and the first to feature "Frank Capra" on theater marquees.

1931   May 8, Capra is invited to become a member of the Academy of Motion Picture Arts and Sciences (AMPAS); October 17, is elected to the Academy's board of governors. July 20, *The Miracle Woman* opens; based on the play *Bless You, Sister* by John Meehan and Robert Riskin, it is the first occasion where Capra and Riskin are connected creatively, though Riskin refuses to work on the screenplay. Riskin does participate in the writing of Capra's next film, *Platinum Blonde.* (Altogether, Capra and Riskin shared screen credit on twelve films.)

1932   *Forbidden,* scripted by Jo Swerling from a story by Capra, opens January 9. February 1, Capra and Lucille are married in Brooklyn. August 4, *American Madness* opens. October 18, Columbia and MGM arrange for

Capra to direct *Soviet,* from a script by Jules Furthman, at Metro, though the film is canceled after executive Irving Thalberg suffers a heart attack.

1933   January 11, *The Bitter Tea of General Yen* opens, the first film to play a regular run at Radio City Music Hall. October, Capra is elected AMPAS secretary. September 7, *Lady for a Day* opens.

1934   February 22, *It Happened One Night* opens. February 26, *Lady for a Day* receives four Academy Award nominations (for Best Picture, Actress, Directing, and Writing-Adaptation). March 21, Frank Warner Capra (Frank Jr.) is born. *It Happened One Night* is honored (in September) as the Venice Film Festival's "most entertaining show." November 29, *Broadway Bill* opens. In November and December, Capra twice undergoes abdominal surgery. "Frank Capra Tells All" appears in the December 16 issue of the *New York Times.* December 20, the Screen Writers Guild selects Riskin's *It Happened One Night* as the outstanding motion picture story of 1934.

1935   *It Happened One Night* is listed among the top ten foreign films of 1934 in the *Kinema Jumpo* (Tokyo) critics poll. February 27, *It Happened One Night* wins Oscars in each of its five nomination categories: for Best Picture, Actor, Actress, Directing, and Writing-Adaptation. April 24, John Capra is born. October 9, Capra is elected AMPAS president.

1936   "A Sick Dog Tells Where It Hurts" appears in the January *Esquire.* April 12, *Mr. Deeds Goes to Town* opens. "Mr. Capra (Humanist) Shares a Bow" appears in the April 19 issue of the *New York Times;* "Sacred Cows to the Slaughter" appears in the July issue of *Stage. Mr. Deeds* is screened at the Venice Film Festival. October 22, Capra re-elected president of AMPAS. November 22, a rough cut of *Lost Horizon* is previewed in Santa Barbara.

1937   *Mr. Deeds Goes to Town* is rated among the top ten foreign films of 1936 in the *Kinema Jumpo* critics poll. February 7, *Mr. Deeds* receives five Academy Award nominations (including Best Picture, Actor, and Writing-Screenplay). March 2, *Lost Horizon* officially premiers in San Francisco. March 4, receives best-directing Oscar for *Mr. Deeds.* August, applies for membership in the Screen Directors Guild (SDG) and sues

Columbia for breech of contract, though cost-overruns and editing conflicts on *Lost Horizon* are among other issues involved (the dispute is settled in November). September 16, Lucille (Lulu) Capra is born. October 4, is elected to SDG board.

1938   February 6, *Lost Horizon* receives seven Academy Award nominations (including Best Picture); March 10, *Lost Horizon* wins Oscars for Film Editing and Art Direction. April 1938, Capra becomes chair of the SDG committee negotiating a basic labor agreement with the producers. May 15, is elected SDG president. (May 26, the House Committee on Un-American Activities [HUAC] is created.) Capra's picture is on the cover of *Time* magazine's August 8 issue ("His Stories Cannot Match His Story"). August 23, John Capra dies. September 1, *You Can't Take It with You* opens, the first of three films Capra made with James Stewart, likewise with Edward Arnold. (October 14, U.S. Army Intelligence opens a file on Capra.)

1939   Capra's "Ce sont les films qui font les stars" appears in the January 4 issue of *Cinémonde*. February 5, *You Can't Take It with You* is nominated for seven Academy Awards (including Best Writing-Screenplay and Cinematography). February 16, Capra threatens to resign as AMPAS president unless the producers settle with the SDG (an agreement is finalized on March 13). February 23, *You Can't Take It with You* wins the Oscar for Best Picture, and Capra for Best Directing. April 2, "By Post from Mr. Capra," advocating a cinema of directors (versus producers), appears in the *New York Times*. May 21, is reelected SDG president. October 2, forms Frank Capra Productions, Inc., with Riskin. October 17, *Mr. Smith Goes to Washington* previews at Constitution Hall; is released October 19.

1940   *You Can't Take It with You* is listed among the top ten foreign films of 1939 in the *Kinema Jumpo* critics poll. February 12, *Mr. Smith Goes to Washington* is nominated for eleven Academy Awards. February 21, Frank Capra Productions contracts with Warner Bros. to produce *The Life and Death of John Doe*. February 29, Lewis R. Foster wins the Best Writing-Original Story Oscar for *Mr. Smith*. December, Capra retires from the AMPAS presidency.

1941   February 12, Thomas Capra is born. Gary Cooper, as "John Doe," appears on the cover of *Time* magazine's March 3 issue. March 12, *Meet*

John Doe premieres in New York, Los Angeles, Miami, and Oklahoma City, though its ending is considerably changed by the time of its national release on May 3. May 19, relinquishes the SDG presidency. May 23, Rosaria Capra dies. August 1, signs with Warner Bros. to direct *Arsenic and Old Lace,* from the Joseph Kesselring play, though the completed film is not released theatrically until after its Broadway run has closed. December 12, Capra agrees to join the Army Signal Corps to make the *Why We Fight* series, though he is not sworn in until January 29, 1942. December 29, Frank Capra Productions dissolves, in the wake of *Meet John Doe's* weak box-office and weighty tax liabilities.

1942   February 9, Richard Connell and Robert Presnell receive an Oscar nomination in the Writing-Original Story category for *Meet John Doe.* February 11, Major Capra departs Los Angeles to report for duty in Washington, D.C.; is eventually (June 6) given command of the 834th Signal Service Photographic Detachment, Special Services Division. July 13, Capra's unit moves to Hollywood; August 13, is promoted to Lieutenant Colonel. In addition to the seven *Why We Fight* features (which were required viewing for all Army personnel) and many additional orientation films, units under Capra's supervision during 1942–45 produced fifty issues of the *Army-Navy Screen Magazine* and forty-six (classified) issues of the *Staff Film Reports,* which were reedited as thirty-four *Combat Bulletins* for troop viewing.

1943   March 4, *Prelude to War* receives one of four Academy Awards in the Documentary category; is released theatrically on May 13. August and September, works in London on *Tunisian Victory* for the War Department's Bureau of Public Relations; the 834th is transferred from Special Services to the Army Pictorial Service (APS). November 12, *The Battle of Russia* is given theatrical release. December 24, is promoted to Colonel; December 26, officially assumes command of the Special Coverage Section, Western Division, APS, though Capra had been functionally in command since mid-November. In addition to continuing to supervise projects already begun, Capra bears responsibility for organizing combat photography units, including those of George Stevens and John Huston.

1944   February 7, *The Battle of Russia* is nominated for an Academy Award in the Documentary-Feature category. March 16, *Tunisian Victory* is released theatrically. April 21, *The Negro Soldier* is released theatrically. May 11, Capra is named an assistant chief of the Army Pictorial Service. September 1, *Arsenic and Old Lace* is released.

1945   February, writes "Pioneer Women." April 10, Capra and Samuel Briskin incorporate Liberty Films (William Wyler and George Stevens eventually become partners). May 10, *Two Down and One to Go!* is released theatrically (*On to Tokyo* is also released in May). June 14, receives the Distinguished Service Medal. August 23, Liberty Films signs a distribution deal with RKO. September 1, buys the rights to "The Greatest Gift," by Philip Van Doren Stern, from RKO, along with screenplays by Dalton Trumbo, Clifford Odets, and Marc Connelly. *Hitler Lives?*, produced by Warner Bros. using APS material (sources differ as between *Here Is Germany* and *Your Job in Germany*), is released theatrically in late 1945. (According to American Film Institute catalogers, *War Comes to America* is also released theatrically.)

1946   March 7, *Hitler Lives?* receives an Academy Award in the Documentary-Short Subjects category. May 20, is elected to the SDG board. Capra's "Il faut savoir faire un film avant de le commencer" appears in the June 25 issue of *Cinémonde*. December 21, *It's a Wonderful Life* opens in New York City's Globe Theater. *Seeds of Destiny*, a segment of the *Army-Navy Screen Magazine,* is distributed theatrically.

1947   February 5, *Arsenic and Old Lace* receives the Belgian Challenge International du Cinema Trophy as the best film of 1946. February 10, *It's a Wonderful Life* is nominated for five Academy Awards (including Best Picture, Actor, Directing). March 10, Liberty, MGM, and Paramount strike a deal under which Capra will direct Spencer Tracy and Claudette Colbert (replaced at the last minute by Katharine Hepburn) in a film version of the Howard Lindsay and Russel Crouse stage play *State of the Union*. March 13, *Seeds of Destiny* receives an Academy Award in the Documentary-Short Subjects category. May 5, "Breaking Hollywood's 'Pattern of Sameness'" appears in the *New York Times*. May 16, Liberty Films is sold to Paramount Pictures.

1948   *It's a Wonderful Life* receives the Foreign Film award from the Circulo de Escritores Cinematagráficas (Madrid). April 7, *State of the Union* is previewed at Loew's Capital Theater in Washington, D.C., with President Truman attending; is released April 22. May, Capra retires from the SDG board.

1950   April 8, *Riding High* is released. May 16, is reelected to the SDG board; May 21, *It Happened One Night* ranks among the top ten films of the last fifty years in an SDG-sponsored critics poll. Though he is absent from the August 18 meeting where the vote is taken, Capra's name is attached to a public statement in which the SDG board explains its motion proposing that all members sign a loyalty oath. September 5, seconds a motion by Cecil B. DeMille to inform producers of guild members "not in good standing" for failing to sign the oath, though at a subsequent meeting Capra votes *against* making the blacklist provision "part of the official bylaws." (These are but a few of the gyrations Capra went through—including twice resigning from the SDG board—during the battle between the DeMille and Joseph L. Mankiewicz factions.) Volunteers to return to active duty during the Korean War, but Army Intelligence (G-2) concludes by November 21 that Capra is "possibly subversive," which effectively bars him from serving, though Capra is not aware of the G-2 finding until later.

1951   March 20, Capra's Paramount contract is settled, though his last Paramount film, *Here Comes the Groom,* does not open nationally until September 6. May, is reelected to the SDG board. Asked in the spring to participate in a Defense Department think tank, Project VISTA, Capra agrees, though obtaining security clearance is problematic; in a letter dated December 14, Capra is informed that the Army-Navy-Air Force Personnel Security Board (ANAFPSB) cannot consent to his request, specifying a list of charges—among them that he has associated with left-wing writers—against which he is given ten days to reply. (He mails his 225 page response on December 29.) December 31, *Westward the Women,* based on Capra's "Pioneer Women" though directed by William Wellman, opens. During 1951, if not earlier, according to McBride, Capra served both the FBI and the State Department as "a political informant," though in his role as a member of a State Department committee on film propaganda, it was his duty to clear screenwriters politically for department projects.

1952   January 5, the ANAFPSB grants Capra conditional security clearance "specifically limited" to Project VISTA. Is first approached about doing the Bell System Science films. February 11, *Here Comes the Groom* garners two Academy Award nominations, one for Robert Riskin and Liam O'Brien in the Motion Picture Story category; March 20, "In the Cool, Cool, Cool of the Evening" wins the 1951 Oscar in the Music-Song category.

1953   December, is appointed to the board of the Fallbrook Public Utility District (Capra wins election to the seat in 1954, and resigns on June 6, 1955).

1956   April, signs with Columbia to remake *Lady for a Day,* though script problems cause Cohn to drop the project. November 19, *Our Mr. Sun* is broadcast on CBS television.

1957   March 20, *Hemo the Magnificent* is broadcast on CBS. September, starts working on *Joseph and His Brethren* for Columbia. October 25, *The Strange Case of the Cosmic Ray* is broadcast on NBC television.

1958   February 12, *The Unchained Goddess* is broadcast on NBC. Supervises instructional shorts in connection with an experimental high school physics curriculum.

1959   February 7, receives the SDG's D. W. Griffith Award for lifetime achievement. May 26, is reelected SDG president (serving through 1961). June 17, *A Hole in the Head* opens.

1960   April 4, "High Hopes," the theme song of *A Hole in the Head,* receives the 1959 Academy Award for Best Music-Song.

1961   December 18, *Pocketful of Miracles* opens.

1962   February 26, *Pocketful of Miracles* receives three Academy Award nominations (Best Supporting Actor, for Peter Falk; Best Music-Song, for "Pocketful of Miracles"; and Best Costume Design-Color, for Edith Head and Walter Plunkett).

1963   In Madrid, prepares to film *Circus,* replacing Nicholas Ray, but is himself replaced by Henry Hathaway (the film eventually appears as *Circus World,* starring John Wayne).

1964   March 27, signs with Columbia to direct *Marooned,* from the novel by Martin Caidin; released in 1969, it is directed by John Sturges, though

Frank Capra, Jr., remained as associate producer and Capra himself received a percentage of profits. As first chairman of the Directors Guild of America's Creative Rights Committee, helps negotiate a contract with the producers giving directors the right to a "Director's Cut." *Rendezvous in Space,* made for Martin Marietta, premiers at the New York World's Fair on September 10.

1966   May 24, effectively retires from directing when he instructs his agent to negotiate the end of his participation in *Marooned.* Starts writing his autobiography, though his initial effort is deemed too downbeat by friends.

1971   June, *The Name Above the Title* is published by Macmillan; is offered as an alternative selection by the Book-of-the-Month Club.

1977   Capra's "'One Man, One Film'—The Capra Contention" appears in the June 26 *Los Angeles Times* in rebuttal of a piece by screenwriter David Rintels claiming that Capra denigrated Riskin in asserting his "one man, one film" credo.

1982   March 5, receives the American Film Institute's Life Achievement Award.

1984   May 16, is made an "American Honorary Member" of the American Academy and Institute of Arts and Letters. July 1, Lucille Capra dies.

1985   August, suffers his first of several strokes.

1986   July 14, is awarded the National Medal of Arts; is too ill to attend the White House ceremony.

1989   September 19, the Librarian of Congress selects *Mr. Smith Goes to Washington* among the first twenty-five films to be placed on the National Film Registry.

1990   October 18, *It's a Wonderful Life* is added to the National Film Registry.

1991   September 3, Capra dies in La Quinta, California.

1993   December 14, *It Happened One Night* is added to the National Film Registry.

1995   October, *It Happened One Night* ranks 92nd among the "All Time Best 200" films in *Kinema Jumpo*'s centennial-of-cinema critics poll.

1998   June 16, the American Film Institute announces its list of The 100 Best American Movies on CBS-TV. *It's a Wonderful Life* ranks 11th, *Mr. Smith Goes to Washington* 29th, and *It Happened One Night* 35th.

2000   December 27, the *Why We Fight* films are added to the National Film Registry.

FILMOGRAPHY

As Gag Man or Writer
COMEDY SHORTS

1924

Cradle Robbers; Jubilo, Jr.; It's a Bear; High Society; Every Man for Himself; Little Robinson Corkscrew; Riders of the Purple Cows; The Reel Virginian; All Night Long

1925

A Wild Goose Chaser; Boobs in the Woods; Plain Clothes; Breaking the Ice; The Marriage Circus; Super Hooper-Dyne Lizzies; Good Morning, Nurse!; Sneezing Beezers!; Cupid's Boots; The Iron Nag; Lucky Stars; Cold Turkey; Love and Kisses; There He Goes

1926
Saturday Afternoon

1927
Soldier Man (produced 1925), *Fiddlesticks* (produced 1925)

Information in parentheses following titles is in producer/distributor order. Material within brackets is variously conjectural, while "uncr" indicates that participation is reported as uncredited in Joseph McBride's *Frank Capra: The Catastrophe of Success*. All films are in black and white unless otherwise indicated.

1928
The Swim Princess, Smith's Burglar

1929
Smith's "Uncle Tom" (produced 1927)

FEATURES

1920
THE PULSE OF LIFE (Tri-State Motion Picture Co.)
[Director: W. M. Plank]
[Script: **Frank Capra**]
Cast: Peggy Lawson, W. Montgomery, Denison Standing, **Frank Russell
[Capra]**
6 reels

1926
TRAMP, TRAMP, TRAMP (Harry Langdon Corp./First National)
Director: Harry Edwards
Story: **Frank Capra**, [Arthur Ripley], Tim Whelan, Hal Conklin, J. Frank Hol-
liday, Gerald Duffy, Murray Roth
Titles: George Marion, Jr.
Cinematography: Elgin Lessley
Editing: Harold Young
Cast: Harry Langdon (Harry Logan), Joan Crawford (Betty Burton), Edwards
Davis (John Burton), Alec B. Francis (Amos Logan), Tom Murray (Nick
Kargas)
6 reels

1927
HIS FIRST FLAME (Mack Sennett Studios/Pathé; produced 1925)
Director: Harry Edwards
Story: Arthur Ripley, **Frank Capra**
Titles: A. H. Giebler
Cinematography: William Williams
Cast: Harry Langdon (Harry Howells), Natalie Kingston (Ethel Morgan), Ruth

Hiatt (Mary Morgan), Vernon Dent (Amos McCarthy), Bud Jamieson (Hecter Benedict)
6 reels

[THREE'S A CROWD (Harry Langdon Corp./First National)
Director: Harry Langdon
Adaptation: James Langdon, Robert Eddy
Story: Arthur Ripley, **Frank Capra** (uncr)
Cinematography: Elgin Lessley, Frank Evans
Cast: Harry Langdon (The Odd Fellow), Gladys McConnell (The Girl), Cornelius Keefe (The Man), Henry Barrows, Frances Raymond
6 reels]

1951
WESTWARD THE WOMEN (MGM)
Producer: Dore Schary
Director: William A. Wellman
Script: Charles Schnee
Story: **Frank Capra**
Cinematography: William Mellor
Editing: James E. Newcom
Music: Jeff Alexander
Cast: Robert Taylor (Buck Wyatt), Denise Darcel (Fifi Danon), Hope Emerson (Patience Hawley), John McIntire (Roy E. Whitman), Julie Bishop (Laurie Smith), Lenore Lonergan (Maggie O'Malley), Henry Nakamura (Ito)
116 mins.

Documentaries

1921
Documentary of the visit of the Italian warship *Libia* to San Francisco
Producer: The Italian Virtus Club of San Francisco
Director: **Frank Capra**
Titles: **Frank Capra**, Giulio DeMoro

1940
CAVALCADE OF THE ACADEMY AWARDS (Academy of Motion Picture Arts and Sciences/Warner Bros.)

Supervisor: **Frank Capra**
Director: Ira Genet
Script: Owen Crump
Cinematography: Charles Rosher
Commentary: Carey Wilson
Cast: **Frank Capra**, Walter Wanger, Bob Hope, Sinclair Lewis, Hattie McDaniel
B&W and Color
30 mins.

1952
THE FALLBROOK STORY (Fallbrook Chamber of Commerce [uncr])
Producer: Charles Peters
Director: **Frank Capra** (uncr)
Script: Ed Ainsworth
Cinematography: Lee Garmes (uncr)
Cast: Cecil B. DeMille, Don Porter, Floyd Ahrend, Diane Kettering, Mary M. Melsheimer, George F. Yackey, Goodwin J. Knight
Color
32 mins.

1954
CAREERS FOR YOUTH (California Institute of Technology)
Producers: **Frank Capra**, Charles Newton (uncr)
Director: Edward Bernds (uncr)
Script: **Frank Capra**, Charles Newton (uncr)
Cast: Dr. Lee A. DuBridge
Color
28 mins.

WHY WE FIGHT

1942
PRELUDE TO WAR (United States War Department, Special Service Division/ Twentieth Century-Fox)
Producer: Lt. Col. **Frank Capra**
Script: Capt. Anthony Veiller, Maj. Eric Knight, Robert Heller

Editing: Capt. William W. C. Hornbeck
53 mins.

1943
THE NAZIS STRIKE (United States War Department, Special Service Division)
Producer: Lt. Col. **Frank Capra**
Script: Capt. Anthony Veiller, Maj. Eric Knight
Editing: Lt. Henry Berman
42 mins.

DIVIDE AND CONQUER (United States War Department, Special Service Division/Warner Bros.)
Producer: Lt. Col. **Frank Capra**
Script: Capt. Anthony Veiller, Maj. Eric Knight
Editing: Lt. William Lyon, Maj. William Hornbeck
58 mins.

THE BATTLE OF BRITAIN (United States War Department, Special Service Division)
Producer: Lt. Col. **Frank Capra**
Script: S. K. Lauren, Capt. Anthony Veiller, Maj. Eric Knight
Editing: Lt. Merrill White
54 mins.

THE BATTLE OF RUSSIA (United States War Department, Special Service Division/Twentieth Century-Fox)
Producer: Lt. Col. Anatole Litvak
Supervisor: Lt. Col. **Frank Capra**
Director: Lt. Col. Anatole Litvak
Script: Capt. Anthony Veiller
Editing: Maj. William W. C. Hornbeck, Lt. William A. Lyon, Marcel Cohen
83 mins.

1944
THE BATTLE OF CHINA (United States War Department, Signal Corps/Twentieth Century-Fox)
Producer: Col. **Frank Capra**

Script: Maj. Anthony D. Veillier, James Hilton, John Gunther, Joseph Sistrom
67 mins.

1945
WAR COMES TO AMERICA (United States War Department, Army Pictorial
Service/War Activities Committee, RKO)
Producer: Col. **Frank Capra**
Script: Col. **Frank Capra**, Maj. Anthony Veiller, Sgt. Irving Wallace
Editing: Maj. William W. C. Hornbeck, Capt. Merrill G. White
67 mins.

OTHER WAR DEPARTMENT FILMS

1943
SUBSTITUTION AND CONVERSION (United States War Department, Special
Service Division)
Producer: Lt. David Miller
Supervisors: Lt. Col. **Frank Capra**, Lt. Col. Anatole Litvak
6 reels

KNOW YOUR ALLY BRITAIN (United States War Department, Special Ser-
vices Division)
Producer: Maj. Edgar Stevenson
Supervisor: **Frank Capra**
[Director: Anthony Veiller
Script: Anthony Veiller, Eric Knight, Jo Swerling
Editing: William Hornbeck]
45 mins.

1944
THE NEGRO SOLDIER (United States War Department, Special Service Divi-
sion/War Activities Committee)
Supervisor: Col. **Frank Capra**
Director: Capt. Stuart Heisler
Script: Carleton Moss, Jo Swerling
43 mins. (a 20 mins. version was also distributed)

TUNISIAN VICTORY (British Army Film Unit, U.S. Army Signal Corps/British Ministry of Information, Office of War Information, MGM)
Producers: Lt. Col. Hugh Stewart, Lt. Col. **Frank Capra**
Directors: Lt. Col. Hugh Stewart, Lt. Col. **Frank Capra**
Script: J. L. Hodson, Capt. Anthony Veiller, Capt. Roy Boulting, Capt. Alfred Black, Capt. John Huston
76 mins.

1945
YOUR JOB IN GERMANY (United States War Department, Army Pictorial Service)
Supervisor: Col. **Frank Capra**
[Script: Ted Geisel
Editing: William Hornbeck, Elmo Williams]
15 mins.

TWO DOWN AND ONE TO GO! (United States War Department, Army Pictorial Service/Office of War Information, War Activities Committee)
Producer: Maj. Anthony Veiller
Supervisor: **Frank Capra**
[Script: Anthony Veiller
Editing: William Hornbeck]
Color
9 mins.

ON TO TOKYO (United States War Department, Army Pictorial Service)
[Supervisor: Col. **Frank Capra**]
15 mins.

THE STILWELL ROAD (United States War Department, Army Pictorial Service, British and Indian Film Units)
Producer: Col. **Frank Capra**
Script: Capt. Oppenheimer, Lt. Col. Alex Bryce
Editing: Maj. Ludwig, Sgt. Mann
51 mins.

KNOW YOUR ENEMY—JAPAN (United States War Department, Information and Education Division)

Producer: Col. **Frank Capra**
Script: Joris Ivens, Pvt. Carl Foreman, Col. **Frank Capra**, Maj. Edgar Peterson, Maj. John Huston
Editing: Maj. Aaxton, Lt. Bracht, Elmo Williams
63 mins.

HERE IS GERMANY (United States War Department, Information and Education Division)
Producers: Col. **Frank Capra**, Maj. Edgar Stevenson
Script: William L. Shirer, George Ziomer, Ernst Lubitsch, Sgt. Gottfried Reinhardt
Editing: Bud Sheets, Dorothy Spencer
52 mins.

1982
OUR JOB IN JAPAN ([United States War Department, Information and Education Division]; produced 1946)
[Producer: Col. **Frank Capra**
Superviser: Ted Geisel
Script: Carl Foreman, Ted Geisel]
18 min.

SCIENCE DOCUMENTARIES

1956
OUR MR. SUN (Frank Capra Prods., N. W. Ayer & Son/Bell Telephone, CBS-TV)
Producers: **Frank Capra**, Donald Jones
Director: **Frank Capra**
Script: **Frank Capra**, Aldous Huxley (uncr), Willy Ley (uncr)
Cinematography: Harold Wellman
Editing: Frank Keller
Animation: United Prods. of America
Cast: Eddie Albert, Lionel Barrymore, Dr. Frank Baxter, Marvin Miller, Sterling Holloway
Color
59 mins.

1957
HEMO THE MAGNIFICENT (Frank Capra Prods., N. W. Ayer & Son/Bell Telephone, CBS-TV)
Producers: **Frank Capra**, Donald Jones
Associate Producer: Joseph Sistrom
Director: **Frank Capra**
Script: **Frank Capra**
Cinematography: Harold Wellman
Editing: Frank P. Keller
Animation: Shamus Culhane Prods.
Cast: Richard Carlson, Dr. Frank Baxter, Sterling Holloway, Marvin Miller
Color
59 mins.

THE STRANGE CASE OF THE COSMIC RAYS (Frank Capra Prods., N. W. Ayer & Son/Bell Telephone, NBC-TV)
Producers: **Frank Capra**, Donald Jones
Associate Producer: Joseph Sistrom
Director: **Frank Capra**
Script: **Frank Capra**, Jonathan Latimer, Charles Stearns (uncr)
Cinematography: Harold Wellman, Ellis Carter, Edison Hoge
Editing: Frank P. Keller, Raymond Snyder
Animation: Shamus Culhane Prods.
Cast: Richard Carlson, Dr. Frank Baxter, Bil and Cora Baird's Marionettes
Color
59 mins.

1958
THE UNCHAINED GODDESS (Frank Capra Prods., N. W. Ayer & Son/Bell Telephone, NBC-TV)
Producers: **Frank Capra**, Donald Jones
Associate Producer: Joseph Sistrom
Director: Richard Carlson
Script: **Frank Capra**, Jonathan Latimer
Cinematography: Harold Wellman
Editing: Frank P. Keller
Animation: Shamus Culhane Prods.

Cast: Richard Carlson, Dr. Frank Baxter
Color
59 mins.

1964
RENDEZVOUS IN SPACE ([Graphic Films Corp., Frank Capra Prods.], Martin
Marietta Corp.)
Producer: **Frank Capra**
Director: **Frank Capra**
Script: **Frank Capra**, Jonathan Latimer
Cast: Danny Thomas, Tom Fadden, Benny Rubin, Charles Lane, Andy Clyde,
James Coburn
Color
18 mins.

As Director

1922
FULTA FISHER'S BOARDING HOUSE (Fireside Prods./Pathé; produced
1920–21)
Producers: G. F. Harris, David F. Supple
Director: **Frank Capra**
Script: **Frank Capra**, Walter Montague, from Rudyard Kipling's poem "The
Ballad of Fisher's Boarding-House"
Cinematography: Roy Wiggins
Cast: Mildred Owens, Ethan Allen, Olaf Skavlan, Gerald Griffin, Oreste Serag-
noli
1 reel

THE VILLAGE BLACKSMITH (Fireside Prods.; produced 1920–21)
Producers: G. F. Harris, David F. Supple
Director: **Frank Capra**
Script: **Frank Capra**, Walter Montague, from Henry Wadsworth Longfellow's
poem
1 reel

THE LOOKING GLASS (Fireside Prods.; produced 1920–21)
Producers: G. F. Harris, David F. Supple

Director: **Frank Capra**
Story: F. B. Lowe
Script: **Frank Capra**, Walter Montague
1 reel

THE BAREFOOT BOY (Fireside Prods.; produced 1920–21)
Producers: G. F. Harris, David F. Supple
Director: **Frank Capra**
Script: **Frank Capra**, Walter Montague, from John Greenleaf Whittier's
poem
B&W and color
1 reel

1926
THE STRONG MAN (Harry Langdon Corp./First National)
Director: **Frank Capra**
Script: Tim Whelan, Tay Garnett, James Langdon, Hal Conklin, Robert Eddy
(uncr), Clarence Hennecke (uncr), [Arthur Ripley, **Frank Capra**, J. Frank Hol-
liday, Murrary Roth]
Story: Arthur Ripley, [Harry Langdon]
Titles: Reed Heustis, [Harry Langdon]
Cinematography: Elgin Lesslcy, Glenn Kershner
Editing: Harold Young
Cast: Harry Langdon (Paul Bergot), Priscilla Bonner (Mary Brown), Arthur
Thalasso (Zandow the Great), Gertrude Astor ("Gold Tooth"), William V.
Mong (Parson Brown), Robert McKim (Roy McDevitt)
7 reels

1927
LONG PANTS (Harry Langdon Corp./First National)
Director: **Frank Capra**
Script: Robert Eddy, Clarence Hennecke
Story: Arthur Ripley, **Frank Capra** (uncr)
Cinematography: Elgin Lessley, Glenn Kershner
Cast: Harry Langdon (The Boy), Alan Roscoe (His father), Gladys Brockwell
(His mother), Priscilla Bonner (Priscilla), Alma Bennett (The Vamp), Betty
Francisco
6 reels

FOR THE LOVE OF MIKE (Robert Kane Prods./First National)
Producer: Robert Kane
Director: **Frank Capra**
Script: Leland Hayward, J. Clarkson Miller, from the story "Hell's Kitchen"
by John Moroso
Cinematography: Ernest Haller
Cast: Ben Lyon (Mike), George Sidney (Abraham Katz), Ford Sterling (Herman Schultz), Claudette Colbert (Mary), Hugh Cameron (Patrick O'Malley)
7 reels

1928
THAT CERTAIN THING (Columbia Pictures)
Producer: Harry Cohn
Director: **Frank R. Capra**
Script: Elmer Harris
Titles: Al Boasberg
Cinematography: Joseph Walker
Editing: Arthur Roberts
Art Direction: Robert E. Lee
Cast: Viola Dana (Molly Kelly), Ralph Graves (A. B. Charles, Jr.), Burr McIntosh (A. B. Charles), Aggie Herring (Maggie Kelly)
7 reels

SO THIS IS LOVE (Columbia Pictures)
Producer: Harry Cohn
Director: **Frank Capra**
Script: Elmer Harris, Rex Taylor
Story: Norman Springer
Cinematography: Ray June
Editing: Arthur Roberts
Art Direction: Robert E. Lee
Cast: Shirley Mason (Hilda Jensen), William Collier, Jr. (Jerry McGuire), Johnnie Walker ("Spike" Mullins), Ernie Adams ("Flash" Tracy), Carl Gerard (Otto), William H. Strauss ("Maison" Katz)
6 reels

THE MATINEE IDOL (Columbia Pictures)
Producer: Harry Cohn

Director: **Frank R. Capra**
Script: Elmer Harris, Peter Milne, from the story "Come Back to Aaron" by Robert Lord and Ernest S. Pagano
Cinematography: Phillip Tannura
Editing: Arthur Roberts
Art Direction: Robert E. Lee
Cast: Bessie Love (Ginger Bolivar), Johnnie Walker (Don Wilson), Lionel Belmore (Col. Jasper Bolivar), Ernest Hilliard (Wingate), Sidney D'Albrook (J. Madison Wilberforce), David Mir (Eric Barrymaine)
6 reels

THE WAY OF THE STRONG (Columbia Pictures)
Producer: Harry Cohn
Director: **Frank Capra**
Script: William Counselman, Peter Milne
Cinematography: Ben Reynolds
Cast: Mitchell Lewis (Handsome Williams), Alice Day (Nora), Margaret Livingston (Marie), Theodore von Eltz (Dan), William Norton Bailey (Tiger Louie)
6 reels

SAY IT WITH SABLES (Columbia Pictures)
Director: **Frank Capra**
Script: Dorothy Howell
Story: **Frank Capra**, Peter Milne
Cinematography: Joseph Walker
Editing: Arthur Roberts
Art Direction: Harrison Wiley
Cast: Helene Chadwick (Helen Casell), Francis X. Bushman (John Caswell), Margaret Livingston (Irene Gordon), Arthur Rankin (Doug Caswell), June Nash (Marie Caswell), Alphonz Ethier (Mitchell)
7 reels

SUBMARINE (Columbia Pictures)
Producer: Harry Cohn, [Irvin Willat]
Director: **Frank R. Capra**
Script: Winifred Dunn, Dorothy Howell

Story: Norman Springer
Cinematography: Joseph Walker
Editing: Ben Pivar
Music: Ernest Luz
Cast: Jack Holt (Jack Dorgan), Ralph Graves (Bob Mason), Dorothy Revier (Bessie), Clarence Burton (Submarine commander), Arthur Rankin (Boy)
93 mins.

THE POWER OF THE PRESS (Columbia Pictures)
Producer: Jack Cohn
Director: **Frank Capra**
Script: Frederick A. Thompson, Sonya Levien
Story: Frederick A. Thompson
Cinematography: Chet Lyons, Ted Tetzlaff, Joseph Walker (uncr)
Editing: Frank Atkinson
Art Direction: Harrison Wiley
Cast: Douglas Fairbanks, Jr. (Clem Rogers), Jobyna Ralston (Jane Atwill), Mildred Harris (Marie), Philo McCullough (Blake), Wheeler Oakman (Van)
7 reels

1929
THE YOUNGER GENERATION (Columbia Pictures)
Director: **Frank R. Capra**
Script: Sonya Levien, Howard J. Green, from the play *It Is to Laugh* by Fannie Hurst
Cinematography: Ted Tetzlaff, Ben Reynolds
Editing: Arthur Roberts
Music: Bakaleinikoff
Cast: Jean Hersholt (Julius Goldfish), Ricardo Cortez (Morris Goldfish), Lina Basquette (Birdie Goldfish), Rosa Rosanova (Tilda Goldfish), Rex Lease (Eddie Lesser)
75 mins.

THE DONOVAN AFFAIR (Columbia Pictures; released in both sound and silent versions)
Director: **Frank R. Capra**
Script: Howard J. Green, Dorothy Howell, from the play by Owen Davis

Titles: Howard J. Green
Cinematography: Ted Tetzlaff
Editing: Arthur Roberts
Art Direction: Harrison Wiley
Cast: Jack Holt (Inspector Killian), Dorothy Revier (Jean Rankin), William Collier, Jr. (Cornish), Agnes Ayres (Lydia Rankin), John Roche (Jack Donovan), Virginia Browne Faire (Mary Mills), Edward Hearn (Nelson)
83 mins.

FLIGHT (Columbia Pictures)
Director: **Frank R. Capra**
Script: Howard J. Green, **Frank R. Capra**
Story: Ralph Graves
Cinematography: Joseph Walker, Joseph Novak, Elmer Dyer
Editing: Gene Milford, Ben Pivar, Maurice Wright
Cast: Jack Holt (Panama Williams), Ralph Graves ("Lefty" Phelps), Lila Lee (Elinor), Alan Roscoe (Major), Harold Goodwin (Steve Roberts), Jimmy De La Cruze (Lobo Sandino)
110 mins.

1930
LADIES OF LEISURE (Columbia Pictures; released in both sound and silent versions)
Director: **Frank Capra**
Script: Jo Swerling, from the play *Ladies of the Evening* by Milton Herbert Gropper
Titles: Dudley Early
Cinematography: Joseph Walker
Editing: Maurice Wright
Music: Bakaleinikoff
Cast: Barbara Stanwyck (Kay Arnold), Ralph Graves (Jerry Strong), Lowell Sherman (Bill Standish), Marie Prevost (Dot Lamar), Nance O'Neill (Mrs. Strong), George Fawcett (Mr. Strong), Juliette Compton (Claire Collins)
98 mins.

RAIN OR SHINE (Columbia Pictures)
Director: **Frank R. Capra**

Script: Dorothy Howell, Jo Swerling, from the book of the musical *Rain or Shine* by James Gleason and Maurice Marks
Cinematography: Joseph Walker
Editing: Maurice Wright
Music: Bakaleinikoff
Cast: Joe Cook ("Smiley" Johnson), Louise Fazenda (Frankie), Joan Peers (Mary Rainey), William Collier, Jr. (Bud Conway), Tom Howard (Amos K. Shrewsbury), Dave Chasen (Dave), Clarence Muse (Nero)
87 mins.

1931
DIRIGIBLE (Columbia Pictures)
Director: **Frank R. Capra**
Script: Jo Swerling, Dorothy Howell
Story: Lt. Commander Frank Wilber Wead, James Warner Bellah (uncr)
Cinematography: Joseph Walker, Elmer Dyer
Editing: Maurice Wright, Harry Decker
Cast: Jack Holt (Commander Jack Bradon), Ralph Graves (Lt. Frisky Pierce), Fay Wray (Helen Pierce), Hobart Bosworth (Louis Rondelle), Roscoe Karns (Sock McGuire), Clarence Muse (Clarence)
102 mins.

THE MIRACLE WOMAN (Columbia Pictures)
Director: **Frank Capra**
Script: Jo Swerling, Dorothy Howell, from the play *Bless You, Sister* by John Meehan and Robert Riskin
Cinematography: Joseph Walker
Editing: Maurice Wright
Cast: Barbara Stanwyck (Florence Fallon), David Manners (John Carson), Sam Hardy (Hornsby), Beryl Mercer (Mrs. Higgins), Russell Hopton (Bill Welford)
91 mins.

PLATINUM BLONDE (Columbia Pictures)
Director: **Frank R. Capra**
Script: Robert Riskin, Jo Swerling, Dorothy Howell
Story: Harry E. Chandlee, Douglas W. Churchill

Cinematography: Joseph Walker
Editing: Gene Milford
Cast: Robert Williams (Stew Smith), Loretta Young (Gallagher), Jean Harlow (Ann Schuyler), Louise Closser Hale (Mrs. Schuyler), Halliwell Hobbes (Smythe), Walter Catlett (Bingy Baker)
89 mins.

1932
FORBIDDEN (Columbia Pictures)
Director: Frank R. Capra
Script: Jo Swerling
Story: Frank Capra
Cinematography: Joseph Walker
Editing: Maurice Wright
Cast: Barbara Stanwyck (Lulu Smith), Adolphe Menjou (Bob Grover), Ralph Bellamy (Al Holland), Dorothy Peterson (Helen Grover), Myrna Fresholt (Roberta, baby), Charlotte V. Henry (Roberta, 18)
87 mins.

AMERICAN MADNESS (Columbia Pictures)
Director: Frank R. Capra
Script: Robert Riskin
Cinematography: Joseph Walker
Editing: Maurice Wright
Cast: Walter Huston (Thomas Dickson), Pat O'Brien (Matt Brown), Kay Johnson (Phyllis Dickson), Constance Cummings (Helen), Gavin Gordon (Cyril Cluett)
76 mins.

1933
THE BITTER TEA OF GENERAL YEN (Columbia Pictures)
Producers: Walter Wanger, Frank Capra
Director: Frank R. Capra
Script: Edward Paramore, from the novel by Grace Zaring Stone
Cinematography: Joseph Walker
Editing: Edward Curtis
Music: W. Frank Harling

Cast: Barbara Stanwyck (Megan Davis), Nils Asther (General Yen), Toshia Mori (Mah-Li), Walter Connolly (Jones), Gavin Gordon (Dr. Robert "Bob" Strike), Richard Loo (Captain Li)
88 min.

LADY FOR A DAY (Columbia Pictures)
Director: **Frank Capra**
Script: Robert Riskin, from the story "Madame La Gimp" by Damon Runyon
Cinematography: Joseph Walker
Editing: Gene Havlick
Music: Bakaleinikoff
Cast: Warren William (Dave the Dude), May Robson (Apple Annie), Guy Kibbee (Judge Henry D. Blake), Glenda Farrell (Missouri Martin), Ned Sparks (Happy McGuire), Walter Connolly (Count Romero), Jean Parker (Louise), Nat Pendleton (Shakespeare)
95 mins.

1934
IT HAPPENED ONE NIGHT (Columbia Pictures)
Director: **Frank Capra**
Script: Robert Riskin, from the story "Night Bus" by Samuel Hopkins Adams
Cinematography: Joseph Walker
Editing: Gene Havlick
Music: Louis Silvers
Cast: Clark Gable (Peter Warne), Claudette Colbert (Ellen Andrews), Walter Connolly (Alexander Andrews), Jameson Thomas (King Westley), Roscoe Karns (Oscar Shapeley)
105 mins.

BROADWAY BILL (Columbia Pictures)
Director: **Frank Capra**
Script: Robert Riskin, Sidney Buchman (uncr), from the story "On the Nose" by Mark Hellinger
Cinematography: Joseph Walker
Editing: Gene Havlick
Cast: Warner Baxter (Dan Brooks), Myrna Loy (Alice "The Princess" Higgins),

Walter Connolly (J. L. Higgins), Helen Vinson (Margaret Brooks), Douglass Dumbrille (Eddie Morgan), Clarence Muse (Whitey)
90 min.

1936
MR. DEEDS GOES TO TOWN (Columbia Pictures)
Producer: **Frank Capra**
Director: **Frank Capra**
Script: Robert Riskin, Myles Connolly (uncr), from the novel *Opera Hat* by Clarence Budington Kelland
Cinematography: Joseph Walker
Editing: Gene Havlick
Art Direction: Stephen Goosson
Music: Howard Jackson
Cast: Gary Cooper (Longfellow Deeds), Jean Arthur (Louise "Babe" Bennett), George Bancroft (MacWade), Lionel Stander (Cornelius Cobb), Douglass Dumbrille (John Cedar), Raymond Walburn (Walter), H. B. Warner (Judge May), Ruth Donnolly (Mabel Dawson), Walter Catlett (Morrow), John Wray (Farmer)
115 mins.

1937
LOST HORIZON (Columbia Pictures)
Director: **Frank Capra**
Script: Robert Riskin, Sidney Buchman (uncr), Myles Connolly (uncr), Herbert J. Biberman (uncr), from the novel by James Hilton
Cinematography: Joseph Walker, Elmer Dyer
Editing: Gene Havlick, Gene Milford
Art Direction: Stephen Goosson
Music: Max Steiner, Dimitri Tiomkin
Cast: Ronald Colman (Robert Conway), Jane Wyatt (Sondra Bizet), Edward Everett Horton (Alexander P. Lovett), John Howard (George Conway), Thomas Mitchell (Henry Bernard), Margo (Maria), Sam Jaffe (Father Perrault)
132 mins.

1938
YOU CAN'T TAKE IT WITH YOU (Columbia Pictures)

Producer: **Frank Capra**
Director: **Frank Capra**
Script: Robert Riskin, from the play by George S. Kaufman and Moss Hart
Cinematography: Joseph Walker
Editing: Gene Havlick
Art Direction: Stephen Goosson
Music: Morris Stoloff, Dimitri Tiomkin
Cast: Jean Arthur (Alice Sycamore), Lionel Barrymore (Martin "Grandpa" Vanderhof), James Stewart (Tony Kirby), Edward Arnold (Anthony P. Kirby), Mischa Auer (Boris Kolenkhov), Ann Miller (Essie Carmichael), Spring Byington (Penny Sycamore), Samuel S. Hinds (Paul Sycamore), Donald Meek (Poppins), H. B. Warner (Ramsey)
127 mins.

1939
MR. SMITH GOES TO WASHINGTON (Columbia Pictures)
Producer: **Frank Capra**
Director: **Frank Capra**
Script: Sidney Buchman, Myles Connolly (uncr), from the story "The Gentleman from Montana" by Lewis R. Foster
Cinematography: Joseph Walker
Editing: Gene Havlick, Al Clark, Slavko Vorkapich
Art Direction: Lionel Banks
Music: M. W. Stoloff, Dimitri Tiomkin
Cast: James Stewart (Jefferson Smith), Jean Arthur (Clarissa Saunders), Claude Rains (Senator Joseph Paine), Edward Arnold (Jim Taylor), Guy Kibbee (Governor Hubert Hopper), Thomas Mitchell (Diz Moore), Euguene Palette (Chick McGann), Beulah Bondi (Ma Smith), H. B. Warner (Senate Majority Leader), Harry Carey (President of the Senate)
129 mins.

1941
MEET JOHN DOE (Frank Capra Prods./Warner Bros.)
Producers: **Frank Capra**, Robert Riskin
Director: **Frank Capra**
Script: Robert Riskin, Myles Connolly (uncr), from the story "A Reputation"

by Richard Connell and the treatment "The Life and Death of John Doe" by Connell and Robert Presnell
Cinematography: George Barnes
Art Direction: Stephen Goosson
Editing: Daniel Mandell, Slavko Vorkapich
Music: Leo F. Forbstein, Dimitri Tiomkin
Cast: Gary Cooper (Long John Willoughby), Barbara Stanwyck (Ann Mitchell), Edward Arnold (D. B. Norton), Walter Brennan (The "Colonel"), Spring Byington (Mrs. Mitchell), James Gleason (Henry Connell)
123 mins.

1944
ARSENIC AND OLD LACE (Warner Bros.; produced 1941–42)
Director: **Frank Capra**
Script: Julius J. Epstein, Philip G. Epstein, from the play by Joseph Kesselring, as produced by Howard Lindsay and Russel Crouse
Cinematography: Sol Polito
Editing: Daniel Mandell
Art Direction: Max Parker
Music: Leo F. Forbstein, Max Steiner
Cast: Cary Grant (Mortimer Brewster), Priscilla Lane (Elaine Harper), Raymond Massey (Jonathan Brewster), Jack Carson (O'Hara), Edward Everett Horton (Mr. Witherspoon), Peter Lorre (Dr. Einstein), James Gleason (Lt. Rooney), Josephine Hull (Abby Brewster), Jean Adair (Martha Brewster), John Alexander ("Teddy Roosevelt" Brewster)
118 mins.

1946
IT'S A WONDERFUL LIFE (Liberty Films/RKO)
Producer: **Frank Capra**
Director: **Frank Capra**
Script: Frances Goodrich, Albert Hackett, **Frank Capra**, Jo Swerling, Dalton Trumbo (uncr), Clifford Odets (uncr), Marc Connolly (uncr), Michael Wilson (uncr), Dorothy Parker (uncr), from the story "The Greatest Gift" by Philip Van Doren Stern
Cinematography: Joseph Walker, Joseph Biroc, Victor Milner (uncr)
Editing: William Hornbeck

Art Direction: Jack Okey
Music: Dimitri Tiomkin
Cast: James Stewart (George Bailey), Donna Reed (Mary Hatch Bailey), Lionel Barrymore (Henry F. Potter), Thomas Mitchell (Uncle Billy), Henry Travers (Clarence Oddbody), Beulah Bondi (Mrs. Bailey), Frank Faylen (Ernie), Ward Bond (Bert), Gloria Graham (Violet Bick), H. B. Warner (Mr. Gower), Todd Karns (Harry Bailey), Samuel S. Hinds (Peter Bailey)
130 mins.

1948
STATE OF THE UNION (Liberty Films/MGM)
Producer: **Frank Capra**
Director: **Frank Capra**
Script: Anthony Veiller, Myles Connolly, from the play by Howard Lindsay and Russel Crouse
Cinematography: George J. Folsey
Editing: William Hornbeck
Art Direction: Cedric Gibbons, Urie McCleary
Music: Victor Young
Cast: Spencer Tracy (Grant Matthews), Katharine Hepburn (Mary Matthews), Van Johnson ("Spike" MacManus), Angela Lansbury (Kay Thorndyke), Adolphe Menjou (Jim Conover)
124 mins.

1950
RIDING HIGH (Paramount Pictures)
Producer: **Frank Capra**
Director: **Frank Capra**
Script: Robert Riskin, Melville Shavelson, Jack Rose, Barney Dean (uncr), William Morrow (uncr), from the *Broadway Bill* screenplay and the story "On the Nose" by Mark Hellinger
Cinematography: George Barnes, Ernest Laszlo
Editing: William Hornbeck
Art Direction: Hans Dreier, Walter Tyler
Music: Victor Young
Songs: Johnny Burke, James Van Heusen, Meade Minnigerode, George S. Pomeroy, Tod B. Galloway, Stephen Foster

Cast: Bing Crosby (Dan Brooks), Coleen Gray (Alice "Princess" Higgins), Charles Bickford (J. L. Higgins), Frances Gifford (Margaret Higgins), William Demarest (Oscar "Happy" Maguire), Raymond Walburn (Prof. Pettigrew), Clarence Muse (Clarence "Whitey" White), Douglass Dumbrille (Eddie Howard)
112 mins.

1951
HERE COMES THE GROOM (Paramount Pictures)
Producer: **Frank Capra**
Director: **Frank Capra**
Script: Virginia Van Upp, Liam O'Brien, Myles Connolly, Arthur Sheekman (uncr), Charles Hoffman (uncr), Barney Dean (uncr)
Story: Robert Riskin and Liam O'Brien, based on Riskin's treatment "You Belong to Me"
Cinematography: George Barnes
Editing: Ellsworth Hoagland
Art Direction: Hal Pereira, Earl Hedrick
Music: Joseph J. Lilley, Van Cleave
Songs: Jay Livingston, Ray Evans, Johnny Mercer, Hoagy Carmichael, Giuseppe Verdi
Cast: Bing Crosby (Peter Garvey), Jane Wyman (Emmadel Jones), Alexis Smith (Winifred Stanley), Franchot Tone (Wilbur Stanley), James Barton (Pa Jones)
113 mins.

1959
A HOLE IN THE HEAD (SinCap Prods./United Artists)
Producer: **Frank Capra**
Director: **Frank Capra**
Script: Arnold Schulman, Myles Connolly (uncr), from Schulman's play
Cinematography: William H. Daniels
Editing: William Hornbeck
Art Direction: Eddie Imazu
Music: Nelson Riddle, Arthur Morton
Songs: Sammy Cahn, James Van Heusen
Cast: Frank Sinatra (Tony Manetta), Edward G. Robinson (Mario Manetta),

Eddie Hodges (Ally Manetta), Eleanor Parker (Mrs. Eloise Rogers), Carolyn Jones (Shirl), Thelma Ritter (Sophie Manetta), Keenan Wynn (Jerry Marks)
Color
120 mins.

1961
POCKETFUL OF MIRACLES (Franton Prods./United Artists)
Producer: **Frank Capra**
Director: **Frank Capra**
Script: Hal Kanter, Harry Tugend, Jimmy Cannon (uncr), Myles Connolly (uncr), from the *Lady for a Day* screenplay and the Damon Runyon story "Madame La Gimp"
Cinematography: Robert Bronner
Editing: Frank P. Keller
Art Direction: Hal Pereira, Roland Anderson
Music: Walter Scharf
Songs: Sammy Kahn, James Van Heusen
Cast: Glenn Ford (Dave the Dude), Bette Davis (Apple Annie), Hope Lange (Queenie Elizabeth Martin), Arthur O'Connell (Count Alphonse Romero), Peter Falk (Joy Boy), Thomas Mitchell (Judge Henry Blake), Edward Everett Horton (Hutching), Ann-Margret (Louise)
Color
136 mins.

FRANK CAPRA

INTERVIEWS

An Interview with Frank Capra

HAL HALL/1931

THE TIME IS SOME TWELVE or thirteen years ago. The place is a power house over in Pasadena. The hour is four o'clock in the morning. It is raining in torrents. Nice and warm is that power house, and the engineer in charge smokes his pipe contentedly, while a young Caltech student dozes peacefully on a nearby stool.

"Frank," suddenly barks the engineer, "Better go out and see if that chimney is smoking again."

And the young man thus addressed rises, turns his coat collar up about his neck and trots out into the rain. He has to go a couple of blocks down the street before he can get a good view of the top of the chimney. By the time he has returned to report that smoke was coming in clouds from said chimney he is soaking wet, and cold. That was the third wetting the young man had received in as many nights, for it was the rainy season, and the City Fathers of Pasadena were poison as far as smoke from the power house chimney was concerned. So, the young man, a student of chemical engineering at Caltech, who was working his way through college, and who receives twenty-five cents an hour for working in the power house from three o'clock to seven each morning, starts thinking.

A couple of weeks later he aroused the curiosity, and the ire, of the engineer in charge of the power house when he started installing a peculiar looking gadget in the base of the huge chimney. It consisted of a selenium cell

---

From *American Cinematographer* (February 1931): 20, 38. Copyright © 1931, 2004. Reprinted by permission of American Cinematographer.

on one side of the chimney, and an electric bulb on the other. And when the next rain fell the young Caltech man did not have to go out and get wet, for the smoke would cut off the light and thus operate the galvanometer hooked to the cell, ringing a bell when the smoke would appear. The apparatus was so good that it is still in use in the chimney after all these years.

The young college student was Frank Capra, director of *Flight, Submarine, The Strong Man, Rain or Shine, Ladies of Leisure,* and more recently, the big Columbia lighter-than-air picture, *Dirigible.* And that practical turn of mind which made him devise the smoke detector in order to keep him inside in the wet weather is reflected in his motion picture work and is more or less responsible for the unusual success that has been his in the brief time he has been in the business of making motion pictures.

He has been in the picture game only some six years, and in that time has reached a point that many men never attain, even with political and family "pull" and years of effort. The chief reason for his success, as this writer sees it, is the fact that Capra applies that cold, hard, logical reasoning of the man of science to his work. He abhors affectation, personal aggrandizement, slave bracelets, freak attire and the usual "show" that so many people in this business use to cloak inability—often stupidity.

"People want to see things as they really are," says Capra. "They are not interested in watching candles slowly soften and flop over into a wedding anniversary cake when the erring wife or husband fails to remember the date. This may be subtle symbolism. But candles don't do that in real life. What our audiences want to see are the characters. They want to see what the characters are doing. They do not want the characters blotted out by backgrounds that take up all of the attention.

"After all, the main thing in a picture is the story. If you have no story you have no picture. The degree of the success of the picture depends entirely upon the story. The story is given the audience by the characters on the screen who enact the roles of the characters in the story. Why, then, do a single thing that will take the attention of your audience from these characters and the story they are acting out?

"The suffering woman is the center of attraction, say, in one scene. The audience is interested in her and what she is doing, and what she is going to do. If you suddenly take their attention away from that woman by a kaleidoscopic whirling of unusual background the audience naturally shifts attention to the background and the story suffers. So, I have always submerged the backgrounds and centered everything on the players. Reality is what is wanted in pictures, not symbolic touches and beautiful settings for mere beauty's sake.

"This naturally brings me to the subject of photography. Photography is one of the most important elements in a picture, naturally. But to my way of thinking, the finest photography is not that which makes the audience forget the players and gasp at the sheer beauty of the setting, instead it is the photography that merges itself, so to speak, in the general atmosphere of the story. Photography that is not calling attention to itself is the finest photography. A cinematographer should know the story long before starting, and should get the mood of the story in his mind, and then keep his photography in the mood of the story from start to finish. A cinematographer can do more than any other individual in portraying the mood of the story, or he can do just the opposite. The good cinematographer portrays that mood, lights his picture so that the audience doesn't realize he has lighted it, gets over the proper effect so that the audience doesn't realize he has done it. In other words, the audience should never realize that a director has directed the picture or that the cameraman has photographed it. That is why "directorial touches" and photographic splurges should be kept out of pictures. Excellence in direction is reached when the audience never thinks of the director's work. Excellence in photography is achieved when the audience forgets photography. Excellence in the actor's work is attained when the audience forgets the player is John Smith, the star, and thinks of him as a living character on the screen. I feel that the time is past when a director can make a series of photographic settings of rare beauty and foist them on the public. The public wants reality and life and story. That is why a player who is not handsome or beautiful, but who is a real actor or actress, is such a success when given the chance."

Capra has his own ideas regarding dialogue. He doesn't like too much of it, and what there is must be good. Rather a wise thought.

"I believe," says Capra, "that there is too much small talk in a lot of pictures. Players chatter away at a terrific pace and most of the time say practically nothing. No wonder you see audiences squirming in their chairs. Sound is the greatest advance the industry has seen. But sound, like color, has its place. On the stage the characters are not always chattering like magpies. Usually the most tense moments of the drama are moments of absolute silence. The same is true in pictures. Dialogue where needed—and of the best—that is what is needed. But where the story can be carried without it—do not have conversation.

"The stage has been an institution that has come down through the ages. It will go on through the ages. The reason is because the writers of plays must give a play that holds interest. The same holds for the screen, although a lot of people do not seem to realize it yet. It takes time to write a story and a screenplay. If you rush it you will have a poor picture. You cannot make pictures as you make soup, by recipe.

"And, as to players. Too much attention is being paid to the matter of voices. Less elocution, more real acting, and our pictures will be better. Picture people seem to have the idea that a butler must have a voice of a certain quality. So they pick the butler by voice. I've heard a lot of butlers in my time, and I have yet to hear two of them with twin voices, if you get my meaning. But on the screen they all sound as though they were trained in the same school of elocution.

"The same with other characters. The voice, as long as the player can speak clearly enough to get across, should be forgotten. Just because a man plays the part of a gutter rat does not mean that his voice should be of a certain type. No two gutter rats sound alike. So why have them sound alike on the screen? Do you get my thought?"

We did, thoroughly. And, may we say here, that Mr. Capra touched a spot that has been a sore one with us. No wonder he has made successful pictures. He thinks intelligently.

And—just another angle to this business of picture making from this young man. It has to do with costs, and supervision.

"You ask me why Columbia has so many good pictures," said Capra in reply to said question. "Well, I think the chief reason is because they give a director such a free hand in his work. They demand quality and results. But they give you a chance to produce them. And this makes for lower cost, also. For a director realizes he is more or less on his own as far as the picture goes. If he can give a good picture at a low cost he has scored doubly. Naturally, if he is using his head, he will see that there is no waste."

Rather a good thought there for the industry.

Capra Foresees Satirical Cycle: Many Subjects Ripe for Ridicule

RUTH MORRIS/1932

LOOKING FORWARD TO THE coming film year, Frank Capra prophesies a cycle of satirical films. Columbia's director, author and ex-gag man believes that laughter, waiting to be released, is just around the corner of any boxoffice cagey enough to capitalize on the present state of public mind.

"Someone is going to evolve a great film out of the depression," enthuses the brighteyed boy who would like to give hard times a pictorial kick-in-the-pants. "Satirical treatment of a plutocrat, insanely trying to conserve wealth and finding happiness only when he is reduced to the breadline, will strike a responsive note in the mass mind. When that picture is made, it will inaugurate the cycle that follows in the wake of any successful film.

"The Man in the Street has had so many dogmas crammed down his throat that he is prepared to revolt against current under estimation of his intelligence. He's fed up. Politics, prohibition, patriotism, big business, high-powered advertising, are subjects ripe for ridicule."

Mr. Capra cites *Of Thee I Sing* as a successful example of the public's reaction toward a humorous exposé of the chicanery and subterfuge in politics and of an existent satirical attitude that waited for a clever producer to commercialize its potential boxoffice!

Ballyhoo, the magazine, accomplishes similar results with the advertising medium by chuckling at overstatement that masquerades as serious fact. The

From *Variety,* 2 February 1932. Reprinted by permission of Reed Business Information. Permission conveyed through Copyright Clearance Center, Inc.

anti-prohibition protagonist at whom newsreel audiences howled recently is another proof to Mr. Capra that the world will flock to a film that laughs down hypocrisies.

Dramatic pictures shorn of theatricalism are the next consideration in a discussion of films attuned to the mood of 1932.

"Emotional dramas," Capra thinks, "will narrow down to small casts and concentrate on two human beings who find tender mitigations in the everyday problems of life. *Bad Girl* struck the note that audiences want today—tender, compassionate emotion. Good boxoffice pictures must project some great love—not necessarily of one human for another. The love may be for nature, a career, an art, a country, but it must be deep and true, humanized by everyday occurrences that translate its basic truth to the average fan."

Switching from a discussion of stories, Mr. Capra refuted the theory that a director is best equipped to direct a story of his own creation. The director who authors his own film lacks judgment and perspective on his work. Creation and projection of a story should be by separate departments co-operating on an exchange of ideas, each department checked and guided by the criticism of the other. But Capra feels that collaboration should be limited to those two and not spread throughout the studio and confused by numerous assistants and supervisors.

Just returned from a European tour, Mr. Capra thinks that the British film industry is defeating its hope of competing against American product. British audiences have to be lured to native releases with double feature bills that offer one American film. Instead of studying the American product and extracting the ingredients that appeal to British audiences, producers are blindly proceeding on the wrong tack. Their films are derived from London stage productions, ingrown and emotionless. Instead of producing pictures that are down to earth they are trying to impose a flavor of West End society on the British public. Capra states it won't do.

Frank Capra Thinks Audience Should Help Create Film Story

LEO FREEDMAN/1933

THE MOTION PICTURE from its inception has been a medium of action. Even before talking pictures the multitudinous captions—such as "Came the Dawn"—were censured by the public. The advent of the speaking as well as lisping sound track made the film-conscious audience raise its hands in apprehension.

"You must be very careful," the quick-to-offer-advice bystanders shouted in unison, "not to permit the dialogue to displace action."

And so, since the birth of the articulate film, the dialogue has been relegated to a position secondary to the action. Hollywood writers and Hollywood directors have listened to the chant, "Less dialogue—more action" until they react involuntarily to the phrase. Now Frank Capra, director of *Lady for a Day,* Columbia's first picture of the new season, which will open for an extended run at the Music Hall Thursday evening, September 7, opens a revolution with the statement that the films, instead of having too much dialogue, haven't half enough. He says that when pictures are choked into lifelessness it is not because of the dialogue but because of the wrong kind of dialogue.

Mr. Capra comes forth with the statement, which will disturb Hollywood, that what is needed is not less, but more, dialogue. And better dialogue. He is emphatic about the last requirement. Not only that. He maintains that we need a different kind of dialogue. Motion pictures require conversation totally different in its psychological influence from the dialogue used in books or in plays.

For years Hollywood has been working to improve motion pictures. Most of the innovations have had to do with the law of optics and the improvement of photographical equipment. There have been occasional attempts to tell stories on the screen so as to indicate the mentality of the performer as well as his actions. Now comes a change in the writing and directing modus operandi.

Mr. Capra has just completed his first picture under a technique which he calls the "stimulation of the imagination."

"We might give it a more high sounding name," he said, "but that wouldn't improve our theory."

Action alone, Mr. Capra feels, is not the solution of the motion picture director's problem. "The movement of an actor across a room to close a door is action," he explains, and asks, "but what good is it? The real action, the important action, is not what takes place on the screen, but what happens in the minds of the audience.

"There was a time in motion pictures when it was thought necessary to show every step in the story," Mr. Capra states. "I think all of us realize that that time has passed. We have come to recognize that in each sequence in the development of the story there are only two or three instances, two or three gestures, which are important to the telling of the story.

"Unfortunately, we cannot show these important contributions and nothing else, for if we did so the story would develop too jerkily for entertainment. What we need, therefore, is to supplement the essential action with dialogue that will suggest action; even the action we employ must suggest more action—action which will be hilarious and more dramatic than we can record on celluloid. The imagination is a greater artist than either the writer or the director. What we aim to do is to make greater use of the audience's imagination. We hope to stimulate the mental activities of the motion picture patron so that the play and story to which the theatergoer reacts is a combination of what has been created on the screen and what has been created in his mind.

"The more perfect our work has been the more of the story will be created by the audience. In other words, all we are doing is leading the audience on to write the play for themselves. It is a new technique. I feel that our first attempt has been outstandingly successful. It may be beginner's luck, but I am convinced that the 'stimulation of the imagination' offers possibilities obtainable by no other method or technique of motion picture story telling.

"This new technique, this stimulation of the imagination, allows a greater scope for dramatic stories than we have ever had before. I am sure that if we attempted to tell the story of *Lady for a Day* by one of the older and established techniques it would have lacked much of the entertainment value it now has."

When Robert Riskin and Mr. Capra discussed the screen adaptation of Damon Runyon's story, they felt that the novel should make the perfect motion picture, since it was filled with action. They soon realized, however, that although they might be able to show most of the action within the scope of ten reels, the important part of the story, the elements which elevate the story above the average, could not be portrayed in its entirety. And piecemeal it meant little.

For a while they were stumped. The need for action had been drilled in them so long that they were hesitant about throwing the established doctrine into the river.

After endless consultations they decided that the play required more dialogue and less action, but not the kind of dialogue that had been used before. They agreed that they wanted dialogue which would stimulate the imagination of the audience so that they would understand and appreciate the action that must have taken place in the scenes they were unable to show.

The theory underlining the "stimulation of the imagination" technique is that all the dialogue used in the motion picture must suggest action. Action remains the goal, but the action is obtained through the use of dialogue. Action, it appears, has succeeded in winning over its worst enemy.

The individual theatergoer, inasmuch as his imagination plays an important part, becomes co-author and co-creator with the writer and director.

Public Doesn't Want to Think, Says Capra

PHILIP K. SCHEUER/1934

WHEREVER MOVIES ARE DISCUSSED, the length and breadth of the land, the name of one recent comedy-drama is sure to come up. This is as true of Hollywood as it is of Hohokus—sooner or later the talk will get around to *It Happened One Night,* produced by Columbia, starring Claudette Colbert and Clark Gable, and directed by Frank Capra. Capra and Columbia's previous collaboration, *Lady for a Day,* was hardly less conspicuous in its success. But *It Happened One Night* cinched them for immortality.

What sort of chap is this director and where did he come from? And how does he do it?

Frank Capra is an Italian—born in Palermo May 18, 1897—youngest of seven children; he is short, 5 feet 4 inches; dark, with a mop of black hair; terse-speaking, with a grim grin . . . and he doesn't know "how he does it."

"I'm no analyst," he said last week in answer to my question. "I can't explain it. Maybe—they (*Lady for a Day* and *It Happened One Night*) came along at the psychological moment. Maybe they had that universal some-thing. Maybe every man pictured himself as the hero of *It Happened One Night*—a happy-go-lucky tramp, feeling the wanderlust."

He shrugged.

"They prove, though, it's the entertaining qualities that carry a picture. Certainly neither story would stand critical analysis; each was full of holes, if you wanted to look for them. So far nobody has gone to the trouble—not

From the *Los Angeles Times,* 3 June 1934, sec. 2, pp. 2–3. Reprinted by permission.

even the critics. Like everybody else, they seem to have just been swept up and carried along."

It Happened One Night ran eleven weeks in Seattle—in these parlous times. Capra prizes a letter from a linotype operator in that city. The linotype operator wrote that he takes his family once every week to a picture show. The first week the Capra film was showing they elected it for inspection. The following week, when a vote came up, they decided unanimously on a repeat visit. The next week, the same, and for three more. Six in all. Six paying trips to see Frank Capra's *It Happened One Night.* He answered the linotype operator's letter, thanking him. That was typical.

"People don't want to think," Capra went on. "Neither do they want a story to be charted for them in advance. Surprise played an important part in both our pictures. It isn't easy to create, surprise; it's darned hard. We were lucky.

"We have one advantage at this studio. We take time to select a story; one we can get hepped up over. We don't have to write it to fit star personalities; Columbia hasn't enough of them for that, anyway. It's the story, the treatment, that counts. Then we go out and get the players to fit.

"No, it isn't easy," he admitted. "We're two months late in starting *Broadway Bill*—that's our next—right now. The people we want, most of them, are under contract to other studios. So far, we've got Warner Baxter for the lead."

Keeping up the company morale is important, Capra said. He does not believe in too many rehearsals; they take the edge off a scene. His scripts are written by Robert Riskin; and while together they manage to work out most of the details, some of these have a way of suggesting themselves on the spot—pure inspiration.

It was like that with the "Man on the Flying Trapeze" sequence in *It Happened One Night,* for instance. The original idea was merely to have a couple of ex-vaudevillians or hill-billies—fellow bus-passengers of the principals—haul out a banjo or two and strum a musical background for the main action. The community sing which subsequently reached the screen grew out of so simple a script direction as this, and provided one of the high points of the film.

Broadway Bill will be Capra's third production in this inimitable vein, discovered for *Lady for a Day.* He has no intention of sticking to comedy-drama indefinitely; "I am anxious," he explained, "to try a musical." Some of his best stuff, he contends, went into *The Bitter Tea of General Yen,* his last serious talkie. It was a dissertation on the diverse viewpoints of East and West, with Nils Asther as a reckless Chinese commander and Barbara Stanwyck as the righteous American missionary who falls into his clutches. Not over-successful, the fate of this picture bore out Capra's declaration that the great mass of paying patrons are not intellectually inclined.

One of the prime Capra tenets is to keep a film clean; smut, he insists, is the way of the lazy writer, the slothful director, the misguided producer. But he holds no brief for censorship, believing that the industry at large should not be made to suffer for the sins of the few. Let critics and editorial writers attack objectionable pictures by name, indicting those involved in its making; and let them base their attacks on artistic grounds rather than moral ones—otherwise, he asserts, they may defeat their purpose by attracting patronage to the very films they would condemn.

"If all else fails," he grinned, "it should not be too hard to shame producers into reforming. They all think they're geniuses, you know."

Capra's large family moved to Los Angeles in 1903. Newsboy, "pipe-crawler" for Western Pipe and Steel Company, student at Manual Arts High School and Caltech, scholarship winner, second lieutenant in the Coast Artillery, tutor to Anita Baldwin's son, and finally gag-man for Mack Sennett comedies—so Frank passed boyhood and youth. He has directed three features starring Harry Langdon, including *The Strong Man;* an early silent film with Claudette Colbert, *For the Love of Mike;* the first Columbia talkie, *Younger Generation;* a bunch of Columbia near-epics, *Flight, Submarine and Dirigible;* Joe Cook's *Rain or Shine;* and such Columbia social dramas as *Forbidden, The Miracle Woman* and *Ladies of Leisure,* all with Barbara Stanwyck. The night following the preview of *It Happened One Night,* a certain producer is quoted as having stated, "I'd give $1,000,000 for the contracts of Bob Riskin, Sam Briskin (supervisor) and Frank Capra." But there were no takers.

The Master of the Human Touch

PAULA HARRISON/1935

FRANK CAPRA DOESN'T BELIEVE in publicity for directors, nor that fans are interested in the men who make their movies. I knew it was through an objective sense of fairness that he had consented to see me. And out of this knowledge I'd built up an image of an ogre who swallowed magazine writers with his orange juice each morning.

True, I couldn't reconcile that image with the sunlit gaiety of the moods reflected in his pictures. It must be, I argued, drawing an imaginary line, that on this side of the line stands everyone else's Capra, warm and approachable, Capra, the director and boss, the friend and colleague—while on the other side, all alone, stands my Capra, stern and forbidding.

When I finally met my ogre I saw a pair of dark eyes that held nothing more terrifying than a faintly quizzical smile—and a face for which the Europeans have a word, though we have none—"sympathetic" they call it in their various languages, when they mean a face to which people are drawn instinctively. Olive-skinned, vigorously moulded, quiet on the surface, it had a vibrant quality which made it seem more alive, even in repose, than does the average face in animation. Not the face of a fire-eating dragon, at any rate, but of a man who should prove easy to talk to—provided you stayed within the bounds of what, legitimately, concerned you.

He made no bones about discussing his dislike of interviews. Walking back and forth, a slight frown between his eyes, he talked with characteristic straightforwardness.

From *Motion Picture*, July 1935, pp. 55, 76.

"Publicity's part of an actor's job—not a director's. A director's job is to make pictures the best he can—apart from that, I don't believe the public gives a rap about him. Besides, my story's been told so often—'from rags to riches'—that sort of thing—'poor boy makes good.' What's the sense in ringing the changes on the same old theme? All it brings me is a flood of mail.

"Every time the name of my birthplace appears in print, I get hundreds of letters from the hometowners who want me to read their scenarios or put their children into pictures. If I tried to answer half of them," he concluded grimly, "I could make up my mind to shut up shop, and devote the rest of my life to correspondence."

So reasonable was his point that I felt an uncontrollable impulse to say, "You're right, Mr. Capra," and give the interview back to the Indians. In self-defense, I changed the subject—and Capra changed. Suddenly he was the man I'd heard about—friendly, responsive—with a genius for putting the other fellow at ease. It was as though the sun had come out and banished a chill in the atmosphere.

For now he was talking about pictures—on which topic he could discourse gladly and freely to anyone. I could all but hear the sigh of relief with which, seating himself, he plunged into clear waters.

"How do I choose my stories? I'll tell you. I ask myself two questions. First, has it possibilities for entertainment? Then, has it an idea to put over, anything to say? If the answer is yes to both questions, I ask myself another. Would you like to work on it? If I feel I would, then I feel—I hope"— he corrected himself, dark eyes and white teeth flashing in a smile that was all the more disarming for being so unexpected—"I hope the audience will like it, too—one must please the audience, you know."

He sits quietly and talks quietly, yet creates an impression of power under control which is curiously stimulating to the listener. He says what he has to say, and stops—no dangling phrases, no "you see-s?" or "you know what I mean-s?," no bids for agreement or approval. Yet there's nothing dogmatic about his ideas—merely the sense that he's thought them out clearly enough to present them with clarity and force.

"For example," he continued, "what struck me about "Night Bus"—the Samuel Adams story from which we made It Happened One Night—was the novel background—the fact that the action took place along a bus route. That's why we took it. In more conventional surroundings, it might have been just another boy-and-girl romance, but the background seemed to hold new entertainment possibilities that made it worth doing. Incidentally, I think I enjoyed that picture more than anything I've done. The script was so beautifully written—the cast so perfect—everything went so smoothly—" There was a gleam of reminiscent pleasure in his eye.

It Happened One Night has been called by the movie trade "an object lesson in the making of motion pictures as they should be made." I've read the story from which it was taken, so I know how much of its grace and sparkle was injected by Capra and Robert Riskin, the writer with whom he works. Each insists on crediting the other with its responsibility. It doesn't matter. The point lies in their perfect collaboration. They spend weeks in shaping the script before anything is put down on paper; they concentrate their efforts on those down-to-earth incidents which warm the hearts of people the world over by the human touch that makes them kin with all mankind.

"It's those incidents, I think, that make the story," Capra told me. "Those are the things people remember long after they've forgotten everything else. The catch, of course, lies in creating the incident. It's not easy. Sometimes you don't find what you want till you're actually shooting—sometimes not then. You know it's wrong, but you don't know how to make it right. You watch and wait, you rack your brains and finally—if you're lucky—you get it.

"In the original script of *Broadway Bill,* for instance, the horse didn't die. I kept worrying about the finish—afraid it was going to be just another horse-race. I kept wondering what we could do to make it different and still sound. It wasn't till we were on location that the idea popped. Fortunately," he observed with perfect simplicity, "I'm so situated here at the studio that I can make what changes I like without asking permission." It was as though a ruling monarch, in all modesty, had declared himself fortunate to be able to govern his people without permission.

Ever since seeing *It Happened One Night,* I'd been wondering what it was that Capra had done to Clark Gable. He'd been popular enough before that—but with a limited popularity. For every dimple-worshipper, there had been three heretics who couldn't see him for dust. Those three and thousands of others had been completely bowled over by the breezy reporter of *It Happened One Night.* "Can this be Gable?" they may have murmured during the earlier scenes, watching suspiciously for the return of the he-man. By the time the famous thumbing sequence rolled round, they didn't give a whoop whether he was Gable or not—they loved him.

Capra refused to take any credit for the change. "That's what Gable's really like," he informed me. "Like the fellow he played in that picture. The part was made to order for him. Why do they put him in the other kind of story? Because this kind's so hard to find, so hard to write." So hard to direct, he might have added, but didn't. "It's airy, insubstantial, a bubble. If it floats, fine, if not, you haven't anything to fall back on.

"With a more dramatic story, you don't gamble so heavily. If the audience doesn't like the characters, it may still be interested in the action. From that angle, *Broadway Bill* was a better risk than *It Happened One Night*. *Lady for a Day* wasn't. In *Lady for a Day* you had to concentrate on humor and human appeal, and handle your sentimental values with the lightest possible touch, else you'd have had a maudlin mess instead of a hit.

"But there isn't any formula. You can build up a picture according to the most logical theories in the world, and still have a flop. What I try to do is to treat my characters, not as types, nor props to carry the action, but as human beings. Make them real people and they're bound to get the sympathy of the other people watching the screen.

"I'm going to do a picture on Washington, for instance. To most of us he's a dead hero, a man with a halo round his head. We take a holiday on his birthday, we revere his memory, or think we do—but if the truth were told, he bores us. He's nothing much more than a picture in a boat crossing the Delaware. But Washington was a flesh-and-blood person, alive in the world as you and I are alive today. He had to eat and dress and wash behind the ears. There's nothing irreverent about showing him that way. On the contrary, it's the finest kind of tribute. History's killed him, fossilized him. The screen can bring him back to life, let us really know him."

Capra's eyes were alight and his voice vibrant with enthusiasm. He'd advocated the human touch so persuasively that I couldn't help but realize why his pictures are so irresistible—embroidered as they are with simple realities.

He Has the Common Touch

FRANK DAUGHERTY/1938

THERE'S NOTHING INVOLVED about director Frank Capra's conception of drama or comedy. His stories usually involve a simple and direct sort of character with a set of persons and circumstances a good deal less direct. He triumphs by reason of his uncompromising forthrightness. And of these characters of Capra's, Mr. Deeds of *Mr. Deeds Goes to Town* is, of course, the archetype.

If you try to apply this definition of Capra formula to *Lost Horizon,* you are in deep water. Capra himself was troubled by *Lost Horizon.*

"I wasn't sure of that picture," he said, "until we had previewed it and were certain that it was headed for success. Tibet seemed a long way to ask people to go to find a solution of their problems, whatever they were. And, of course, that's about all the answer the picture gave to the situation it posed. I was relieved to have the solution of my next picture, *You Can't Take It with You,* occur nearer home. In fact, the title gave the solution to the whole problem.

"I was convinced when I saw the stage play," he said, speaking of the same George Kaufman–Moss Hart story, "that here was a great idea told through comedy."

His analysis of the picture possibilities of the play received little approval with his studio at first and none at all from the authors. But he understood the stage and the cinema approach as two divergent ways of treating a theme. On the stage *You Can't Take It with You* was a satire on current folkways and events in the United States; in its movie version it became a rose-colored endorsement of nearly everything the play had laughed at.

Capra was not necessarily breaking new ground when he fashioned the picture in this manner. He had behind him the lessons of *Mr. Deeds Goes to Town,* his own film and one of the most successful motion pictures ever made. Eugene O'Neill's *Ah, Wilderness!* was similarly adapted in tone to the screen audience, and *Stage Door,* a drama by the authors of *You Can't Take It with You.* In the last-named play what had been more or less cynical views of the sentimental American scene became, by virtue of more sympathetic treatment in pictures, successful comedy drama with practically no over-tones of disapproval. This relates to Capra's basic formula of box office.

"You can't make sport with an audience's cherished beliefs and have a very wide audience," he says. And he elaborates on the theme by pointing out that most of the tongue-in-cheek themes flourish and fade usually within the small circle of the Broadway theater when they do not receive a movie glossing.

Born in Sicily, Frank Capra came to America at the age of six and began his Americanization as a newsboy on the streets of Los Angeles. The same simple directness of approach which makes his pictures memorable gave direction and success to his own early efforts. Despite a good deal of economic difficulty, he graduated from high school at sixteen, two years too young to enter California Institute of Technology, from which, nevertheless, he was graduated some years later with a degree in science and a scholarship.

Hollywood had by this time become the working ground of a group of curious people who went about all day making a form of outdoor drama and recording it with a camera—trying to make an art medium of what had been only material for Broadway's penny peep shows. Capra had been editor of his college literary magazine; he turned his hand now to writing for the movies.

His earliest efforts were with the company which was later to become Columbia, his present studio. His most important schooling was under a master of screen comedy whose methods even today stamp the whole field of film comedy—Mack Sennett. While with Sennett, Capra first worked with Harry Langdon, and later directed some of the best films that comedian made.

Capra does not produce anything new. He simply makes the best pictures he can with the materials at hand. Although his method had been slow in bringing him recognition, it has proved to be the best way he could have worked. For today he is in the forefront of his profession, with a long list of worthy pictures that includes *Lady for a Day, Submarine, It Happened One Night, Mr. Deeds Goes to Town, Lost Horizon, You Can't Take It with You.*

He has not yet made a color picture. He believes that color is still too novel and distracting for the films. Soon he plans to make his first western picture and his first musical. "Westerns," he says, "developed from the adaptability of the camera to the scene in which movies first flourished—the West."

His next picture will have a political theme. He wants to show one of his honest people—say a cowboy senator in the guise of Gary Cooper—against the artificial background of the two august bodies of government we know as the houses of Congress. He thinks the gentleman from Montana as he would fashion him might be enlightening to the Congressmen. But even if the picture becomes satire, he says, it will have no villains. There should be a laugh in it somewhere for the satirized.

It is sometimes said of Capra that he develops stars, that Gable, Jean Arthur, and others, owe their first real success as comedians to him. Even Cooper, it must be admitted, has greatly developed since *Mr. Deeds.* But Capra modestly disclaims the personal effect.

"If I can take credit for the good players which crowd my pictures," he said, "it is because there are so many good players in Hollywood from which to choose." He laughed.

"I used to look at European films and wish it were possible to get actors such as the French and Russians have in their pictures. They seemed completely fresh and natural. It was only after I traveled in France and Russia that I learned that directors in those countries envy us our great company of accomplished actors quite as heartily as we envy them theirs.

"'You have such wonderful actors, even for the smallest parts!' they told me. 'No wonder Americans make good pictures.'

"I've come to think they're right."

Capra's pictures, more than most others made in Hollywood, have led the way back toward the technique the screen abandoned when it left off making silent pictures. Dialogue is cut to a minimum, a mobile camera again gives fluid motion to what had almost become a static screen. The last two or three

years, he thinks, have done much in these ways for the betterment of pictures.

Each of his own pictures costs him nearly a year of labor. He can't make
them faster, even when he tries, and it is a source of wonder to him that
sometimes other directors shoot creditable efforts in five or six weeks.

"Maybe you can't make them faster," I said, "because you have your own
way in your studio. Directors less highly paid, with less authority, have to do
what they're told." He didn't smile.

"I was the same," he said, "when I was getting $25 a week and even the
wardrobe people were ordering me about the lot."

This may partly explain why a Frank Capra picture can never be described
as "just another movie."

Une Conception de la Beauté

MARCEL DALIO/1944

MARCEL DALIO IS A well-known actor who has a place of his own in the French Theater and Screen. He is probably best remembered by American audiences for his portrayal of Rosenthal, the French-Jewish prisoner, in Jean Renoir's *La Grande Illusion*. On the stage, Mr. Dalio shared honors with Louis Jouvet. In this country, awaiting the recognition he richly deserves, he has been seen briefly in many Hollywood flickers, including *The Song of Bernadette* and *Wilson*. Aside from its informative qualities, this interview with Frank Capra is of interest because it can be traced back, and belongs, to a "style of thought" which was widely in fashion in French film magazines.

Burbank, peaceful California village, nestled near a verdant foothill; an aerodrome hub, from which the great silver Douglas aircraft are launched and sail toward New York or San Francisco.

A green door with crossbars, a rustic sign: "Frank Capra Productions."

Neither policeman, nor door-keeper, nor blonde operator wearing pilot headphones before an ebony console illuminated by firefly lights.

You enter as if to an old mill, and after having given your name to a smiling male secretary, you yourself knock at the door of the great "Lord of Hollywood," the only one among them all to have prevailed three times in the competition of the American Academy of Motion Pictures.

From *Salient* (New York) No. 3 (December 1944). The original headnote is in English. The remainder of the text is translated from French by Sylvia Rucker.

The most cordial greeting, of the greatest simplicity. "If I have agreed to grant you this interview, and to receive you here in my office, it is because I treasure unforgettable memories of my visit to France in 1936. I had the impression there of being as well understood as I am here, perhaps even better understood. They love my films there as much as yours. Our films, in fact, are as alike as brothers."

Frank Capra expresses himself in very pure French. While he speaks, I stare at him attentively: He has extraordinarily dark eyes, as black as the black enamel of Egyptian masks, which his sculptured head, his strong jaw, his high and open forehead, his masculine beauty also evoke.

"What do you want to know about me?"

"Your beginnings."

"The only odd fact of my life: I was a science student at Caltech in Pasadena. I intended to become an engineer, and I admit that my demanding studies did not inspire me. A friend of mine, a good amateur photographer, sought out my advice. He had read in a newspaper the tempting announcement of a San Francisco producer who, wanting to make a film, was advertising for skilled technicians, cameramen, directors, assistants.

" 'Would you go, if you were in my shoes?'

" 'Without hesitation. To prove the point I'll go with you.'

" 'No kidding! What will you be? An extra or assistant?'

" 'Are you kidding: a director.'

" 'But you know nothing about that.'

" 'And the others know more than I do?'

"This was, after all, in 1923.

"On seeing us, the 'producer' was convinced—I have always wondered why—that we were two experienced filmmakers. He discussed only salaries, royally offered me $75, and seemed as astonished by my acceptance as I was by his offer."

"Do you remember the name of the film?"

"Sure, it was called *Fulta Fisher's Boarding House* and was only one reel. The film's backer, a wood and charcoal wholesaler, had entrusted the task of making a cinematic adaptation of a story by Kipling."[1]

---

1. A more literal translation of this sentence would read: "The producer, a wood and charcoal wholesaler, had entrusted to his accountant the task of making a cinematic adaptation of a story by Kipling." Evidently Capra garbled something in this sentence—the facts, his

"Why are you smiling?"

"Because, believing that my inexperience would be obvious to real actors, I cast ordinary passersby, choosing those who had great faces."

"And that worked?"

"More or less. . . . It's neither better nor worse than other films from that era."

"And afterwards?"

"After that, things got a bit more serious. First there were farces with Mack Sennett, then comedies with Hal Roach, then the real films, the ones you know."

"Of all your films, which is your favorite?"

"*Mr. Deeds Goes to Town,* and also a forgotten film, *Lady for a Day,* which goes back to 1933."

"All people of taste share your opinion. As far as I'm concerned, *Mr. Deeds Goes to Town* was an exceptional success."

"Yet it's very simple."

"It is exactly the simplicity that makes it beautiful. Are you the author of the story?"

"That depends on how you understand 'author.' I bought the rights to a detective story that recounted, in detail, the mysterious murder of a twenty-year-old multi-millionaire assassinated at the opera. From this woolly story the figure of Mr. Deeds stood out, a simple young man, naive but likable, because sincere. I had the luck to cast Cooper in the role. In reshaping the character, little by little I modified the plot completely, so that all that remained of the original story was the virtuous Deeds character, who triumphed over all obstacles, and finally overcame the stupidity, bad faith, and maliciousness united against him.

"I'll tell you the secret of my working method: An idea grabs me, I think about it, think more profoundly about it, I search for a plan, and I model the characters on the men and the women I see in the real world."

French, or both. By all accounts, the "producer" who hired Capra was an "oddball Shake-spearean actor" named Walter Montague. I take the "producer" in this sentence to be one of Montague's "business friends" (as Capra subsequently told the tale in *The Name Above the Title*) who bankrolled "Fireside Productions"—probably David F. Supple, according to Joseph McBride's *Frank Capra: The Catastrophe of Success.* Per McBride, Capra probably met Montague in December of 1920; *Fulta Fisher's Boarding House* opened at the Strand Theater in New York on April 2, 1922.

L.P.

"How do you explain the fact that your films, until now, have always been successful both artistically and commercially?"

"You embarrass me. That's a question, I admit, that I've never asked myself."

"Would you like to try to answer it together?"

"While we are on the topic, if you like: The success comes, no doubt, from my concept of beauty. For me, the criterion for beauty is to please everyone; something beautiful is immediately understood, felt, loved. Complicated studies are not needed to be moved by a pretty woman, by moonlight on blooming fruit trees, by a sunset of sapphire and ruby hues, by a clear night sky studded with stars of gold like those that lend so much charm to California.

"Likewise, the fisherman, the peasant, the child, the simple man as well as the refined, all comprehend more or less Beethoven's Fifth Symphony, the love song of Tristan and Isolde, a Gothic cathedral, the Victory of Samothrace, a canvas by Titian or the Sistine ceiling; all will love them equally, because a beautiful thing pleases everyone, and all the more when its lines are very simple. In sum, either beauty is appreciated by everyone, or else it is incomplete or too complicated.

"Far be it from me to compare my films to the masterworks I have mentioned. I have tried to make films that were simple and sincere, and that has brought me the success that you find astonishing; I am astonished myself. . . . But it's my turn to ask a question: How do you explain the public's enthusiasm?"

"Because the characters you create are human and true. They are not marionettes, but living beings. They speak English but could just as well speak Turkish, Italian, or Swedish. Take, for example, in *Mr. Deeds,* the two old sisters from the country who, in the course of the trial of our hero, speak tirelessly in each other's ear, like parakeets. I say that these two characters, to cite only their example, are no more American than European, no more modern than ancient. They are drawn from the universal comic source, the comedy of Molière, of Aristophanes, because it is an exact and truthful portrait, of the kind of old fool we have all known in our villages and in our cities. This illustrates in a striking way the theory that you've elaborated so brilliantly for me.

"A last word: I am always glad to find myself in the presence of a happy man, on whom Fortune smiles. I bet you would be embarrassed to have to make a wish, here, on the spot, without having time to reflect . . ."

"You are mistaken: the flash of a single shooting star would be time enough for me to ask to continue to make good films for as long as possible, for my own pleasure and the public's, my own kind of films, not the studio's! But first we must win the war."

"We will win."

"Surely, but why ponder other projects in the meantime? Come see me after victory. Then we'll chat."

Emotional Appeal Capra's Film Goal

EDWIN SCHALLERT/1946

' ' P EOPLE ARE NUMB after the catastrophic events of the past ten to fifteen years. I would not attempt to reach them mentally through a picture, only emotionally. Anything of a mental sort, anything apart from the purely human, will have to be incidental.''

It was Frank Capra, one of the sagest of movie creators, talking—the same Frank Capra who was bound over to the service practically from the beginning of the war to its close . . .

Frank Capra, who dazzled the public with the complete gayety and charm of his *It Happened One Night* in the midst of the depression period, and gave the public such a lift that many went to see the film two and three times . . .

Frank Capra, who time and again after that rang the bell loud and long with his *Mr. Deeds Goes to Town, You Can't Take It with You* and *Mr. Smith Goes to Washington,* productions that were daringly controversial in their way and thus alive, and at the same time vastly entertaining.

Capra is back in the popular running again, although during wartime he was never entirely absent. He exerted control over some of the most brilliant and interesting documentaries. He was a guiding influence over a dozen and one projects that helped to enlighten the public concerning what the conflict was about. And he has returned from that long period of detached service apparently ready to put his finger right on the popular pulse again.

He will crystallize his ideas in a first feature called *It's a Wonderful Life*—a

From the *Los Angeles Times,* 3 March, 1946, sec. 3, pp. 1, 3. Reprinted with permission.

title that is surprisingly literal in its significance. It aims to tell just why "life is wonderful," no matter how futile it may seem superficially.

The picture is a very free adaptation of a thought contained in a Christmas book, *The Greatest Gift,* written by Philip Van Doren Stern.

The subject belonged to RKO, and several different adaptations had been written, but nothing on which the company would take a chance.

Capra organized Liberty Films after the war, and affiliated with the studio, and they asked him to look over the possibilities of their purchase. It looked perfectly okay to him, fitting right in with the mood of today.

The picture is about a man who thinks his life has failed miserably and who finally expresses the wish that he had never been born. Some sprite out of another world takes him up on the wish and he then personally views in a kind of dream what would have happened if he had not lived.

It seems that he had forgotten, as many people do, the truly good deeds he had done. For example, he rescued his brother from drowning as a child and that boy's action later in wartime saved several hundred other people. All this might not have happened if he hadn't courageously pulled his brother out of the water in the first place.

Capra has simple methods of reaching a perfectly obvious but elusively splendid destination. He eliminates what he can't tackle.

"I would not know how to make a picture that would illuminate the bigger problems of today," declared this man, who was able by direction to bring something of the scope of a mighty war before the eyes and minds of theatergoers. "I don't think that it is well to approach those problems too directly, in any event.

"There are just two things that are important and one is to strengthen the individual's belief in himself and the other, even more important right now, to combat a modern trend toward atheism which is very much present in the world.

"Improving the individual and bringing a more hopeful outlook on life to him is the only way that you can improve the nation, and ultimately the world. It is the individual that must be built up in his beliefs, his hopes, his aspirations and then as a matter of course will you find the new world we all talk about developing in the larger way.

"The one thing that Americans are against in principle is regimentation. They demand and need the right to think for themselves. I believe that this

is true also of the English and the French, and that they will not be responsive to a system of government that does not give them that freedom.

"Regimentation will not make great headway here nor there as a conse-
quence, but nevertheless people will have to be stirred individually to combat influences that may produce catastrophes far greater in their effect than
those the world has already endured.

"I think first that we must entertain in pictures and then convey our message, whatever it may be, to the individual, but achieve this quite incidentally."

What Capra says probably spells the really big box office that he has
already proved he could command, but neither does it ignore the finer
values.

State of the Union to Pace Election

PHILIP K. SCHEUER/1947

NEXT YEAR WILL BE A presidential year. Tomorrow, producer-director Frank Capra will put before the cameras *State of the Union,* a comedy-drama about a man who almost runs for president. Capra expects to get it before the people in April or May—just ahead of the national conventions. He hopes it will help them—the people and the delegates too—to appreciate the state of the Union in a presidential year.

Capra admits this will be tough, perhaps the toughest job he's ever tackled. True, he has the prestige of the smash stage hit by Howard Lindsay and Russel Crouse, the *Life with Father* playwrights, behind him. He has a cast headed by Spencer Tracy, Claudette Colbert, Angela Lansbury, and Adolphe Menjou, plus all the resources of the MGM studio, before him. And he has already decided he will shoot at a "terrific pitch"—even more terrific than that which wowed 'em in such Capra triumphs as *Mr. Deeds Goes to Town,* an Academy winner; *You Can't Take It with You,* another; *Mr. Smith Goes to Washington, Arsenic and Old Lace,* and *It's a Wonderful Life.*

So far, so good. But, says Capra, the stage is one thing, the screen another. "Everything's easy in the theater; the audience brings a lot to it, including a will to overlook that make-believe proscenium arch. But a play can't be filmed as it is; it simply would not be acceptable.

"I don't know whether that is because the movie audience is more difficult or the medium is so different. Probably a little of both!

"*State of the Union* is a satire on—a burlesque of—the great game of poli-

---

From the *Los Angeles Times,* 28 September 1947, sec. 2, pp. 1–2. Reprinted by permission.

tics. In the theater everybody accepted it good-naturedly as such. It defended the democratic system while kidding it. But today, with democracy and totalitarianism struggling for supremacy, that system is being attacked on all sides.

"That's why ours is going to be a delicate operation. If we make a picture that seems to run down democratic processes, we play into the hands of their detractors. Our job will be to make all the criticisms expressed add up to praise—and as I say, it's going to be tough!

"However, we'll stress the personal angle more than the play did. Our story is about a man finding himself, his soul, against the background of a campaign year. He is Grant Matthews, a self-made man who 'started out with a screw driver, a wrench and two years of high school—and built Matthews Aircraft!'

"He gets into politics quite accidentally. Fed up with the double talk at a manufacturers' convention (this is before the picture opens) he has gotten up and let 'em have it with both barrels. His speech has attracted national attention; so much so that Conover, a politician, sees him as a Republican 'dark horse.' We take it from there.

"Tracy is a natural for the part of Matthews, the best casting we could have made if we'd had the whole field to choose from. He will play a man who sees ideals with one eye and ambition with the other. His wife Claudette wants him to see ideals with both and his friend Angela Lansbury feeds his sense of ambition. That's the crux of our conflict.

"Actually, he never really runs or even announces himself a candidate. When he is ready to throw his hat in the ring, he's out."

The *Times*'s Bill Henry assisted as technical adviser. "What he did was really review the picture before it got on the screen," Capra said, "keeping us straight politically and"—with a chuckle—"helping us avoid pitfalls like condemning newspapers generally instead of specifically."

The dialogue (from a script by Capra and Anthony Veiller) will be as topical as possible under the circumstances, touching on the Taft-Hartley Act, high prices, foreign policy—anything that isn't likely to get dated before 1948. Capra is even toying with the idea of recording extra "wild" sound tracks, up to the minute in content, for quick substitution in key runs—much as Lindsay and Crouse did with lines in the play.

"Our script isn't preachy," Capra grinned, "but it does tend to be speechy. Matthews will make a speaking tour (in montage form) and say something pithy at each of seven or eight spots. How much he'll say will depend on how much audiences will stand for!"

Frank Capra's movies have long reflected his patriotism and humanity. (During the war he became a chief of the Army Pictorial Service, emerging with the rank of colonel and a D.S.C.) At fifty he is as unshaken as ever in his belief that the two, love of country and of his fellow men, are compatible ideals.

"I am an American," he said seriously. "I believe in the American system of government and in free enterprise. For the record, I am and have been a Republican—probably because I'm congenitally against those who are 'in.' I don't believe in too much power for anyone or any group.

"I do believe in putting up a fight for whoever happens to be the underdog at the time. If there is anything 'leftist' in this, it's in what people read into it. I am against the inequalities of this world, but I think that sooner or later they will be resolved under a system like ours, where the people are TOLD, and not under totalitarianism, where they are not.

"And don't ever believe that the attacks on our pictures abroad are due entirely to their lack of quality. Those pictures are also great salesmen for the American system!"

Popular Art: Frank Capra

ARTHUR B. FRIEDMAN/1957

Q: *I understand you were born in Palermo, Sicily, in 1897, and emigrated to this country at the age of six; that you settled in Los Angeles with your mother and father and six older brothers and sisters. I understand that when you first came, you sold newspapers to help support your family?*

FRANK CAPRA: That's right. We all had to get to work very fast, because we were all very poor. I started selling newspapers at the age of six. As a matter of fact, I've been making my own living since the age of six, one way or another.

I graduated from high school rather young, and wasn't able to go to the university of my choice, California Institute of Technology, until the year following my graduation. I had to take some time off to make a little money, but I finally got there all right. I worked while in college. I waited on tables and I had the laundry agency at the dormitory. I also was the editor of the school paper for the last two years. I managed to do all right. I managed to make my way through college without too much effort—in fact, with a lot of fun.

Q: *You received a scholarship and won a letter of recommendation for the National Research Council for work you did on an incendiary bomb?*

CAPRA: That's right. That was for World War I; before we were in the war, I was put to work on a research problem for an incendiary bomb, and I did

From Reminiscences of Frank Capra (August 1960), in the Columbia University Oral History Research Office Collection. Reprinted by permission.

manage to do the research work on it for Dr. Noyes, a famous scientist from MIT who put me on the project. I don't know if it was ever used, but Dr. Noyes was very satisfied with the results of the research we did on it. I was specializing in chemical engineering.

Q: *Why were you interested in this field? And why the change?*
CAPRA: Well, it's very simple. I couldn't get a job. I graduated during wartime and went into the armed services in World War I, and I was in service about thirteen months. Then after being discharged, there weren't many jobs around for chemical engineers. As a matter of fact, I spent about eight years really after that before I had a regular job of any kind.

Q: *What work were you doing at the time you answered the newspaper ad, put in by this man Montague in San Francisco?*
CAPRA: At that time I think I was selling mining stock. I also sold photographs, house to house. I tutored quite a bit. Between selling photographs house to house and selling mining stock and various other jobs, that kept me going for a little while.

This occasion you speak of, with Montague—this was the start of my career in motion pictures. I read an ad in a newspaper—no, it wasn't really an ad, it was an article—saying that they were going to start making motion pictures with some company out near Golden Gate Park. For some reason or other, I thought perhaps it was a chance for me to get a job. So I went out to see the man, and told him I was from Hollywood. That was the magic word, and when I saw his eyes open, I thought: I'd better play this up a little more. I *was* from Hollywood, in a sense, but I was not from the motion picture industry, of course.

I asked him what he was going to do, and he told me a few things he was going to do. He was going to picturize poems from various well-known poets, illustrating them on the screen with pictures. It didn't make much sense to me really, but I needed a job, and I found out very quickly that I knew more about motion pictures than he did—and I didn't know anything. This was about 1923.

The first picture was *Fulta Fisher's Boarding House*, based on a Kipling poem.

I had talked this man into letting me make this picture for him. I don't really know why he fell for it, and I don't know why I got in, but since I was "from Hollywood," he gave me carte blanche—complete confidence. So I had the problem of hiring people, cameramen and actors and so forth, who mustn't find out that I didn't know anything about it, you see. I hired local cameramen, newsreel cameramen, and local actors that I picked up on the street, who had never acted before. It was simply a bar-room scene with a very dramatic incident in it. So the director not knowing anything and the actors not knowing anything, we were even. We were all on the same basis, and we made a picture out of the poem, which played at the Strand Theater along with one of Harold Lloyd's pictures, and got some excellent reviews.

This was my start in motion pictures, and I said to myself: I guess this is my racket.

That picture cost $1700 to make, and the owners got a check for $3500 for it.

Q: *What made you leave this gentleman and return to Los Angeles?*
CAPRA: I didn't make any more films with him, but I did decide to find out something about the film business, and being technically minded, the first thing I wanted to find out was: what was film and what made it valuable in the first place? So I got a job in the laboratory. I worked in the laboratory in San Francisco for about a year, developing and printing films and learning something about editing and about film techniques, as that would be applied to the camera and the laboratory.

Then a motion picture company came up on location, with a director by the name of Bob Eddy, and Dan Mason, who used to star in the Toonerville Trolleys. They worked on location, making a series of comedies, and I got on with them as a prop man. I worked with them for the full series of twelve pictures, and went up from prop man to writer, and to assistant producer with the company. Then when they came back to Los Angeles, I came with them.

Q: *Was Arthur Ripley with them in San Francisco?*
CAPRA: No, he was at Mack Sennett's. My first job when I got back to Hollywood was in *Our Gang* comedies for Hal Roach. I was with them for about six months, and I was writing their material. The way they worked there, the director was Bob McGowan—he was the only one that handled these kids, and he was very jealous of his ability to handle these kids and never wanted anybody on the set with him. So I never saw Bob McGowan work with the

kids—in fact, I very seldom saw Bob McGowan at all. The procedure was that they worked two weeks on a picture, shooting it, and then two more weeks preparing the next one. I saw him during the two weeks he was preparing, but during the shooting I didn't see him very much, if at all.

Now, I had never been assigned an office at Hal Roach. As a matter of fact, I had a hard time convincing [them] that I was working there. There was a gateman there who didn't like me, for some reason or other, and everytime I tried to get into the studio, he'd throw me out. I had a terrible time getting in. And after I did get in, I had no place to go—no office—and I didn't know anybody except this Bob McGowan, and he didn't introduce me to anybody. So I used to wander around the back lot, sitting on lumber piles with a piece of paper and pencil and trying to make up little gags for these kids to do, which I'd hand to Bob McGowan at noon, at lunch. He'd take them from me and stick them in his pocket, and that's all. I never knew what happened to them.

Well, one of these times when I was sitting on a lumber pile, Will Rogers came along and asked me what I was doing. I said, "Well, I'm writing material here."

"Writing material for who?"

I said, "The *Our Gang* comedies."

He said, "You're a writer?"

I said, "I think so."

He said, "Then why aren't you in an office."

"I haven't got an office."

"Got a typewriter?"

"No, I haven't got a typewriter."

"Well," he said, "that's a terrible way to treat a person round here. Tell you what you do—you come into my dressing room. I got a typewriter there, and I don't use it much, and after [I'm] dressed and made up in the morning, you can use it for the rest of the day."

I thought this was just wonderful of Mr. Will Rogers to take pity on me, and I did go into his dressing room and used it as an office. When I'd hear him coming, I'd sneak out, so I wouldn't be too much in his way.

I never did get an office at Hal Roach. My office was Will Roger's dressing room, by courtesy of Will Rogers.

Then I got a job with Mack Sennett as a writer. (I didn't work for Harry Cohn until later.) At Sennett's I guess I must have written thirty or forty of the two-reel comedies. That's where Arthur Ripley was at the time, and that's where I met him.

There was a comedian called Harry Langdon whom Mr. Sennett had discovered, and from the very first picture that Harry Langdon made for Sennett, I was assigned to him as writer, and I wrote all his material. Then, when Harry Langdon became so big—he was an enormous hit—he went out and formed his own company, to make features. And he took me with him as his director. So I made three pictures with Harry Langdon, *The Strong Man, Tramp, Tramp, Tramp,* and *Long Pants.* That was in 1926–27.

From there, I went to Columbia pictures and worked for Mr. Cohn, and after that I guess I worked for Harry Cohn some twelve years. (No, the report that he originally recommended me to Sennett I don't think is true.)

Q: *I understand Mack Sennett had "the Tower" where a number of writers worked together . . .*

CAPRA: You may be interested in how Mr. Sennett handled his writers. You must understand that Mr. Sennett had as his model and hero a section-hand boss for whom he used to work as a water boy. He never had much education. This was a very tough Irishman that he admired, and he patterned his life after this Irishman. When he was making these films (he started out as an actor and then became a producer), at all times he kept this section-hand boss in mind as the archetype that he would like to become.

Now, he was a most peculiar gentleman, with a great deal of creative ability. He didn't like books. He wouldn't let you bring a book into the studio at all. For some reason, he hated people that read books—he didn't trust them. Writers, of course, he associated with books, and writers were a sort of anathema to him, and yet he knew he needed them—and liked them very much, as a matter of fact—except that he was never sure of himself around them. They were too smart.

So he had a tower in the middle of the studio, which was four storeys high—a real tower, with windows on all sides. On the first floor were the studio managers, but the second floor were the studio executives, on the third floor the accountants, and on the very top was a room with windows on four sides—a very large room, maybe 25 × 25—and there he kept the writers, "the prisoners of Edendale," as they called themselves.

Now, in order to get up there, they had to go by every executive, and in order to get out they had to go by every executive, so it was a very difficult thing to do—to go out. He figured we would come at nine o-clock in the morning, go up there, come down at twelve, go up at one, and stay till six, and we kept those hours.

Naturally, sometimes, there'd be ten or fifteen writers in there, all working on various subjects, and all talking with each other, and of course there were moments when people went to sleep a little bit. Mr. Sennett had a habit of coming up that very narrow stairway in his stocking feet, and if he caught you asleep, you were through.

In order to circumvent that, the writers connived with the head carpenter to raise a riser on the stairs about one-half inch—one of the risers which was about halfway up was about a half inch higher than the rest of them. This solved all the problems for the writers, because when Mr. Sennett got to that one, invariably he tripped on the riser, and everybody would wake up and get into a thinking position.

Q: *Harry Langdon is considered a master of pantomime—how much did a writer contribute to that?*

CAPRA: This is one of the truly tragic and untold stories of Hollywood— Harry Langdon. You're right when you say that he was one of the greatest pantomimists that we've ever had—actually one of the funniest men we've ever had. But before he came into pictures, he had a small act in vaudeville— quite small, he was no great hit, but he made a living at it. So when he came to Mack Sennett, and I was assigned to him for his material, to write his material—here I wish somebody else could say this besides me, but you asked me—I say it was the material that made Harry Langdon, because the material had a theme behind it. The characterization that we evolved for Harry Langdon was one in which he had no ally but God. He had no brains, he had only goodness, and only goodness got him out of every situation. He was the naive elf, and as long as he maintained that character, he was very successful.

Now, the tragic part of it is that as long as he used this character—which he didn't have before he went into motion pictures, it was evolved for him and written up for him, and actually he didn't understand it—he was a hit. Then when he became so big, and he began to read all these wonderful things about him[self], I think he began to believe that it was his own art- istry—which no doubt it was—but it was not his own interpretation of his character, not a character that he had evolved himself. So he didn't really know his character, though he could play it.

So, at about the time we finished the third picture, *Long Pants,* he decided that he would produce and direct himself. Now, there are many successful actors who have done this successfully, but there are also many who have not, because it's very difficult for an actor to have an objective viewpoint when he is doing subjective work, like acting. That's right, they sometimes don't understand just exactly what they are doing, and certainly they can't stand off and look at it.

So he began to make some pictures on his own, and he lost this character-ization—this little man whose ally was God. When he lost that, he lost his humor. His downfall was faster than his rise, and his rise had been phenome-nal. So he made I think two or perhaps three more pictures, and then his contract was cancelled. He went down to two-reel films again, and from that to no films, and he died shortly after that—I'm sure his downfall contributed to his early end.

Q: *Charlie Chaplin has claimed he feared no comedian save Langdon.*
CAPRA: I think that's quite true. Every comedian in the motion picture business then—in the motion picture profession—felt Harry Langdon was the great one—including Chaplin. I'm not trying to say that Langdon was as great as Chaplin, but Chaplin had enormous respect for him, and every time we previewed one of Langdon's films, all the comedians—Chaplin, Lloyd, Keaton and many others—all came to watch him, because they thought he was marvelous and they wanted to learn from him. He was a great panto-mimist—you could hold a camera on his face for five minutes, and he would just keep the audience in stitches, doing absolutely nothing.

Q: *I've been told that in the Sennett days, stories, etc. came out of a group effort in the Tower. [Alva] Johnston in the* Saturday Evening Post *said: "Capra finally worked out a definite characterization for Langdon." Were the gags and story ideas a group effort, or not?*
CAPRA: Well, sometimes they were and sometimes they weren't. Generally one or two writers were assigned to one picture—not a group of ten or twelve. One or two, and they would discuss an idea and finally come up with some kind of a basic idea that could be made into a two-reel comedy. Now, this could be written down into one, two, three pages of copy, and that's all. Sometimes it was never written. Then it was told to Mack Sennett. If he liked the idea, you would go on and develop the gags and the scenes for it. After

you had developed enough of these gags and scenes so it looked like a picture could be made out of it, then he would assign the director and the comedians to that story. There was never anything written in the way of a script as we know it today—there was never a formal script written.

Q : *I believe Felix Adler told me [that] when he was at Sennett's as a writer, he'd seen Sennett use Langdon as an elegant character, nasty to people and so on. According to Adler, he had worked in vaudeville earlier with Langdon and had seen Langdon do a more "innocent" act, and told Sennett he thought he had Langdon figured wrong with this "elegant" character, and Langdon should get back to what he had been doing earlier.*
CAPRA : That could very well have happened. I'm not sure whether I was assigned to the very first picture Langdon made or not. I recollect that I was, but he could very well have made one picture before I got with him. However, I don't remember Mack Sennett making him an arrogant or a thinking character—as far as I'm concerned, the character I worked on for Langdon was always a non-thinking, wispy, innocent character.

Q : *You were associated with Langdon in his production of* Tramp, Tramp, Tramp, Long Pants, *and* The Strong Man, *the three films that marked him as a great comedian.*
CAPRA : Yes, I was. That's right. Especially the second one, *The Strong Man.* I did both the writing and the directing on those.

Q : *In 1927, you and Harry Langdon came to the parting of the ways; could you tell us how that happened?*
CAPRA : Very simple: he fired me. Why? Well, because he wanted to get away from this character that we had established for him, and he would not take my advice as a director or as a writer anymore. I could see that the reviews had kind of gone to his head. They called him "the sad comedian." They used to say there was more pathos in his comedy than comedy, which was true; there was a great deal of pathos in his characterization—but the pathos came out of fun. Well, he took this very literally, and he wanted to do sad scenes instead of funny scenes, and we parted on that issue. It was strictly on the issue that I thought the pathos came out of comedy and it should always be funny—then out of his comedy would come the pathos

and he did not agree. I don't think he realized that his pathos came out of his fumbling efforts.

I think perhaps he had a lot of advisers. But when a man gets that big—he rose very fast, and he didn't know how to handle it, he'd never been big before—and so he quickly acquired hangers-on who would want to cash in on him and tell him what to do and be part of his success. Perhaps some of these people did influence him in that direction, but I don't think so. I think it was just plainly that he didn't have the actual capacity to understand his character.

Q: *I take it you don't think Langdon had the depth to do as Chaplin did—conceive the ideas, write the stories, etc.?*
CAPRA: I think he had the creative depth to do it, but he didn't have the intellectual depth that it takes to conceive and direct and produce—and he didn't have the mechanical ability that Chaplin has to produce a motion picture, to think it through. Chaplin is a thinking comedian—he is in effect Jack the Giant Killer, in his character. He is the little shrimp everybody picked on but he got himself out of it by his thinking. Langdon got himself out of situations by his naive approach, his goodness. Chaplin is a very versatile man, and has produced, created, thought up his own character and his own situations—and nobody else could have done it for him. I don't think Langdon is in that class at all. But as a pantomimist, as a man to do bits of business in pantomime, as a straight out-and-out comic, I think Langdon is tops in the world.

Q: *You finished your last film with Langdon in 1927; then you did* For the Love of Mike.
CAPRA: Yes. I got a job in New York—that was done in New York. It was the last of a series of pictures that Robert Kane was making for First National, and he had very little money left. I was hired to direct the picture, and I'll tell you right now, I have yet to be paid for that picture.

As a matter of fact, the actors—Ford Sterling and Claudette Colbert (that was her first picture)—refused to work unless they were paid money for that day's work. So the gentleman who produced *South Pacific*—Leland Hayward—was the business manager for that outfit, and he had to come around every morning and pay these actors their daily stipend or they wouldn't go on to work. Of course, they forgot to pay me, and I never did get paid for that picture. Ben Lyons was on it, with Claudette Colbert, and I must say that was one of the most terrible pictures that was ever made.

Q: *What was the matter with it?*
CAPRA: I dunno—it just stunk.

Following this, I came to work for Harry Cohn. In those days, [Columbia] was a very small one-horse outfit on Gower Street, which was then called Poverty Row. You wouldn't be caught dead there—unless you were hungry. It was a quickie operation. Harry Cohn and his brother.

Q: *Their problem was to make films so quickly they could circumvent the distribution set-up and get their product out to the exhibitors?*
CAPRA: Well, I suppose that was it. I don't know a great deal about the distribution set-up, but they were a very small outfit, and they did have a great deal of difficulty getting into the major theaters. As a matter of fact, they hardly did get into the major theaters. They made pictures for the cheaper houses that changed every day, and they had more pictures to show than the good houses that had one picture a week.

Q: *I believe when you came there, you directed nine films in a year?*
CAPRA: I think that's correct. I'm not sure of that number.

Q: *What was your job in those days?*
CAPRA: Well, my job was actually the same as I'm doing now. I have never worked on a picture in which I didn't produce and direct it, and perhaps even write it. Those pictures—*The Younger Generation, Way of the Strong, Power of the Press,* etc.—I had to conceive them and produce them and direct them.

The first picture I made for Columbia was *That Certain Thing,* with Ralph Graves, and I remember what I got for that picture: it was $1000 for writing and directing it.

Q: *Not long after that, you were making $25,000 a year for a series with Ralph Graves and Jack Holt.*
CAPRA: Capra: Yes. That series began with *Submarine* and *Flight,* a Marine corps aviation picture, and another one called *Dirigible,* which was a lighter-than-air service picture (1931).

Q: *I understand another director, [Irvin] Willat, had started on* Submarine, *Cohn was dissatisfied with him—that's how you got on it?*

CAPRA: Yes. Unfortunately what happens is that a director can't get off on the right foot for the first week or two, and the film he produces in that first week or two doesn't come up to his normal standards, for some reason or other, and the producer loses confidence in him and wants to change directors. That happened at that time, and for me was a very enormous step, because it meant going into a much bigger picture with a larger budget. I was very sorry for Mr. Irvin Willat, because he was a very well-known director, but for some reason or other his material didn't please Mr. Cohn, particularly his first weeks' work. So I was assigned to that picture, and it was quite successful in the end. With that picture, *Submarine,* I made the leap from the quickies to the program pictures.

Q: *I understand you contrived to take the make-up off of Graves and Holt and make them appealing as heroes, even though tough men—an innovation?*

CAPRA: Yes, that's right—and I've done that ever since; wherever it can be done, wherever there are no very distinguishable blemishes to hide, I insist that actors wear no make-up. It was quite an innovation at that time, and the cameramen certainly didn't like it, but I think the end result proves that I wasn't too far wrong on that.

Q: *How would you explain your confidence in your craft at this time, to defy the others in this particular instance, considering you were very young and new to program pictures?*

CAPRA: I don't know that I can explain it—except that I was never endowed with a lack of nerve. If I thought something should be, then I insisted it should be that way, even if I had to stick my neck out. Anyone has to do that, who's a creative person. If you want to play it safe all the time, you're not going to get very far; but if you insist on carrying out your ideas and sticking with them and taking full responsibility for them, then what happens is that if those ideas turn out to be right, you also get the credit for innovations, and you get the full credit. If you stick your neck out and succeed, then you're much better off than if you play it safe. Of course, I've been sticking my neck out all the time. So far I've been lucky, and the ideas that I've had have turned out all right. But you can go a long way on a few successes, because then it means that you are capable of making successes any time you start, even though you don't actually make it this particular time.

Q : *I imagine producers will tolerate experimentation in someone who has successes—not with others.*

CAPRA : Yes—the principal assets we have in our industry (which is the wrong term, it should be a profession actually, from the production side)— the principal assets are individuals. It isn't studios, offices, buildings—it's individuals. It's the creative ability of a few hundred individuals that make motion pictures in Hollywood. The executives, studio producers and so forth—they bank on individuals. They just have to trust themselves to individuals. There's no model to follow, there is no production line—each individual has to make his own picture. The greatest of these assets, of course, in individuals, is enthusiasm. They bank on the ability that a man has to create something, and they have to ride with it, and that's all there is. That's all the assets they have—the creative ability of a few individuals.

Q : *One such individual was Jo Swerling—would you tell the incident about* Ladies of the Evening?

CAPRA : We had bought a property called *Ladies of the Evening,* a script, and I was about to start on it. I have a habit of giving a script to many people to read, to get their reactions. Sometimes I'm afraid of it—sometimes I'm sure in my own mind, but I'd like to get reactions because what they say opens up my own ideas. So we gave this script *Ladies of the Evening* to a group of writers at Columbia, and among the group were six or seven brand new writers that Mr. Cohn had brought out from New York. They'd never worked in pictures before. Among these characters was a short, stubby, aggressive little man called Jo Swerling who smoked White Owl cigars and never sat down, kept walking up and down—he was a newspaperman—and he was called in. He had read the script, and he was called into Mr. Cohn's office in my presence and the presence of others and asked what he thought of it, and he said, "I think it stinks."

Everybody else had been saying they were quite pleased. This man said, "I think this is terrible. Anybody who'd make this is an idiot."

Yes, I'd had a hand in writing the script. So I instantly became attracted to this man, because here was an individualist, and individualists of course are what we need. So I asked him why he thought it wasn't good, and he told us. I asked him "What would you do with it?" and he told me a few things that he would do with it, and I said to Mr. Cohn, "Let's put this man onto writing this film—which we did, and he turned out an excellent script. It was known as *Ladies of Leisure,* in which Barbara Stanwyck starred.

I don't know that I brought anything out in Barbara Stanwyck. She's a wonderful actress to begin with. I just made the most of it. I discovered a little trick, perhaps, that helped bring her natural ability out. Very early I discovered that you could not rehearse with her, because she did her best scenes in rehearsals. The first time she did a scene, it was the best scene you could get out of her—which is not usually the case. Having discovered this, or realized this was the case, I never rehearsed with her. I rehearsed with everybody else in the scene, but I just told her where to be and what to do. The mechanics of the scene I explained to her, but never rehearsed the actual scene with her, and only had her do the scene when the camera was actually playing on her, because I knew that would be the best scene she'd play. That, in a sense, brought out some of her best abilities, but I didn't teach her anything.

Q: *Have subsequent directors of Miss Stanwyck worked similarly?*
CAPRA: I don't know. I don't know that I ever mentioned it to anybody else. I made about four pictures with Barbara Stanwyck, and I found this worked consistently so I used it, and I'm not sure that anybody else has ever used it. If they have, I'm sure she probably would have told them about it.

Q: *You felt she lost basic spontaneity by continuing rehearsals?*
CAPRA: Something happened to her when she had to repeat a scene. This was inexperience, mostly. I think now she's so experienced that she can do a scene many times and do it equally well each time, but those were her early days when she didn't know what a camera looked like, and in rehearsal she put everything into it—and she didn't have much left for the actual scene.

Rain or Shine, made about this time, was a musical comedy that starred Joe Cook—it was a stage musical and we put on a movie version of it. I guess you could call it a musical, yes.

The Miracle Woman, 1931, with Barbara Stanwyck, followed.

Q: *Then you directed in 1931 also* Platinum Blonde, *with the lady known by that title, and it was one of the first in which Loretta Young appeared.*

CAPRA: One of the first, and a man who would undoubtedly have become a big star, Bobbie Williams, but he died shortly after the picture from a ruptured appendix—he really would have become a remarkable light comedian. *Platinum Blonde* was Jean Harlow's second—she'd done *Hell's Angels* before that. Jean Harlow was a wonderful person to work with. Yes, she's become a legend.

I supposed she had what Marilyn Monroe has—if you know what Monroe has, you know what Jean Harlow had. It's an indefinable quality of sex, attractive appearance—she was badly cast in that picture. She didn't know what a society girl was like, which is what she played in it. She was a very wonderful person—she wanted to learn all the time. I remember trying to tell her to go home—she'd never go home when her scenes were finished, she'd always stick around the set, sit around, watch the others, trying to learn how to become an actress. I never directed her in any other picture.

Q: *Apparently in the years to this point, you had learned a great deal as a director that would later serve you well. How would you summarize your career to this point, in terms of what you were learning of your craft?*
CAPRA: Well, as I told you before, I was searching around for something to do, and I had an awful lot of stuff stored in me—never having had a real job—and finally, finding something that I could really do, I just went to work at it. I knew, from the first time I made a picture, that this was to be my career, really, and I knew I could be good at it. I had enormous confidence. There was nothing that I wouldn't tackle. I would say that most of it was due to just plain hard work and confidence. I was sure I could do anything, and I wouldn't turn down anything. No matter how hard it was, I would tackle it.

Q: *You didn't move along one groove—you did all kinds of things . . .*
CAPRA: I'm glad to hear you say it, of course. Everybody is glad to hear he isn't in a rut. But perhaps it's the fact that I like to pioneer things. I like challenges. That might explain at least part of it.

Q: *Do you think there's any correlation between your early interest in chemical research (curiosity, etc.) and your sense of experimentation in film techniques and directing?*
CAPRA: I would think so, definitely—because having had a technical training, a scientific training in the disciplines of science, I had studied and had

an organized mind. Perhaps my mind was a little more organized than the minds of others in my position. For instance, when sound came in, it threw an awful lot of people, but it didn't throw me at all. I immediately used it, took it, understood it. A great many practitioners of our craft aren't mechanical, and aren't in a sense physical. Those physical things I probably would understand a great deal better than some of my brother directors, and I was not afraid to use them.

I would say definitely that my early training in science, and the disciplined mind in facing problems objectively, helped me a great deal.

Q: *Following the Jean Harlow film, you made a controversial film called* American Madness *in 1932 that didn't do very well at the box-office and had adamant and mixed critical comment. I think Walter Huston was one of the stars.*
CAPRA: Yes—Walter Huston, Pat O'Brien, and Miss Cummings. This was a Depression story, during the bank run, showing a banker who believed in people rather than in the money he had in the vault. I know this was a little controversial, because it was about a headline newspaper story—it was topical at the time—and showed a bank run, and perhaps many people thought that you shouldn't show bank runs, because it might be catching. But nevertheless, I think it was one of the best pictures I made. It had a lot of speed. It was one of the first pictures on the rough speedy side, where everything was just slam-bang, slam-bang. It came off, in a sense, because of that technique of speed and that tempo.

Q: *Was this basically a comic technique, developed with Langdon?*
CAPRA: No. Of course, timing is the same in everything. You have to have timing in comedy, in drama, in slam-bang or anything else. Timing is something that I don't know how to explain. It's something you either have or you haven't got. It's when to do the right thing at the right time. Directors have it, actors have it, great generals have it—it's there, from someplace, and I don't know as I can explain it. This means pacing the whole film, too, and pacing it at such a speed—a speed beyond the normal—so that it achieves another quality that (in the case of *American Madness*) did attract attention at that time.

I feel it was one of my better films because I tried something, and it came off, and any time that happens, you like it, you see. You like your own children when they're nice and healthy.

Q: *You followed this with another film that was controversial, in terms of what it achieved—an experiment—in* The Bitter Tea of General Yen.

CAPRA: Yes. *The Bitter Tea of General Yen* was an attempt to tell a love story between a Chinese warlord and a frustrated American missionary. I don't have to tell you, the ingredients are already there for trouble, because you have the racial question, you have the religious question—you have those cards stacked against you, race and religion—and to try to tell that kind of love story, I think I just flew over my head on that. I thought I did pretty well, but I'm not sure but what those two problems aren't insurmountable, no matter what I could do with the picture. It came off, in my mind, as an artistic triumph, but it was certainly not a public success.

Q: *In terms of the public, it might have been ahead of its time. Would such a story have a better reception now?*

CAPRA: I think it would, because I think the audience has been more conditioned—the world is getting smaller, thanks in great measure to our films that play all over the world. I think *The Bitter Tea of General Yen,* if it were shown today to the public, would be more acceptable than it was at the time—as a theme, and as a picture.

I didn't write *The Bitter Tea of General Yen.* It was a book originally, and I did not write the script for that. A writer by the name of Jules Furthman wrote that script.[1]

Q: *Did you feel he was over his head?*

CAPRA: No—if anybody was over his head, it was me, because even though somebody else writes it, he pretty well writes it to suit me or I wouldn't make the picture.

Q: *How did you find a working formula, to get along with a writer assigned to your films?*

CAPRA: We generally got along very well. It's a matter of confidence in each other and of recognizing each other's ability and not stepping on each other's creative toes. Teams have been very successful in Hollywood. There's something chemical about a team—they think alike, they react alike—and

---

1. The writer of record on *The Bitter Tea of General Yen* was Edward Paramore. Capra worked with Furthman on *Soviet,* an aborted MGM production. L.P.

when two such people work together and understand each other, they get along very well. Teams have been very successful in Hollywood—director-writer teams, or two writers in a team. I don't know what it is—perhaps one acts as a sounding-board for the other, and vice versa; they act as audiences for each other.

Q: *Do you, as a director, dominate the script?*

CAPRA: Yes, I always have. In a sense, when a script is completed, whether I write it or somebody else writes it, it's mine, in the sense that I have to absorb it and like it in order to interpret it on the screen. Even though somebody else wrote it, it becomes yours before you're through with it. The director has to be responsible for everything that goes on the screen, if he's also the producer, and in this case I am the producer and the director so I have to be responsible for that script, no matter who wrote it.

Q: *Your team with Robert Riskin has always had happy results—as in* Lady for a Day, *based on a Runyon story. How did you and Riskin first get together?*

CAPRA: I think he worked on *American Madness*. I don't remember whether he wrote the whole script or just a part of it, but I think that was the first time we got together.

Riskin is a superlative dialogue writer. He writes scenes beautifully, and he has a great ear for what people should say and do under certain circumstances. The way we worked with Bob Riskin was that in most cases—not all of them, but the majority of cases—I would lay out the scenes, and he would write the scenes in dialogue form, and he was absolutely superb in dialogue.

I think his coming onto *Lady for a Day* came about through his work on *American Madness*. I don't recall the details, but I'm sure we instantly clicked the moment we talked and worked together. I'd only known him a bit here at the studio before that. I think he came out just a short time before—I believe at the same time Jo Swerling did.

Lady for a Day was a sentimental sort of film. This was followed in 1934 by *It Happened One Night*—the Oscar, the Academy Award.

Q: *This is usually credited as being the first of the "zany" comedies—how does that word strike you?*

CAPRA: It strikes me all right.

Q : *I'd heard that Gable, as a tough-guy hero, was on his way down, and that this showed him for the first time as a light comedian.*

CAPRA: That was the case, of course, but it wasn't premeditated. The genesis of *It Happened One Night* is just another strange Hollywood story that is very difficult to believe.

No one in the studio seemed to like the script. We had very great difficulty casting it. I'll tell you right now that the starring female role was offered to five or six of the best known actresses and they all turned it down cold. First, we had Robert Montgomery in mind, because there was a deal whereby Columbia had borrowed Robert Montgomery from Metro. Robert Montgomery read this script and he found something else to do immediately. Nobody liked this script.

Gable at the time had some difficulties with Metro, and in order to discipline him and make him become a good boy again—I think he wanted more money or something—they offered Mr. Cohn Clark Gable for this part. Well, it was all right with me, but I'd never seen Mr. Gable do any comedy—but still I thought, "Well, if we can't get Robert Montgomery we'll use Gable." I think we were a little disappointed, though, because we knew Montgomery could do comedy.

Well, Mr. Gable—he was being sold down the river, he was being sent to Siberia, to the salt mines—to come to Poverty Row for a film, from the great big MGM. I remember he came into my office for the first time, and I think he'd had a couple of drinks. He had his hat down over his eyes and he was in no mood to talk. I asked him, "Mr. Gable, shall I tell you the script or do you want to read the script?"

He said, "I don't give a damn what you do with the script!"

I thought, well, this is going to be fine! So I gave him the script and said, "Here, you read this," and he put the script under his arm and walked out. He was in a mean mood. He wasn't happy. But he hadn't even read it then, and he read it, and he re-read it, and he got happier, I guess, as he read the script. Because when we started shooting the picture, after the first couple of days, he realized the fun of the picture, and he joined in with it, and his spirit absolutely dominated that film.

With Claudette Colbert, it was slightly different. We got her at a time when she was on vacation, and by doubling her salary we got her to play the part. She didn't particularly want to read it or know anything about it, and she didn't like the picture when she'd finished. I think the poor girl had a vacation coming and somehow we'd taken up all of her time, and I think she was very surprised when she won the Academy Award for it. But Gable I think understood the show right from the very beginning, when he got into it. I don't know of anybody in the world who could have done it better than Gable. We were just fortunate. The old man with the whiskers had his hand on us with that picture, that's all.

Q : It Happened One Night *seemed to be filled with this improvised directorial hand—would you comment on that?*
C A P R A : Well, sometimes things look improvised—and sometimes they are improvised—but I'll tell you, in most cases they're pretty well thought out. I don't know what you're referring to—there were many scenes, like the piggy-back scene—well, that was in the script. That we thought out before. The hitch-hiking scene—I think that was thought out on the set—where she raised her skirt and stopped the car—which became almost a national ride-catching gesture—an institution, afterwards.

This is going to be a very poor explanation of what you call directorial improvisation, which you say is my hallmark—a poor explanation, if there is any explanation—but being a producer of the film as well as director, and in many cases the writer, the script—to me—is fluid. I don't take it as gospel or as Bible, and I don't stick to it word for word, scene for scene. I take advantage of the characters—if I find that an actor goes a certain way, I go with him. If I find that a situation can go on longer than it is in the script, I take advantage of that and develop it and develop it. This comes from early comedy training, where we had no script, and where we just got a couple of people together and developed scenes, as long as we could think of various things to do. I really think that's just early comedy training.

Q : *Of course,* It Happened One Night *put everybody associated with it on top. Then you came out with another hit in 1934, with Warner Baxter,* Broadway Bill. *Many people have observed here a pattern in your casting technique—that the people cast were true to type.*
C A P R A : I suppose that comes from *Fulta Fisher's Boarding House,* where I was afraid to use actors. I believe that actors, if they're given a little aid and a little leeway, get along much better than they are normally supposed to. The trick is to get that best scene from that actor at the right time, so that it can go onto the screen, even if it's just twenty seconds—but that twenty

seconds that that actor works must be his top. Now, if you can skim the top from that actor's performance, and you have him give the top performance on every scene, and never let him down below his top that he's able to give, you'll get a fine performance. If his scenes go up and down, from top to medium to below standard (for his capability), you have an uneven perform-ance. The trick of a director is to get only the peaks.

Q : *What is your relationship to top performers, who perhaps have confidence in their own ways—how do you manipulate them to get these peaks from them?*
CAPRA : Well, first of all, you must get their complete confidence. They must absolutely believe in you. And they must know that you like them; they must know that you love them; they must know that any mistakes they make, it's perfectly all right. There must be an understanding between the actor and the director that is open—everybody's hair is down—so that there's no fear, unnecessary distrust or mistrust, on either side. And when that happens, when an actor is completely free and frank and completely free of any fetters of any kind, personality-wise—no personality fences between the actor and the director—many wonderful things happen. The director is an audience. He is the actor's only audience, in motion pictures.

At this point, I'd say that most of the films I'd worked on up to this time were comedies—were for entertainment purposes—and that entertainment was the major aim in every one of the films I'd worked [on] up to this time. Later on, something else crept in. Yes, that began with *Mr. Deeds Goes to Town*, 1936.

Q : *For which you got another Oscar. What was the change that happened here?*
CAPRA : Well, the change that happened—I don't know if it was deliberate, I can't point to any single day when it happened—was this. Having achieved a certain amount of success in this medium, I began to ask myself: why shouldn't I say something, as well as entertain? Many a person has broken himself upon this rock—when you try to bring messages into motion pic-tures, you are then tampering with something that you may not be able to handle. I don't know that my message was a very open and deliberate one, or a very obvious one, but I began to think in my own mind, philosophically, that perhaps I could use this ability to create and ability to produce motion pictures for something that would transcend entertainment a little bit.

Now, having always been a positive person in my philosophy, I began to think in terms of the triumph of the individual. I don't know what brought that on. Probably Hitler brought that on, I don't know. But I began to react against these totalitarian institutions, against the one man dominating individuals, shooting people in large numbers, and I suppose subconsciously I began to put up the fight for man as an individual, and the triumph of the human spirit over obstacles.

I certainly did have a hand in the writing and conceiving of *Mr. Deeds. Mr. Deeds Goes to Town* started, of course, as a book written by a very well known man, high up in Republican circles; it was a book about a young man who had inherited a great deal of money, including an opera house in New York, and the story of his troubles and tribulations with this opera house when he went to run it, being as he was a small town individual.

We threw all that part away. We just took the part where a small town man inherited twenty million dollars, and he was a very happy man, didn't want the money, didn't know what to do with it—the trials and tribulations of a man who inherits a great deal of money. That's the genesis of that story. From there on, it was all invention.

Q: *What do you suppose made this film the box-office attraction that it was?*
CAPRA: Yes, it's done well in every country in the world. I suppose it is basically the triumph of the individual human spirit over every kind of obstacle, be it money, be it larceny, be it whatever you want. I just think it's the story of the individual—the triumph of the individual, as against the tragedy of the individual.

Q: *This has been called "the fantasy of good will," and you're given credit as its prime promulgator. Also, Alistair Cooke said: "Capra is a great talent all right, but I have the uneasy feeling he's on his way out. He's starting to make movies about themes instead of people—Mr. Deeds is tremendous because the idea is taken charge of wholly by one person and one glorious part, Mr. Deeds himself." He says you emphasize theme—you say you were motivated by your interest in promoting the idea that the individual counted.*
CAPRA: I think he's quite right when he says you may be on your way out when you handle themes instead of people—you really can break yourself upon that rock, when you start with "messages."

However, I had a pretty good message to tell, and if I could tell it with entertainment, and if I could do it with humor and warmth and comedy, I thought myself on pretty safe ground. I think the results show I was on safe ground.

Q: *You had a diversion from this kind of film—emphasizing respect for the dignity of the individual, as in* Mr. Smith Goes to Washington—*also with* Lost Horizon, *in 1937.*
CAPRA: Well, diversion in method, perhaps, but not in substance. I would say that *Lost Horizon* was an extrapolation of that same theme. I think the theme—subject—is basically consistent with the theme of *Mr. Deeds.*

Q: *While the opening scene was magnificent, some critics felt that when you dealt with the utopia, there was a loss in what they'd come to expect, in terms of "Capra style." Were you aware of that?*
CAPRA: Yes. I was aware of it, and I was a little disappointed in *Lost Horizon* myself. It was my idea entirely to do it, but I was disappointed in the way it came out, because I'd hoped for more. Although it's been said that it's one of my best pictures (and perhaps I'd have to agree with them), I thought that the main part of the film—I should have done better, somehow. I got lost in architecture, in utopia, in the never-never-land, and it was only toward the end of the picture that I got back on track with human beings and individuals, where I began to feel that the story dealt with human beings again. This is common, for one who wants to exploit a theme, and gives the theme too much of a part in the story.

In this case, I myself was disappointed in the film itself. I thought it should have been better than it was. I wavered several times. I shot several endings, before I decided exactly how to end it.

One very dramatic thing happened in that. We were making tests for the High Lama in *Lost Horizon,* and I really wanted someone who looked very, very old and wouldn't have to be made up too much (with my fetish against make-up), so in looking around, we did find a very old-time actor who lived somewhere in the San Gabriel Valley, who was around eighty years old and a very well known actor. We did take a test of this man, and he was absolutely superb. We thought we'd found the man. But this was the first part this man had had offered to him in some twenty years, and being an actor, he came and he did the scene, he had an agent and everything else, he had all the trappings of an actor—except that he'd never expected to act again, and this was such a shock when he got the part that something in him broke, and he died the next day.

If there's an actor's heaven, I suppose he died happily. He died trying out for a role.

Q: *You followed this film in 1938 with another smash hit,* You Can't Take It with You. *Some critics claim in this sentimentality took over; Otis Ferguson in the* New Republic *wrote: "Capra has not yet returned from Tibet." He thought* You Can't Take It with You *was " . . . simply Shangri-La in a frame house."*

CAPRA: Well, I think "Shangri-La in a frame house" is a very good objective for a film. I don't see anything wrong with that. He was praising the film, as far as I'm concerned.

Q: *In* Mr. Deeds, Mr. Smith Goes to Washington, It's a Wonderful Life, *et al.—these protagonists seem to exemplify the "little man" theme, the premise on which Langdon blossomed.*

CAPRA: That could be quite true—as to these characters being somewhat the same, or prototypes of something else, reminiscent of Langdon—perhaps the critics are right on that. As I mentioned, I've always been interested in the triumph of the individual, in his ability to survive, in his ability to evolve towards a goal of some kind—some people call it God. That's been my primary interest in developing characters and making stories about an individual who's surrounded by difficulties and triumphs over them, due to his moral character and his personality. In that respect, I think those criticisms were right: these characters were types of the same individual.

Q: *Do you think this advanced your career, in that it stamped the work as a "Capra film"?*

CAPRA: Well, it didn't hurt my career, because after all careers are based on making successful movies, and these were all quite successful. They were well liked by audiences all over the world, not just by Americans. One thing I was surprised to find was this: I thought this sort of picture would not be understood elsewhere, as they were so American in type and character. I was greatly surprised to find they were very well understood in foreign lands, and very well liked, well received all over the world. So whatever these characters were, they struck a common chord universally, in the hearts of the audiences. I would say that's some kind of success.

Q : Meet John Doe *in 1941 seemed to be one of the most controversial, particularly in its ending. What were some of the problems?*

CAPRA: Well, the ending of that film was a problem. We tried several endings. I don't think we were ever satisfied with any, but we finally chose the one we were least dissatisfied with. There is probably something wrong with the film somewhere in the middle, or the ending wouldn't have been as difficult, for it was very difficult really to put an end on that thing and a Q.E.D. on the story. In general, I think if you can't end something satisfactorily, then perhaps the construction somewhere in the story is wrong. The motives have gotten tangled up and you don't really know what you're coming out with at the end, and you don't know how to finish it: so perhaps there's something wrong with the story basically. Riskin wrote this one. This film was made and produced and owned by Bob Riskin and myself. We made it as an independent film. We made it with our own money and with borrowed capital. Strangely enough, from our own financial standpoint it was the most successful film we ever made, although it was not nearly the box-office success that many of the other films were. This was because of our personal tie-up with the financing. It just shows you how remunerative these films were, if you own a film and it isn't too much of a hit yet it still makes a lot of money. I don't know what moral you can draw from that.

Q : *This was on the eve of the war. Then you went into service and became associated with the brilliant* Why We Fight *series in 1942. How was that series conceived, and how did you become connected with it?*

CAPRA: The series was conceived in the mind of General George Marshall, then chief of staff. I had volunteered my services one year before Pearl Harbor, because I thought something might be coming up, and if I could be of any use, I'd volunteer my services. I was making a picture called *Arsenic and Old Lace*, just about to finish it, on December 7th. On December 8th I got my orders to report. I asked for a short stay to finish the picture, which I was allowed—four weeks—and then I reported to Washington. I didn't know what my duties would be, or why I was wanted exactly, but after a very short time in Washington I found out.

I was sent for by General Marshall, then chief of staff, and he outlined for me what he would like me to do. He wanted a series of films made which would show the man in uniform why he was fighting, the objectives and the aims of why America had gone into the war, the nature and type of our enemies, and in general what were the reasons and causes of this war and why were 11 million men in uniform and why must they win this at all costs.

I was thrilled by this assignment—it was quite a challenge—even though I didn't know how exactly I'd bring it about, but I instantly saw what he wanted. He wanted an orientation type of film, a series of films which would be a part of the mental training of our soldiers as to just what they were doing in uniform, and why they were called away from their jobs and told to carry a gun, and why they must win this war.

It was quite a challenge, and I was very happy with the assignment. Now I had to get together a group of individuals, crews and film. I was allowed to recruit Hollywood personnel. I thought: this is a type of film that I've never been associated with. Very few people in Hollywood had made so-called documentary films, or historical films, or films that were based on fact. They'd had very little experience with it. Yet I thought perhaps I should go only for professional filmmakers, because I couldn't see where an information film would be too different from the telling of a story. We were telling history, instead of telling a story, and we'd like to do it dramatically.

So I recruited probably seventy-five to 100 top filmmakers in Hollywood, and got them into uniform—although we did use quite a few civilians for part-time jobs and selected jobs. Then we began to accumulate the enemy films and news reels and American films and so forth, and we told the story—an historical story—from the invasion of Manchuria in 1931 to the bombing of Pearl Harbor, about ten years. We tried to tell in detail, with motion pictures, the history of those ten years, and what brought about our entry into World War II.

That series was called the *Why We Fight* series, and it was a series of seven films. It took seven films to tell the story of those ten years.

Then we made another series of films called *Know Your Enemy,* in which we took the Japanese and told their history, from as early as we could find it, using their own film for the purpose—same thing with Germany and Italy. Then we initiated another series called *Know Your Ally,* in which we told them about the British, the French, the Australians, the Canadians, the rest of our allies.

These were the films that were made between 1942 and 1945.

We had full power over selection and editing, because there was no precedent for this. General Marshall just put it in my hands to get it done.

Q: *You took a personal hand in many of these operations?*

CAPRA: I took a personal hand in all the operations—conceiving, the writing, the editing, the cutting, to the final completion of the films. The difficult part of it was that in most cases we had to know the policy—what was the policy of these nations in these times, what was our policy during this particular period of ten years—and that was difficult to obtain. We went through all the State Department sources, all the sources we could go to, and we didn't get a clear explanation at any time of exactly what our policy was, probably because we didn't know. Policy was being made as events took place, and events went faster than our policymaking. So in a great many of those cases, we had to make up our own policy and actually that's what we did: we made up the policy of the United States and had it approved. These pictures were approved by the State Department, by the O.W.I. [Office of War Information], by the President of the United States, General Marshall, the Secretaries of War and State—but they were approved after the policy was made, and in very few instances was anything changed in these pictures. That was one of our hardest things, to try to foretell or recreate what our policy was at various instances during these ten years of fluid historical events.

They had never had to crystallize it, you see—never had to put it into a few words, as you must do for a film. Since these films were going to soldiers, and since what they were seeing they would have to believe and accept as the absolute truth—and it should be the absolute truth of the events that had occurred—we were in many cases forced to outline and state a policy which probably was never stated before, only because we had to crystallize it in our minds, in doing it.

Q: *In terms of testing them for their purpose, did you ever preview any of them for soldiers?*

CAPRA: No, not exactly preview. There was an evaluation made of these films by the research department of the Army as to exactly what their effect was on the thinking of the soldiers. I know of one instance in which they took the film *The Battle of Britain*, which showed the time when Britain was being bombed and undergoing its worst year, and they took it to an island in the Caribbean where there were soldiers stationed who would be stationed there for at least a year, and they questioned these soldiers, through a questionnaire, through trick questions, to find out their attitude on Britain, before the film was shown. Then they showed the film to half of the soldiers, and then went back six weeks later and re-questioned the soldiers, including those that had seen the film and those who had not, to see if attitudes on Britain had changed. They found a marked change in attitude among the soldiers that had seen the film. So this in a way showed that the messages of the films were getting across, and I must say that as far as we know, soldiers liked to see these films. They liked them very very much; because they were presented in dramatic form by professional moviemakers.

I might tell you a little incident about Mr. Churchill. He was a great fan of these films, thought they were just tremendous. I was in London on an assignment once, and I was surprised with a call that came to me: "The Prime Minister wants to see you," the P.M., as they called him. Mr. Churchill being, in my opinion, probably the greatest man of our time, this was quite an exciting event to me, so I went to see him. He said, "Have you got some photographic equipment here?"

I said, "I can get some, Sir."

He said, "I'd like to make a little foreword to this series of film, and I'd like then to insist that they be shown in public theaters in Great Britain."

I said, "This is wonderful. When can we do it?"

He said, "Any time."

I said, "Well, I can be here tomorrow morning."

So we made an arrangement that if I could get the equipment there the next morning at 10 Downing St., he would be ready. That night I got some of my British friends and British movie people, borrowed equipment from them, took it to 10 Downing St. through the back, through the windows and so forth, and I was ready for the Prime Minister at ten o'clock in the morning. I photographed him giving a foreword to these films, about a four minute speech in which he lauded them and called them "the best statement of our cause" that he'd ever seen or heard.

Then these *Why We Fight* films were released to the British public in their theaters, with his foreword on it, and parenthetically I might say that he gave me a British medal called the Order of the British Empire. That's how much he liked the films as a statement of our cause.

I had the Legion of Merit about 1943, and the Distinguished Service Medal was given to me by General Marshall himself. I'm very, very proud of that.

Q: *How do you feel about what you've done, to this date, in the motion picture industry? Do you feel you've reached some of the goals you were reaching for?*

CAPRA: That's quite an ambitious question. I'm afraid my answer won't be nearly as ambitious as the question.

Personally, I don't know as I have any tremendous goals, or ever have had any. It's just on a day-to-day basis. It's a long story, from those early days to now, but I think it was made possible because of our great country, America—those things are possible in America.

Q: *Why do you suppose General Marshall called on you?*
CAPRA: Well, I wish you'd ask General Marshall that one! I suppose first of all they called on me because I had volunteered, and secondly, I was known as a person who made pictures on his own, and didn't need an organization and was a sort of independent producer, a producer and director in control of all of the elements of the picture he was making. In other words, I was more or less a self-contained studio within myself, or was at least able to function as such. Other than that, I don't know why he called on me.

Q: *I was wondering whether you felt that the theme of the dignity of the individual man had become so associated with Capra that this might be some reason why they thought you'd have a feeling for this assignment?*
CAPRA: It might be. It could very well be. But I think during wartime everybody was thinking a little more realistically, rather than idealistically. I think they just wanted a man who could play it by ear in a rough and tumble way and make good at it. They perhaps thought back to my early days when I was making my way around without too much, and maybe that had something to do with it. Anyhow, they were looking for individuals who would take charge and produce results.

Q: *After that,* It's a Wonderful Life *and* State of the Union; *and in 1949, a remake of* Broadway Bill *as a musical, called* Riding High *with Bing Crosby. Why did you do the remake?*
CAPRA: That's a good question—it would take a long time to answer, because there's no actual motivation behind it. It was an economic situation. Along about that time, the studios began their first panicky withdrawal from expensive films. Everybody was cutting down; as the box-office was losing ground some of the executives thought that the way to meet that would be to cut down on the cost of pictures. I've always been violently against that

theory. My theory has always been that if you make something good they'll come to see it, no matter what happens.

But at that time—this was at Paramount Studio—I was under contract, and I had to finish two more pictures for them, and nothing that I could suggest seemed to please them, because they all meant money. So in order to finish out this contract and get free again and on my own, I took what I thought were two pretty good subjects that wouldn't cost too much money, and made them as fast as I could, in order to free myself from that contract. So the reasons for making *Riding High* and the next one, *Here Comes the Groom,* were purely economic.

Q : *Just released over TV are some documentaries you made for Bell Telephone Co. Did you get a thrill from making these, as with the war series?*
CAPRA: I got a great thrill out of making them. This was suggested to me in 1951. I had decided to take about a year's vacation, since I'd never really actually had a vacation. At this time, I was called by the president of AT&T and was told that he had an idea for television, based on science—a science show of some kind. Science films and science shows had been done many, many times, but never with quite the results that were expected of them. Mr. Craig, then president of AT&T, had the notion that, perhaps if professional people were involved and there was some money spent and some experimentation in the subject, perhaps the science film and science could be made interesting to the public.

I agreed with him completely. So, as part of my vacation, I decided that I would try one for him, on an experimental basis, and made the picture called *Our Mr. Sun,* which is a combination of science and entertainment, and aimed at broad television audiences. In other words, you don't have to bring too much knowledge of the subject to the show to understand it.

They liked it very much, and asked me if I would do a couple more experimental films for them, and I want to tell you these films are all handmade. I never had more than four people at a time working on these films. They were all written, directed and produced by me personally, conceived and done that way, sort of handmade.

So we made these four—one on the sun, one on blood, one on cosmic rays, one on the weather. They are more or less just pilot films, really. Now the Bell Telephone people want a series made, on a regular fixed time and cost schedule, and of course that was beyond me, because I'm not a man for fixed costs and fixed schedules, so my experimentation work and pioneering work ended there. Now Warner Bros. is going on with the series, on a fixed cost basis.

Q : *How do you feel about the inroads of TV and the future of the motion picture industry, in view of what you said, that if the picture is good enough the audience will come?*

CAPRA: Well, I think that still holds. I'm not as pessimistic as a great many in Hollywood are, particularly the executives, and those financially inter- ested in theaters and studios. I must say they face a very difficult problem, as to exactly what to do and what to make. It seems that if you make a picture that people *must* see, it grosses a great deal of money—people just flock to see it. But if you make pictures that [aren't *must* see pictures, people won't go to them], because they get as much entertainment at home or elsewhere as they do in the theater. Consequently not only the poor pictures and the mediocre pictures, but the good pictures also are suffering. Only the very best and the great pictures are succeeding. Well, it would follow that one should only make great pictures, and then the problem would be over. But making great pictures is not done by just wishing it, or done over a desk. I don't know of anybody that ever makes any kind of a picture that doesn't hope it's great and doesn't try to make it as good as he can.

So the problem is now: how do we make nothing but great pictures in Hollywood? There's no solution to that, except that if pictures are made with more time, more money, choice of subjects that are not available on televi- sion, perhaps they may have a chance. But there is no clean-cut formula for Hollywood at the moment, except that it has to compete with television and other forms of entertainment for the entertainment time of people. This is just going to shake out an awful lot of people from our business, and picture studios probably will close up. Perhaps there are too many studios, perhaps too many pictures being made. However, that slack in work in Hollywood has been taken up by films for TV, and there seems to be no lack of employ- ment for the working type of actor and the working type of director and the working type of technician.

Where it probably hits the hardest is in the executive end, and in the vast financial structures that have been built up in theatrical holdings and in motion picture distribution company holdings. They're the ones that will suffer.

From a working man's standpoint—a Hollywood working man's standpoint—the picture is not black at all.

As to releasing films to TV for what some people think is too small a price—I don't know about that. That's an economic question and I can't comment on that.

You asked me a while ago, had I achieved my goals, and I think my answer was that I had no goals. I don't think that is quite true; it's just that I don't particularly like people who go around claiming they have goals and aiming at them.

My change in my career happened before I made *Lost Horizon.* I think I'd made *Mr. Deeds Goes to Town,* and had gotten a couple of Academy Awards. And, as often happens to creative people in this business, they get frightened about making any more pictures. It happens to everybody. You make two or three hits, and then you're just so scared that you can't go on making hits that you don't want to make anything any more.

Some people go on a bat, some people just retire, some people don't make any more, some people go to Europe. My defense against the feeling that I was scared about making another picture for fear it would not come up to the standards of the ones preceding was that I got sick. I think my sickness was really just an attempt to get away from going to work. I was sick for weeks and weeks and weeks, and nobody knew what was wrong with me, except that I didn't want any visitors, I didn't want to talk to anybody, I just wanted to be sick.

Well, a friend of mine—one of the few friends that I let in to talk to me at all—brought somebody with him and he said, "Look, come out here and see this man."

I said, "Who is he?"

"Now, don't ask any questions, I just want you to come out and see this man."

"Well I'm sick, I can't get out of bed."

He said, "You can get out of bed. Just come on in the next room, he's sitting right here."

"Who is he?"

"Never mind. Just come out and talk with him."

So he intrigued me as to who was this person he'd brought, so that I put on a bathrobe and—barely able to walk—went into the next room, and there was a little man about five feet high, with glasses, very unprepossessing kind of a man. I was introduced to him. I forget his name. He said to me, "Mr. Capra, you're a coward."

Just like that: I said, "Well, so. I am?"

He said, "Yes. Yes, you're quite a coward, quite a coward."

I said, "In which way am I a coward?"

He said, "Well, I just heard your radio, and you're listening to Hitler."

I said, "That's right."

"You understand him?"

I said, "No."

He said, "Well, Mr. Hitler has the advantage of talking over the radio to probably twenty million Germans, maybe to the rest of the world. He yells and rants—not over thirty minutes because nobody can stand him over thirty minutes—and he is producing results in the world. He's getting his ideas across, he's promulgating whatever he thinks he's after, and he's influencing people."

He said, "You, Mr. Capra, have much more ability to influence people than Mr. Hitler has. You can speak to them through your pictures for two hours, and in the dark, and you can speak to not twenty million people, but, perhaps 200 million people. And you're not doing it. Therefore I say you're a coward."

He said, "I say you're a coward in another respect. I think you're offending God."

"How come am I offending God?"

He said, "God gave you these gifts that you have, this ability to make motion pictures. Not you—you didn't acquire it—it was given to you. You were given these gifts for a purpose, and it is given to very few to have these gifts, and when you don't use these gifts that were given to you, then you're offending God. You're not only a coward, but in a sense you're against God. Good day—glad to have met you—good-bye—good luck." And he left me.

So my friend looked at me, and I looked at him, and I said, "Well . . . I guess that guy's right."

So I went in and dressed, got up, took my family to Palm Springs for a week, and my sickness just fell off, just as it should have. I never was sick at all. It was just a perverse state of mind, a defensive mechanism, some way to avoid working.

But actually what the man said was, to my mind, very, very true. So when you say personal aims or personal goals, I'll say that you have to make use of the gifts that were given to you.

I never saw the man again. I don't know where he came from, I don't know who he was.

Q: *Do you feel that an educational institution can contribute to the growth of a student interested in filmmaking?*

CAPRA: Certainly—by introducing him to the tools. Now, you may have a gift, but you've also got to have some tools to spade up that garden with. So what the university can do is stimulate the interest and introduce the student to the various tools and the various mechanisms of the creative art of motion pictures. Then the individual is on his own from there on. He's got to have something besides mere knowledge of how to use the tools before he's successful in a creative art.

I don't know how much a university can develop of the creative power within an individual—perhaps a great deal—but there must be some creative power there to begin with, in the individual. You can't just automatically teach anybody how to act. You can't automatically teach anybody composition, as regards to color and form in the way of photography. There must be within that person a sensitivity to that art. You can teach him the tools, and you can perhaps guide him, if he has some spark of creativeness within him; you might guide him toward the end by which he may use that creative power best, perhaps as a cameraman, a director, a writer or whatever—but the person himself or herself must have an inner urge of some kind and an ability of some kind.

Q: *What projects are you working on now?*

CAPRA: I can tell you what we're working on now, and it looks like we'll make it—that is a picture called *Joseph and His Brethren,* based on the Bible story in Genesis. It's a very large subject and will be a very costly film. I'm the producer and director on it, and I hope we make it. I hope it comes off.

Q: *Are you working on anything like the Bell documentaries?*

CAPRA: Well, yes. I'm not actually working full-time on it, but I'm very, very interested in an area of motion pictures that I think in the future will be of great, great importance, and that is educational films—particularly educational films for actual technical use in schools. We hear today [about] the lack of scientific education in our schools, the lack of interest of our pupils, the lack of adequate teachers—perhaps all these things are true—but here's where film can be a great tool and a great asset to the educators, and to science in general.

I'll tell you about a committee that was formed over a year and a half ago, before the Russians put up their Sputniks. The spearhead of this committee and the driving force behind it is a professor of physics at MIT, Jack L. Zacharias. This gentleman, along with many other top physicists in the colleges and educational institutions, was dissatisfied with the knowledge of physics that high school graduates brought with them when they came to college. They wondered whether physics was being taught properly in the high schools. So they investigated. They got a steering committee of twelve or fifteen people, and I was included in that steering committee because of my interest in educational films. To their great surprise, they found that in the thousands and thousands of high schools in the United States, the study of physics was in a great many cases non-existent. Some schools didn't even have a physics course. In other schools, physics was taught by high school coaches or English teachers, without true preparation in the subject. As a result of this, students went to college without very much physics behind them. As a matter of fact, many very bright students were steered away from science because of the inadequate teaching of science.

This committee delved into the textbooks, and they came up with reviews and criticisms of the textbooks used in physics in high schools. They found that the physics that was being taught in the high schools today was in the main physics of fifty years ago. It didn't have any relation to the physics that is going on today. They found also that it was pretty dull, not stimulating at all, so you could see where some bright kid might be scared away from scientific things, from pursuing scientific studies.

So, to better this situation, this committee called upon about a hundred top physicists in the country, mostly university people, and some educational people, and said: can we produce a physics course for high school that will interest more students in physics, and perhaps give them a truer knowledge of what physics is?

So they got together and outlined a one-year course in high school physics, [for] which they would write a completely new textbook, and as an adjunct to the textbook—and a major adjunct to the textbook—they wanted to produce films on the various subjects.

As a matter of fact, this course is now a going thing. The textbook is almost completely written, and about sixty twenty-minute films are to be produced to go along with the textbook, for a one year course in the senior year of high school, in physics. I think the results are just tremendous.

Q : *Who is going to pay for these films?*
CAPRA :   Right—now, who's going to pay? This committee decided they'd need some money, so they went to the National Science Foundation, a government organization dedicated to the promotion of science, and they put up a million and a half dollars. The Ford Foundation was next asked to do something about it, and I think the Ford Foundation has given them $500,000, or somewhere in that neighborhood. A couple of the other foundations added their little contributions, so they have a couple of million dollars to produce these films with, and produce this textbook with, and give it to the high schools as a package.

My interest in this, of course, is trying to help them produce the sixty twenty-minute films on physics. I don't think it'll be too far in the future before the chemistry people will do the same thing, the history people will do the same thing, the geography people and so on. I think you'll find education will take an enormous jump in the schools—as it should, because nothing can teach like films can teach.

I'm very happy to be a part of this kind of an experiment, and I think it offers a tremendous future, not only for high school students and for the country as a whole, but for people that are interested in films, using films, making films for teaching purposes.

I have conducted a one man campaign, at Caltech and MIT and various other technical institutions, to get them to put in a photographic department in their schools. In general, research is conducted by men who take a long time in working out a problem and then eventually they put it all down on paper—long-winded reports, technical reports—and in many cases these reports get put on the shelf, get lost, nobody ever sees them again. What I've been trying to campaign for is that these research people use film to record their researches with, because film will be seen, can be shown, can be shown to many many people—whereas a report can just be lost. It takes a great deal of time to read and very few people can read them, whereas if they photographed their research results as they went along, and then allowed this film to be circulated among all the other institutions, I think research would take a big jump forward.

I think this would apply to almost any kind of research—in biology, physics, chemistry, engineering, anything else. I'm surprised that these major technical institutions have not used film as a medium of communication, to exchange ideas, one with the other. I hope the time is coming when they will use film as well as paper.

I don't feel they've used these media for communication as they should, as they could have, and as they will do very shortly.

Q: *Is there anything you've done in connection with your craft that you wish now you'd done another way or that you may be sorry about?*
CAPRA: I can't say that I would do anything differently, because I was at the top of my enthusiasm on all occasions, in all pictures I was making, and I don't know how you'd improve on that. Looking back, you can look back objectively, but you must always take into consideration exactly what your enthusiasm was at the time you made that. Now, that's very difficult to reproduce and very difficult to evaluate, because enthusiasm is one of the prime assets of the making of any kind of entertainment, or any theatrical enterprise. I don't know why, perhaps because enthusiasm, I think, comes from two Greek words—"en" [and] "theos"—I think they mean "God within," which is a very good description of what enthusiasm is.

I would have to go back and recreate the values of the moment, and that's very difficult to do. So as far as I'm concerned, everything that happened was for the best.

Capra of *Deeds* & *Smith* Sagas Sees Hollywood Now Over-Intellectual

FRED HIFT/1958

IN ITS SEARCH FOR A new approach to capture and hold audiences, Hollywood today is "over-intellectualizing" its subject matter. The primary need is to find the way back to the basic tale, director Frank Capra said in Gotham last week.

Capra, one of yesteryear's top names in Hollywood and director of such "classics" as *Mr. Smith Goes to Washington, Mr. Deeds Goes to Town* and *It Happened One Night,* is returning to the theatrical film scene after a four-year absence during which he produced four full-hour science films for American Telephone & Telegraph Co. for use on television.

This fall he'll shoot *Goodbye Eden,* starring Frank Sinatra and based on the play *Hole in the Head.* It's a comedy-drama for release through United Artists. Only other name cast so far is Edward G. Robinson. Picture will be made in Hollywood and Miami. Earlier, Capra had been set to direct *Joseph and His Brethren* for Columbia. However, with the death of Harry Cohn the project has been abandoned as being too costly.

Perhaps because he has been reared in a different tradition, Capra believes strongly in the basic values; and he disagrees strongly with those who speak of films in terms of an "art" form.

"I'm not sure to which extent 'art' has a place in filmmaking," he said. "The medium certainly is capable of producing art, but I don't think it's really there. We make pictures primarily to entertain. The Europeans seem to

From *Variety,* 16 July 1958. Republished with permission of Reed Business Information. Permission conveyed through Copyright Clearance Center, Inc.

take a different point-of-view, but I think they're off-base. Films aren't pictures that are to be hung on a wall. They have to have three dimensions—two on the screen and the third in the audience. They have to have that, or else they fail. And then who gains?"

Capra said that, to him, some of the Walt Disney films managed to combine the elusive elements of art and popular entertainment.

The director said he didn't think there had been any significant changes at the audience level. "Intelligence doesn't change," he commented. "It's the same now as it's always been. What does change is knowledge and the appreciation of better things. A lot of people tend to confuse these values. Hollywood today seems to feel that it must appeal to a higher level of intelligence. Actually, many of your 'old' pictures gave the audience a more complete show. The accent is on the latter."

Considered particularly deft in his handling of comedy, Capra deplored the lack of laughter on the screen today, but at the same time admitted that comedies "are the hardest thing to make."

"Comedy is really the highest of all the arts," he opined. "To succeed with it, you have to first know the facts and the basis of life on which to comment in a humorous way. Comedy, after all, is based on what should be, not on what is. I think that, possibly, the East-West ideological conflict has tended to unbalance the base of what is and what should be. We've lost that certainty during the last ten to fifteen years, and unless you are quite sure of your base, unless it's steady, comedy is difficult to achieve."

Capra opined that there "wasn't a subject in the world" that couldn't be tackled by the screen. However, he questioned the "gimmick" approach to filming. "Sometimes it works out, but in the long run it doesn't," he said. "You've got to appeal to basic emotions as a general guideline. It's the basic tale that counts, and by that I don't mean that the screen can't convey a message."

Capra's own past work has demonstrated the truth of his remarks. Though his important films, like *Mr. Deeds* and *Mr. Smith,* were basically emotional stories, they had something definite to say. "I've always made films that held out for the triumph of the individual," Capra said. "In my pictures, inevitably, there was hope for the little man, regardless of the odds against him."

Frank Capra: "One Man—One Film"

JAMES R. SILKE AND BRUCE HENSTELL/1971

''MAYBE THERE REALLY WASN'T an America," wrote director John Cassavetes in a recent Hollywood trade journal, "maybe it was only Frank Capra." The thought is indicative of the current attention being given to Capra and many of his contemporaries by those who make films as well as those who study them. Few directors have been as popular with their audiences and fewer still created such explicit representations of the state of mind of those audiences as Frank Capra. The sentimental dreams and wishes of middle class America, that patented blend of "Capra-corn" which critic/historian Richard Griffith called "the fantasy of good will," that's what the 1930s is about, or as Cassavetes would have it, the films are the 1930s.

This year the films are destined to reach new audiences. Major retrospectives of Capra's work are planned for the Museum of Modern Art in New York, the AFI Theater in Washington, D.C. and the Los Angeles County Museum of Art. A source of 16mm prints is published at the end of this paper for those who wish to conduct their own studies. To add another dimension to the films, Capra's outstanding autobiography, *The Name Above the Title* (Macmillan), has recently been published and is highly recommended.

The delightful moving images with which Capra gave us his estimate of the individual and collective American personality were made possible by

---

This seminar with Capra originally appeared in pamphlet form as the third installment in the Center for Advanced Film Studies' "Discussion" series, and is reprinted by permission of the American Film Institute. The "source of 16mm prints" mentioned in the second paragraph has been deleted; so too a bibliography.

his sure and authoritative grip on the techniques of film. In this *Discussion* Capra speaks of how his films move, of how they were edited, tailor-made to the requirements of a large audience. He speaks here of how he drives his films, in the pace of his actors, the rhythm of his editing, to precisely fit each piece of the image to every other piece. His development and use of multiple camera and playback techniques helped him to create that essential even quality his films demanded. For Capra the cardinal sin was dullness. How to avoid it, a cardinal lesson.

This Frank Capra *Discussion* is published by the American Film Institute from a seminar held at the Center for Advanced Film Studies in Beverly Hills on May 26, 1971. The focus of the seminar and the *Discussion* series is the creative process of filmmaking. In the past year many of Capra's films have been shown at the Center and relevant published material made available in preparation. The proceedings were taped by Los Angeles educational television station KCET and later broadcast as part of the series "The American Film Institute Theater," hosted by George Stevens, Jr., director of the American Film Institute. James R. Silke of the Center's faculty led the discussion which included Fellows, faculty, and guests of the Center. After brief introductions the first question was asked: How do you construct a scene?

CAPRA: I start with the actors. We have a scene, a four or five page scene to shoot that day. We read it together—I want everybody to know what they're doing—and then I listen. If it hits my ear, if lines hit wrong, I change them. Then I try different approaches, say this, or try it this way, especially for comedy. Then when that's settled, when we have a good reading of it, we have a rehearsal, a walk-through. Once that's done I use the stand-ins for the actual lining up of lights and cameras so that the actors just don't sit there in the hot lights and tell stale jokes to each other. Then I rehearse the scene as a whole. Get the whole thing worked out in long shot, and maybe take it in a long shot and that, for me, is just like taking it as a rehearsal. I may not ever use the long shot, but it works the bugs out.

SILKE: *What do you mean by bugs?*
C: The natural moves, or unnatural moves; you work it out so you begin to feel they're real people talking really, talking over each other. I don't move the actors just to be moving; if they're not supposed to be moving they just *sit*. You don't let an actor jump up, walk over there, talk, then come back

here and talk and then come back here and sit and talk without a reason. Just movement of actors does not necessarily help the scene. Sometimes it distracts from the scene.

What you need is what they are saying, you need the emotional part. You're photographing emotion not walks. Then I go in and break it up and try and shoot the whole scene with two or three takes. Then maybe individual close-ups and little pieces of it. That's normally my method of shooting.

BRUCE HENSTELL: *Could you tell us what your concept was for Gary Cooper's performance in the courtroom scene of* Mr. Deeds?

C: Well, he didn't have much to do for a long time, he just sat there. He's the greatest sitter. Gary Cooper had a most wonderful face, as you well know, a great expressive face in the sense that you think you see a lot in that face. That's why he was a star, [that] noble face, a face that had integrity written all over it. So he just listened. He was sore at the world, he was so mad he said, "The hell with it, let 'em take my money, let 'em take anything."

Then he started hearing some of the people who were for him and he started to speak. He began to speak as Mr. Deeds would speak and make suckers out of all the phonies he had around him. That was the whole scene.

HENSTELL: *In your book you talk about playbacks. Did this device help your actors achieve this natural quality you desired?*

C: On *Mr. Smith Goes to Washington,* I first used playbacks. I got so tired of going up and shooting a close-up on, say, Jean Arthur, and having the script-girl or someone else read the lines to her from offstage. Generally the actors read them but sometimes, you know, they wouldn't read them, they'd just toss them off. And for the reaction shots she was playing to nothing, she was playing to a blackboard, a chalk mark. And here she is: solid, impaled, stuck there, she can't move this way, that way or this way. She's got to play an emotional scene in close-up with the vigor, tempo, and emotion of the general shot. That's one of the most difficult things for an actor or actress to do.

First of all, you've got nothing to play against except a script-girl reading feed-lines or a chalk mark; you can't overlap those badly delivered lines so she's got to wait until the script-girl gets through, pause and then say her lines. This was horse-and-buggy for me. For a long time I resented this whole idea of shooting close-ups that way. I knew it was wrong. What we should have done is play the whole scene around her with the actors, all over again.

But this we couldn't do because the actors don't like to play when the camera's not on them.

So, I did another thing. I shot the master shot and when I okayed the master shot—when I knew I was going to use it—I transferred the soundtrack to a record, quickly down at the sound department, and brought it back on the stage and put it on a playback, on a loud speaker. With the on-and-off button, I could cut it in and cut it out wherever I wanted, on the playback.

Let's say Jean Arthur is here in this close-up. I'd play the scene, the actual scene, back so she's playing against it, against the actual voices, the actual tempo, the actual vigor of the voices. First thing, she plays the scene like she did in the long shot. She hears herself, she knows the quality of the voice she was using, the quality of the expression, and she's got a real scene to play. When she had to speak a line I just cut off the playback and she'd say that line, and back would come the response on the playback, so she was playing against the scene. This I did forever after in all the pictures that I shot. What happened was you could cut from long shots to medium shots, put in your close-ups, and they looked like they fitted in like a jigsaw puzzle. It never varied in tempo, it didn't jump up and down, and so they were very smooth, flowing scenes. Next time you see *Mr. Smith Goes to Washington* you'll see how beautifully the close-ups fit right in with the long shots and you don't notice the cutting.

s : *Can you describe your use of multiple cameras?*
c : I used multiple cameras almost from the beginning. When sound pictures came, we had to use multiple cameras because of those great big booths the cameras were in. Really had to make a little play out of every scene, a small act out of every scene, which took three or four cameras. The photography was very bad, everything was bad about it, but we had to get it all on one sound track. We had to use one sound track for three or four angles.

We hadn't learned to intercut sound track as easily as we can now. So we had to get three or four angles on one sound track, perforce we had to use three cameras on every important scene: one to take a medium shot, a close-up this way and a close-up that way, that was the usual set-up. It was almost dictated by the fact we used these great big booths and they were so big they couldn't be maneuvered. You set one, two, three and put the actors in front and let them work to the cameras. But when we got the cameras out of the booths, with freedom again, we went back to mobility. The three camera set-up stayed with me because I couldn't match, I had a difficulty matching close-ups to medium shots; getting the action and the sound to match, getting the actors in the same mood. I thought: "Isn't this crazy," that we have to take one shot, then take it over again in close-up and then take it over again in another close-up, then you put them together and the voices would jump, the moods change. Perhaps you did them an hour apart; perhaps a day apart. The actors had something to eat for lunch and they never can do the same scene twice. That was a difficulty.

I used multiple cameras so that I wouldn't have this jump in tempo, jump in voice when intercutting between close-ups and medium shots. Also I used multiple cameras because early I used an actress by the name of Barbara Stanwyck who had had no experience whatever in films, some in theater, a very young woman, very silent, very somber woman. Fires were bursting out of her, but they burned too fast. I found out that she left her best scene the first time she did it, even in rehearsal. It was just wonderful, but then she could never reproduce that scene again. The more you did it, the farther she got from it; she just left it, she was just drained. She gave it all in that one scene. This was a very amazing thing, I had never run across it. Most people get better in rehearsal; she got worse. She had been rehearsing mentally and she threw it all out at once. Therefore, I had to use multiple cameras on her because I'd never get the same scene again if I used different shots, different set-ups. That caused me to use multiple cameras.

STEVENS: *Could you talk a bit about* Lost Horizon?

C: *Lost Horizon* is a very interesting story because it was a very dramatic example of what film was about. I read it on a train, and I told Harry Cohn: "That's my next picture and it's going to cost about two million dollars," and that was about half of Columbia's whole budget for the year. Well, he went for it. I went down to Alameda Street in downtown Los Angeles and looked at some icehouses to explore the possibility of going in and shooting it in an icehouse. They thought we were crazy. We found an icehouse that was piled high with swordfish. We rented it, took the swordfish out, and moved in. We had an enormous amount of problems: film fogged up, the cameras wouldn't run as well and the cables and lights cracked and broke. We were working in 15° weather and we didn't have the mechanics for that. Outside it was 90°. We had these snow machines, which produced ground-up ice, so the actors were walking on snow. It was just real stuff; great! Now, we ran the finished picture, three hours, in a projection room at Columbia. Everybody said, "My God! This is the greatest picture that's ever been made." Oh, the hurrahs, we were walking on air. So Harry Cohn called his New York people to come out and see what he had done. He was a pretty cagey guy too, that's what made him what he was, so he said: "Let's take it out and sneak preview it once. We'll take it to Santa Barbara and if we can knock off those snobs up there with it, we're going to knock everybody off." So we took it to Santa Barbara, Sunday night, raining, and I just knew that it would be the greatest thing that was ever shown to an audience. We sat there, the picture opened, and about five minutes into the picture, they began to laugh. And I didn't know what they were laughing at; there were no laughs intended. Then a little later on there were more laughs and pretty soon they were laughing at the whole damned thing. That was in the first ten minutes. So I got up, went out into the foyer, there was a man getting a drink and I said: "You first," and as he was drinking he said: "Did you ever see such a goddamned Fu-Man Chu thing in your life?" Jesus, I ran out of the theater.

There it was; half the budget of Columbia, two million dollars going down the drain. The audience came out in twos and threes long before the picture was over but finally the rest of them came out. And you could hear them talking: "Goddamndest thing, did you ever see . . ." I went up to Lake Arrowhead alone and walked around those hills for two or three days by myself, trying to figure out what had happened. Finally I got an idea and went back to the studio and had the cutter put the main title at the beginning of the third reel. Then I went into Harry Cohn and said: "Let's preview it again" and he says: "Don't, don't" and I said: "I don't know if it's going to work, but bring your New York guys because we've either got it or we haven't got it."

So we took it to San Pedro, beginning with the third reel, and that version was the picture that was finally shown. They were entranced with the picture, by golly, we all relaxed, and the picture was one some people have said they've seen twenty times. A completely unreleasable picture suddenly becomes something beautiful, something the audience loves, by just throwing away the first two reels. We got back to the studio and had a big celebration, and while they were celebrating I went out to the cutting room and got those first two reels in my hands and went down to the incinerator and threw them in. Being nitrate film there was a hell of a swoosh and it lit up the sky. And that's what happened to those two reels.

s : *You really didn't care for them!*

c : Really didn't care for them. So I have only one piece of advice for you: if the picture doesn't go, throw away the first two reels.

If you saw *Lost Horizon* alone or in a small group—this is philosophically very important for you to hear—a small group loved the picture the way it was. We had an example of that in the projection room. One individual would be entranced by the picture. We showed it to five hundred or a thousand people; no good. The third dimension of a film is a thousand people, a thousand pairs of ears and eyes looking at it, not one pair. There is something about a thousand people that is more acute, more sensitive, more reactive than one person or two persons or three persons.

You must never judge a picture in the projection room with one or two people. The line between the ridiculous and the sublime is very wide to an individual. The more people you get, the finer the line becomes between the ridiculous and the sublime. That's why people in audiences titter at times when they shouldn't, where there's nothing to titter at.

H E N S T E L L : *I found the same to be true of your other pictures, such as* Mr. Deeds *or* Mr. Smith, *that the comedy seems to play better with a larger audience.*

c : Well, *Mr. Deeds Goes to Town* was tailored to a large audience, using previews, in the cutting, in the editing. We previewed probably six or seven times and we'd change it where the laughs were too long or too short, or if something was dull. The film was tailored to a large audience, not to a single person.

I used a tape recorder at previews. The only honest way to ever preview a picture was with a tape recorder. You hang a microphone down from the balcony and you record what comes off the screen and the audience reaction at the same time. . . . You cannot go to a preview and be objective. You're just so damned involved in it. But a tape recorder is completely objective; it records just what happened.

You play that tape back. You fix something in the film, you preview it again and record it again and then you compare tapes; did you fix it or is there something else? You use the tape like a tailor uses marks to build a coat. When finally the tapes are about the same level of response, that's about the best you can do and you release it. That's how I edit films.

H E N S T E L L : *How closely did you work with your film editor? Was he given an editing script to work from or would you actually be in the cutting room with him?*

C: I'd be in the cutting room with him. They couldn't get rid of me no matter what.

HENSTELL: *Did much of your films develop in the cutting room?*
C: Yes. I remember once, in the shooting of *State of the Union,* there's a place there where an actor jumps out of a plane. It was a kind of big, fast-acting piece of melodrama going on. We put it together one way and we thought it was great. [William] Hornbeck was the editor. Then we took it apart and tried it another way and we could never get it back the way we had it at the beginning. After that experience we took the first editing that we did and made a dupe of it fast so we could always go back to it. We had forgotten how the heck we did it. This shows you how important editing is because that scene changed, it was never as good as it had been because mechanically it was not edited as well as it had been.

S: *Could you restructure a whole scene in editing it?*
C: Yes, I overshot purposefully so as to have some leeway. His dad (turning to Stevens) was the master of shooting for cutting. George Stevens made all his pictures in the cutting room; he had enough film.

A fellow like Jack Ford was never interested in editing a film, so he would shoot it so that it could be edited in only one way. He had no leeway. I allowed enough leeway so that we could maneuver with the film. That's why I say that in the cutting room a great deal of creation goes on.

S: *How did you handle pace in your films?*
C: In my pictures people's eyes are riveted on the screen: you can't take your eyes off because something is going to happen.

Usually, you go to a theater and you see a picture and it hangs there after the scene is over. The audience is way ahead of the picture all the time. I don't know why it is that they're constantly ahead of the picture. In the projection room or in front of the movieola, you don't see that the last three or four frames of the film seem to hang. On a big screen they're there so long that they seem like minutes rather than microseconds. Well, I thought it was the size of the heads of the actors on the screen; magnified ten times bigger than they are, they simply communicated faster. Or, perhaps, a thousand pairs of eyes and ears assimilate faster. One or the other. I don't know which it is, but I know it's so. In *American Madness,* for the first time, I purposefully speeded up the shooting of every scene by about 40 percent above normal. Not with the camera but actually with the actors.

STEVENS: *Pacing?*

C: Pace. I just upped the pace. It looked very fast in the projection room but when I got it in the theater it didn't look fast. As a matter of fact it looked very interesting. So I did that in practically all of the pictures I made, except for mood scenes where pace was not a factor. But in normal scenes, I shot them about 40 percent faster than normal and then they seemed to be normal on the screen or at least they didn't seem to be abnormal. There was an urgency to the scenes that seemed to work.

STEVENS: *How did you bring the actors to play those scenes, to bring up the pace.*

C: By rehearsing, kicking up the pace, overlapping lines. Some lines you didn't hear but it was alright. Overlapping movements, cutting out dissolves, jump cutting instead of dissolving from the eighth floor down to the bottom floor; all these things seemed to speed up the pace. I found another trick; the tempo of a scene could be speeded up, not by shouting but by quiet talking. You have a feeling that if you want to hurry something, you want to speed it up, you ought to make it all a little louder. But we can say more words quietly than we can shouting.

I thought films lagged behind the audience and I wanted to catch up with the audience. And this kind of did it. Next time you see one of my pictures just notice the pace: it moves, it *moves.* Since you're telling a story the audience wants it to move, they want to see what comes next. Your father (turning to Stevens) did just the opposite. He got his effects by long, slow paced scenes, which is another way to get effects. George got great effects by just long walks down a hall. You looked at a lady going down a hall and you tried to figure out what she was thinking. That too is useful for effects and he got great effects with slowing down the pace. But I got mine by speeding them up.

STEVENS: *Can you talk about your collaboration with writers in, say,* Mr. Deeds *and* Mr. Smith?

C: Well, the writer I collaborated the most with, in real collaboration because we both seemed to vibrate to the same tuning fork, was Robert Riskin. He was great: great script writer, great dialogue writer, great ear for dialogue, and we'd write everything together. We worked together right from the very start. He'd go off and write and then he'd come back and we'd go over it, then he'd go off and write.

We'd change a script often during the making of the picture. An actor would run away with something and when an actor would run away I'd let him run.

S: *What do you mean by run away?*
C: If there's an actor, like Tommy Mitchell, and you've got him playing a bit part in a picture he's very effective. He can be so effective that you want to use him more. You write something.

HENSTELL: *What did Riskin's scripts look like?*
C: Scenes or master shots; I never worried about camera angles. There's no use breaking the script down into minute things, it's a waste of time. Because you don't know what actor is going to play it, you don't know what the set is going to look like. It doesn't matter what the script is like, the script is just the story.

HENSTELL: *Could you tell us how you worked with your craftsmen?*
C: Everybody does that differently. I never left the set; I stayed right there. While they were working I would get ideas. I never had anything so solidly set that I gave them this or that instruction and walked away. I liked to be part of everything that went on.

I stayed right on the set even though I wasn't in anything. I'd stay there and whistle and go over the scene, over the scene, over the scene in my mind. And in many cases I found all kinds of little things that I could add or subtract, little ways to use the camera more effectively. I never stopped sleeping, drinking, eating the picture; you couldn't stimulate me with anything else. You'd talk to me about something else and I wouldn't listen, I couldn't listen. All I was thinking about was the picture. That's why I never left the set. The minute I'd leave the set somebody would come up and say: "Oh, how about . . ." The hell with it; I wanted to stay right with that scene, right with that daily work; that's the way I worked. That doesn't mean that's the proper way to work because the proper way to work is the one that suits you. No two directors work alike, no two directors shoot the same story alike. I might fall in love with a property that some other director would not be able to do. And vice-versa. I make a statement in my book that there are no rules in filmmaking, only sins, and the cardinal sin is dullness. That's a pretty good generalization.

I don't think that there are stars and bit players or extras. Whatever goes on the screen, whether it's ten seconds or ten minutes, has to be of optimum quality. Star quality. A bit player plays a scene that lasts thirty seconds; that's thirty seconds in that film, that's a piece of the mosaic. Why shouldn't that thirty seconds be as good as every other thirty seconds?

s : *Your extras constantly amaze me.*
c : Sure, they're not extras; they're people. Say you have a dozen extras walking by. Well, they can just walk by. An assistant can say: "Get your ass down there and walk through that scene" and that's it. That's not it; they're people. You find a great difference if you say to an extra: "You're worried about your husband, he hasn't got a job," "You got a new hairdo you want people to see."

Just give them an identity, any tiny bit of identity. They walk through the scene with that identity and they become people, not sheep. It's small, sounds unimportant, but it is not unimportant.

Take a cashier where your star goes to pay a bill. There she is made up, she's a cashier, but she's never been a cashier before; she's an extra, she's Mabel Glotz. You'd better be careful that that cashier doesn't look like an extra. You'd better give her an identity. She may not have a single word to say, but if she's thinking about going out that night and she's looking forward to it, she'll have an attitude. If she's got a sick mother in the hospital, she's got an attitude. She'll become a real person even though she just makes change.

S T E V E N S : *What was the original material that* Mr. Smith Goes to Washington *came from?*
c : The original material was a book.

S T E V E N S : *Did you ever read it?*
c : No. It was a book called *The Gentleman from Montana.* Joe Sistrom came

in and he had made a two-page outline of the book on yellow paper. I read the first page and that's all I wanted to read. My God, it was an idea. And that's all I wanted to read; I never read the book.

I wish I had a picture about the shooting of *Mr. Smith* because that would be a fascinating textbook. We shot on three levels at one time. We had cameras up on Jean Arthur, cameras on Jimmy Stewart way over here, and cameras on Claude Rains fifty feet away.

STEVENS: *This was the set of the Senate Chamber?*
C: Yes, and we were playing a scene with three cameras maybe a hundred feet apart.

S: *That's three different set-ups, then, going at once.*
C: Three different set-ups, because we were on so many levels. If we just took one set-up at a time we'd still be there. It was fascinating to see and hear. Just as if it was in the Senate, the actors were shouting back and forth at each other because they could hardly hear. It looked mighty real. And it was wonderful to edit because you edited on one sound track. All these scenes on one sound track. You could cut back and forth at any point you wanted.

STEVENS: *That picture is a good example to talk about research, pre-production research.*
C: We did a lot of research, went back to Washington, got a lot of plans of the Senate, including the original plans of the Capitol. There were all the details connected with the various desks: Jefferson Davis's desk where somebody kicked a hole in it because he got up and left to join the southerners when the Carolinas seceded, Webster's desk where something had happened. The research on it was just simply marvelous. The reproduction of the set was faithful. You had to be *in* the Senate; if you weren't in the Senate, you didn't have a picture.

STEVENS: *That even works with extras, clothes and all the details right down the line.*
C: Right down the line, right down to the pencils they had, yes.

HENSTELL: *You had a technical background in the sciences that not many other directors had. Did that help you?*

c: Probably helped me in that sound didn't scare me, I knew what was going on. The others were really scared, really frightened.

My status went up instantly because I knew what a microphone was and knew what to do about it. I did have an advantage there especially with the studio owners who were all really thrown. For a short while the soundmen ran everything. They threw actors out. At this time if you didn't have those pear-shaped tones, you went out. Absolutely nutty stuff, crazy stuff. The soundmen would take tests of the stars and say: "He's no good, throw him out, he'll never be alright," and out went Jack Gilbert, the biggest star in the business. He drank himself to death because the soundmen said his voice didn't register like a stage actor's voice.

s: *What'd they say about Jean Arthur?*
c: Jean Arthur? She came in later. But I suppose if she had been there, they'd have thrown her out. Her voice breaks into a thousand tinkling bells.

HENSTELL: *Could you tell us about how the introduction of sound changed your feelings about comedy?*
c: It did add another dimension. But I never quite forgot visual humor. In a scene in *Mr. Smith Goes to Washington,* where Jimmy Stewart is embarrassed, I just played on his hat. That was really a sight gag but quite effective. I just never quite forgot the training, and I fell back on it constantly, of the visual gag.

STEVENS: *I think that's what made a lot of pictures so strong. In long, sound, story films, if something wasn't working, the director with experience in silent comedy had that resource, that ability, to turn a situation with a sight gag.*
c: Particularly in the plot scenes, where somebody was explaining the plot, exposition. Those are the scenes that can be very dull. There's where you have got to use your ingenuity to keep that bubble in the air and not make it dull.

s: *Could you give us an example of that?*
c: Yes. I can think of an example with Jean Arthur. She was telling Jimmy Stewart something about the Senate, how you put a bill across. And that could be pretty stuffy exposition.

So I had her throwing a half-dollar up and catching it while she was talking. And then she missed it and was looking for it under the chair while she was talking. It alleviated the stolidity of the exposition.[1]

HENSTELL: *You did the same thing when you introduced the Jean Arthur character in* Mr. Deeds: *we see her first playing with a rope while talking.*

s: *Is this something that came from Arthur or is this something you figured she could do?*
c: No, it just came out of the scene. There was a scene that I thought was flat. I used these touches to liven up a scene, make them more human, make them so that the actors just don't stand and talk to each other. And that's what I mean, just moving the characters doesn't give you that, but if you have a man pick his nose or something . . .

s: *There are scenes that you play with absolutely no movement and with the performers' backs to the camera, where you don't let us see anything. Do you save those for a particular moment?*
c: Well, when it might be embarrassing to the character.

s: *You play the motel scene in* It Happened One Night *between the two in almost total darkness.*
c: Yes. Love scenes are murder, love scenes are tough. That's where they giggle at the wrong places, when you try to play a love scene. So, generally, I have a reactive character. This is an interesting thing about comedy; you can have a character who represents the audience. He sees what's going on and is amazed by it, moved by it, stunned by it and he reacts. That way you trigger the laugh. You control the audience by asking for the laugh with a reactive character. Then they're not laughing at scenes where you don't want them to. For instance, I could take one of these nude films today, one of these sexy nude films where they roll around in the bed and bite each other and kick each other, and I could make it very funny just by having a reactive character watch. It would make a very funny piece of business. It would destroy completely what the film tries to do. The use of the reactive character in comedy is very important. If you think they're going to laugh, or there is

---

[1] This coin-flip scene occurs in *Mr. Deeds Goes to Town*. L.P.

a chance they'll laugh, stick a character actor there, he bats his eyes, and you get the laugh.

s : *In the Senate scene of* Mr. Smith *you used the press that way. They guide the whole scene, watch the flow of the drama; is he winning, is he losing . . .*
c : They are one with the audience; the Greek chorus.

HENSTELL: *Could you tell us something about casting Jimmy Stewart in* Mr. Smith? *Most people identify Stewart with that kind of role. But he hadn't played roles of that kind prior to* Mr. Smith.
c : No, I had only seen him in one film before casting him in *Mr. Smith*. I had seen him in a thing called *Navy Blue and Gold*[2] and I saw him play one scene, just one scene, one scene which affected me. I forget exactly what the scene was, but that's all I had to see. I never made tests of actors. I think that tests are the unfairest thing. You can't tell anything by a test because they come in, put on make-up, read, make the test. So I'd just talk to the actor, or see him; I'd rather see him in a picture someplace, see him under real circumstances of performing rather than a test.

Then I'd make up my mind and if that's the girl I thought would play that secretary, that's it. I wouldn't care whether she was an actress or not. I could make her do it. I cast every part down to the tiniest parts. But I cast the person, not the acting ability, but the person.

I had a story in mind and I knew the characters. People, in scripts, are just two-dimensional characters. They're not people until you see them in the flesh. It made a great difference for me to be able to think that Ward Bond was going to play this man. Now I had Ward Bond in mind and before I just had a character. When you cast the characters you figure your story in terms of Ward Bond, Jimmy Stewart, and they're people. Now you begin to think of material for them as human beings.

STEVE MAMBER: *Your interest in common man figures such as Smith and Deeds, and your concern with small-town life; do you think that came out of finding stories that people would be interested in or was there something about America you were trying to say?*

---

[2] Sam Wood, 1937; Stewart appeared in Capra's 1938 film *You Can't Take It with You* in advance of *Mr. Smith*. L.P.

C: There was my own youth, things that were involved with that; there was the fact that I had always been a rebel, against conformity; for the individual, against mass conformity. That means mass conformity of any kind. I see mass conformity happening again today, and I just don't like it. I don't like to see these youths conform so to each other. I'd rather see some individuals. That was the common man idea. I didn't think he was common, I thought he was a hell of a guy. I thought he was the hope of the world.

ROBERT MUNDY: *Do you think that the Capra heroes you evolved in the thirties have become less tenable today? The nature of America has changed and the loss of innocence is no longer an issue.*

C: I'm not so sure of that. There's a guy called Ralph Nader who would make a perfect Capra hero. An individual, alone. He is worrying and moving politicians, industrialists, great industries, and he's making them squirm, alone. He's a typical Capra hero and he's working today. No, I don't agree with that; I think that the individual is the way we have leaped forward, the way we have progressed.

HENSTELL: *Could you tell us something about your problems with* Meet John Doe?

C: The plot of *Meet John Doe* was one in which Bob Riskin and I got all mixed up. One of the reasons that we got mixed up was that we started out, not with an innately good man, but with a drifter who didn't give a damn whether he was good or bad.

But the story affected him. It was really a much better story than others we told because the story affected the central character. But the only out for him at the end was to commit suicide. But that I couldn't bring myself to do because that was a negative outlook. So what we were stuck with was an unanswerable, unsolvable story.

It's like St. George slew the dragon and got slain in the act. Unsolved problem. If St. George kills the dragon and gets slain himself—what? For seven eighths of the picture we had a fine, fine thing going for us there; the very end collapsed like a brick sock.

S: *Did you know this all along?*

C: Well we knew we didn't have a finish all along, but I was quite sure we'd find one. We shot five different finishes and tried them out in front of audiences. The last one that we used came from a letter. It said: "I've seen all your finishes and you're all wrong. The only way you can keep him from committing suicide is if the John Does themselves ask him not to." We went right back to the set and shot that finish and that's the one that went in the picture. It was not the right one but it was better than the others. We just weren't good enough to finish our own film, that's all.

STEVENS: *There are two parts to making pictures and you mastered both of them very early. One was the talent and ideas of what was going to go into a film and the other was getting control of the film, getting control of the means. You were able to decide what pictures you were going to make.*

C: I took that responsibility. Actually, most directors who wanted that responsibility could have it. They'd be sticking their neck out, of course. They had to back up everything they did. They couldn't say "the writing was bad" or "he told me to do this" or "the acting was bad." But if you're willing to take full responsibility, even right now, a director can go as far as he wants to, can have all the responsibility he wants to take. He has to say no, he has to argue, and he has to fight, but he can take it. And if he is willing to take the responsibility, and if the picture is bad, he has to take it. If it's good, he gets the credit. All this is part of having enough confidence in yourself, enough courage in yourself, to go out there and stick your neck out.

I worked for a very tough man called Harry Cohn. It was a constant battle, but he never won one single battle with me. I had to win every argument with him, because if you didn't, he lost confidence in you.

He'd challenge you on everything. If you didn't win the argument, he'd throw you out. This was a very crude way to run a studio but he got results by this crudeness on the simple theory that an artist with courage and guts should know more about what he's doing than the sensitive ones who are unsure. And he didn't want any unsure people around him. He wanted people who'd say: "It's going to be this way Harry or go to hell." That's fine.

MUNDY: *It seemed that the pressure from Cohn was more bureaucratic and financial than artistic. I wondered if there were any instances where Columbia made you change the picture from the way you wanted it.*

C: Never. I had to win every argument to stay there and that meant no changes unless I agreed with them. Harry Cohn did not know enough about . . . had no trust in his own artistry of any kind, but he was a great showman, a great gambler. But he'd only gamble on the people he thought knew what they were doing. You had to make him feel that you knew what you were doing even though you didn't, which was most of the time.

MUNDY: *Most directors mention with pride the movie where they first had the right to final cut. But it seems that you had that very early in your career.*
C: Yes. I thought that was the way pictures should be made. I suppose, being a Sicilian, I take a very dim view of authority of any kind. I don't like anybody telling me what to do.

STEVENS: *You hear so much about studios which imposed on the filmmakers. My experience has been that people who really wanted responsibility could have it.*
C: Unless you wanted to fall back on alibis and share the blame with somebody else if it didn't turn out right, then you had to share everything else. But if you took it all on yourself, it's poor but it's my own, you could take it. That's the way pictures should be made. One man—one film.

STEVENS: *What does that mean?*
C: One man makes one film. One painter—one painting. It isn't a committee.

STEVENS: *There's a lot of collaboration involved.*
C: Collaboration but not committee. Not committee responsibility. Collaboration—of course. You've got collaboration with thousands of people really. One man has to make the decisions, one man says yes or no. That man should be the director. And if it isn't, then you get unevenness.

STEVENS: *Were you involved in the budgeting of your films?*
C: Yes, *Ma'am.*

STEVENS: *Could you talk about that? The answer is obvious but why?*
C: Why? Because I knew that a film is a dichotomy of business and art and there's no other way you can figure it. And you have got to make both work. You've got to pay attention to both.

If your film loses money, you're not going to make many more films. Your films have got to be successful. I know you don't think talking of commerce is very important. But don't lose sight of the fact that if you don't make money with your films you're not going to make many films. You might be working in films, but if you're going to be filmmakers, you must pay attention to the money side, the financial side. Writing a book, you know, you buy a typewriter and you buy some paper and that's it, that's the total expense, and the rest of it is your time. Making a picture is hundreds of thousands of dollars, millions of dollars, tens of millions of dollars perhaps, and that's an enormous responsibility. Time is your great enemy, schedules, and budgeting and so forth, and I paid a great deal of attention to that. If you do, you get the picture made on time and don't lose any of the ingredients of the picture, any of the artistry of the picture.

STEVENS: *In other words, the budgeting is a whole series of decisions about where money is going to be spent so that it goes in the direction you want the film to go.*

C: Right. Filmmaking is decision making. That's all you do, make decisions, you make a thousand a day. You have got to make them fast and you have to make them—not by logic, logic isn't connected with filmmaking—they're gut decisions. That's your creativity. You make a decision and you make it fast. And don't worry about it after you make it because that's it. I've often gone back in after a picture started and the whole thing evaporates, just goes off into the air. How can you possibly make anything out of this crap? You have these ups and downs and you go and hide in a room and read it and conceptually it's pure nothing. How did you ever get started in this thing? You want to leave the country fast. And you can't do that, you have got to trust in that original "why did I pick it in the first place?" You have to go back to the original decision making—that you thought it was pretty good at the time—and stay with it. And it'll evaporate at times but you have to trust that first instinct. You have to discipline yourself to trust in those instincts.

STEVENS: *Even in those pictures that turned out to be enormously successful, you had those "loathes" . . .*

C: I should say, you bet.

STEVENS: *How do you account for that?*

C: Well, because you don't know what you've got until the very last minute. Until you've spent all the money and put the picture together, you don't really know what you've got and you worry. You worry because there goes hundreds of thousands of dollars of expense, millions of dollars of expense, and it's all in a few cans of film. It looks very, very cheap for the amount of money you spent on it and you don't know what you've got until you play it before an audience. You really do not know. There's no way of knowing.

STEVENS: *Your optimism about the individual was colored by your own life. You came to a foreign country, made a success of yourself, and were able to control your own destiny.*
C: Well, I fell in love with Americans.

STEVENS: *Pictures today are colored by a different kind of experience.*
C: The pictures today deal with what is going on today and we dealt with what was going on in our day. If we dealt honestly we had a universal picture which was good anytime. If we dealt honestly.

HENSTELL: *What was it in your films that captured so brilliantly the public imagination and made you one of the most successful directors of that period?*
C: I told a form of human comedy. I dealt with serious problems, protest films, but they were done with entertainment. They were done primarily through comedy. That's a very tough thing to do, doesn't always come off. But I was able to make that come off, and that was why they were entertaining.

S: *You started as a gagwriter in the silent period so you're not really writing funny words, you're talking about comic actions. What makes it comedy?*
C: Those were sight gags, as a matter of fact; we didn't write any of them, we only talked. We could only talk to the director and tell him the story. We weren't even allowed on the sets. We thought up gags and told them to the director when he wasn't working. They were sight gags. What is comedy? That's rough, that's rough to try and answer. It's the high-hat on the tramp and all those kind of things; things that aren't as they should be are funny or tragic.

Not always, because some things that are as they should be are very humorous, very touching. The birth of a baby: quite normal, just as it should be. But I defy any person here or any other place to go and look at a little baby just born and not laugh, not feel great about it. I defy you to see any newborn and not smile; a little pigeon, innocence, we laugh at innocence.

And laughter is surrender, laughter is the surrender of all your inhibitions. If you don't like somebody, you can't laugh at them; if you don't like a comedian, he can't make you laugh no matter how funny his lines.

A live little lion cub, a little kitten: very funny. His father: no laughs. It's a surrender. It's victory, it's success. Comedy is success. The Gospels are a comedy. The greatest comedy of all is the Resurrection of Christ; the divine comedy, the victory over death. These are the human values of comedy. And they're not all just slapstick. Comedy is much deeper, much deeper than just slipping on a banana peel. Comedy is the perfume of life. That's why when comedy is warm it lifts. It's a victory, it's a success story. One of the things that I had in my films that people like was this kind of warm lift they got out of this warm comedy. If you fear, if you dislike, if you hate: no laughs. If you like, if you love: laughs.

Capra Today

JAMES CHILDS/1972

JAMES CHILDS: *One thing I've always liked about your films is the way in which you handle crowds. Would you comment on that?*

FRANK CAPRA: Well, crowds to me mean motion, motion means motion pictures, motion means life. This is another expression of optimism: movement, life, energy, vibrancy—men going places and doing things, not drooping off in corners.

CHILDS: *This, then, would explain your use of fine character actors at various levels in your films.*

CAPRA: Yes.

CHILDS: *Of all your films, it seems to me that* Mr. Deeds *and* Mr. Smith *are most indicative of your philosophy of life. Do you see this too?*

CAPRA: I think so, because in a sense Mr. Common Man—Mr. Uncommon Man, rather—Mr. John Doe are all attempts to glorify and tell the story of what we call euphemistically the average man.

CHILDS: *With him were you fighting a war against cynicism?*

CAPRA: Against cynicism, "massism"—mass entertainment, mass production, mass education, mass everything. Especially mass man. I was fighting

From *Film Comment* 8.4 (November–December 1972): 22–23. Copyright © 1972 by the Film Comment Publishing Corporation. All rights reserved by the Film Society of Lincoln Center. Reprinted by permission.

for, in a sense, the preservation of the liberty of the individual person against the mass.

CHILDS: *In that regard, do your films present truth or are they a balm for the human spirit? What do they give to people?*
CAPRA: I think one thing they give to people is hope.

CHILDS: *Hope?*
CAPRA: Yes. You cannot overestimate the fact that there is some reason for their being here—some reason to life, some reason for the creation of life, some reason for the cosmos to be here. Why we're here is not given us to know as yet; but if you follow whatever is biological, if you follow whatever is psychological, if you follow whatever is spiritual, you can find a reason for being. Even the Bushmen worship something. They are not forced to worship; they are not asked to worship. They do it from some inner desire, some great inner desire of the human spirit to worship something over and above their daily lives. Now, what is this drive for some perfection? It is the hope for better things.

CHILDS: *If I had to use one word to describe the dynamics behind your films, I'd perhaps use "perseverance"—which is, of course, something Faulkner used in his Nobel Prize speech, isn't it? Man will . . .*
CAPRA: . . . Persevere. Man will persevere and make this statement of himself come true, eventually.

CHILDS: *"It's a brutal world," Claude Rains says in* Mr. Smith, *which may or may not be true. But why is it the brutes always rule the world? Or put another way, how lasting are the accomplishments of* Mr. Deeds *and* Mr. Smith?
CAPRA: I don't think it matters as long as they're stated. In our free society we have to have every viewpoint stated, and Claude Rains had a perfectly good viewpoint to state when he said, "I decided to compromise in order to get certain things done." This is *also* a statement and perhaps an even more realistic statement than what Smith said. Smith was the idealist. Between the idealist and the pragmatist—somewhere in between—lies the truth, and they are often rubbing against each other. We each have to decide between the compromiser and the non-compromiser. One man gets along and the other says we should do better.

CHILDS: *Would you call Smith a sucker? It seems to me that you give the sucker an even break. "Sucker" is perhaps too strong.*

CAPRA: Yes. Well, he says in a sense, "I'm unprepared for this job. I shouldn't be here because I don't even know how to pass a bill. I'm a neophyte. I'm a child. I don't belong here with you learned men. I'm a child in one way—but I'm a man in another. I don't like to see evil invade this sacred sanctum." He can speak as a child and speak the truth.

CHILDS: *Most of your best heroes are innocent and childlike. Are they extensions of Harry Langdon's film characteristics?*

CAPRA: Yes. Most of these heroes have faith: faith in goodness and in the innate goodness of human beings. They lived that and they believed it. In a sense, this faith activated them and made them survive. Whereas other people say you need long claws and long teeth to survive, these people are saying, "No, you don't; you need compassion and brotherhood to survive." This is what I believe in, this is the way we should survive, this is the way we advance against the people who say, "No, it's the long claw, the sharp claw that survives." And there is the compromiser in between who says, "I will let my claws be cut, but I still want to operate as if I were still in the jungle. I'm a compromiser."

These are the statements that are said in *Mr. Smith*. Take your pick. In a sense, when at the end Senator Paine is defeated and he tries to commit suicide, and says, "Expel me, not him!"—that is a defeat for that particular viewpoint. Maybe you shouldn't go as far as suicide, but he too was once an idealist and then made a decision to compromise. So I don't know who wins at the end there.

CHILDS: *Those who've labeled your films Capracorn, what have they seen in your films?*

CAPRA: These are the critical minds as we know them here in the United States. Their base of operations is the Eastern seaboard and they're more or less allied to the European culture rather than to the American culture, certainly not to a city in Ohio a thousand miles away. So I've never had a very good standing among American intellectuals with my films. Certainly sentiment is an almost *verboten* emotion with the intellectuals. Why that should be I have not an idea, except it's perhaps too common, too ordinary—it's not arcane enough for an intellectual. Perhaps it's too simple.

CHILDS: *Did you deliberately try to make sentiment respectable?*

CAPRA: Certainly. Yes. I see nothing wrong with sentiment. Not respectable, especially, but more respectable. I thought sentiment was part of the warp and woof of life itself.

CHILDS: *Is it possible that a cynicism has imbued most people since World War II—because of the events that took place in it—and makes your kind of film difficult to produce today?*

CAPRA: I don't know if I can speak for the American public as a whole, because I don't think anyone can speak for it. There is no way to computerize the American public. I was in World War II and had an active part. That war left me a pacifist, a confirmed pacifist. I never could understand the brutality of war. I certainly couldn't understand [how], once we killed so many young people to defeat Germany and to defeat Japan, we could be ten years later their best friend. This is idiocy to me. I never understood why at one time we were at each others' throats and the next time we're shaking hands. What happened to all those dead people? What did they die for?

So war has become an abomination to me, because I couldn't understand it. I could understand a man holding up a bank, because he needs money desperately or he's a confirmed crook—and if we catch him he goes to jail. But I couldn't understand sending the flower of each generation off to war and getting them killed, and the next minute we're friends with the people we'd just been fighting. This is cynicism. When those values become distorted, then people have a right to question politicians, to question leaders. Those against the Vietnam War, in one sense, say, "To hell with it! My father got killed in Germany to knock off the Germans and here we are their best friends. What the hell are we in Vietnam for?" That's why I like the young people of today: they question things. They might not always be right, but they question things such as war and bad politics.

CHILDS: *Did you ever consider making a pacifist film?*

CAPRA: I think any film I would have made would have been pacifist, and *Mr. Deeds* and *Mr. Smith* imply pacifism. Probably instead of greed and corruption I would have aimed it at intolerance and war.

CHILDS: *Is there a place for wholesomeness in films or has this quality been usurped by TV entertainment? Is there a place for your kind of film for the mass market?*

CAPRA: Well, I don't like the word "mass."

CHILDS: *Well . . . "market."*
CAPRA: Yes. The human spirit yearns for hope, yearns for compassion, yearns to be allowed to become a brother to his neighbor—yearns for that. I think the public would accept my kind of film today as much as it ever did.

CHILDS: *Some of today's youth would agree. I just left the screening of* Lady for a Day *and it was a smash hit.*
CAPRA: I can only go on that. I think that hope is eternally needed.

CHILDS: *There's always a fantasy quality to your films. Would you call them at all realistic?*
CAPRA: Oh, I don't think so. Not realistic. They're entertainment and they're fantasy and they're comedy, but throughout this fantasy and comedy is woven this idea of "you dirty bastards, get off our necks!" You see?

CHILDS: *Women are very strong in your films. In the "Mr." films Jean Arthur bucks up the two heroes at critical points. Would this have been your influence on the script?*
CAPRA: Perhaps that's a result of a mother complex. I had a very strong mother—a very nice mother. I had a great respect for her ability to do under the worst kind of circumstance and not panic. Women have always been pillars of strength to me. Always. I'm not a feminist, but I'm a real lover of women. I have great respect for women.

CHILDS: *You seem to see their strengths.*
CAPRA: I do see them as strong people. The men are weak by comparison.

CHILDS: *Why are we weak?*
CAPRA: Because we have an imagination, we're poetic. Women are more pragmatic; they think in terms of everyone's welfare. They think in terms of tomorrow and in terms of continuation. Men commit suicide.

CHILDS: *Men are more despairing?*
CAPRA: Men are more despairing. Women do not despair. Woman will put up and make do.

CHILDS: *Do they have more perseverance?*
CAPRA: Yes. I think so.

CHILDS: *What do you think your contribution to motion pictures has been?*
CAPRA: My contribution to motion pictures has been that, throughout my career, I've spoken to millions of people and told them there is hope.

CHILDS: *Are you critical of films today?*
CAPRA: I'm impatient with them when they don't use film for something else besides negativism. People have enough of negative problems in their lives and I think the theater has another function to fulfill and that is to uplift.

CHILDS: *Lastly, "One man, one film." Are you espousing the auteur theory here?*
CAPRA: Yes. It is an art form and one man must create that form.

CHILDS: *Do you really think that your consciousness is the only one imprinted on your films, as say Ibsen's consciousness is imprinted on his plays, as Milton's is on his poetry?*
CAPRA: Yes. This has been so with my films. My films have been one man, one film.

Frank Capra Interviewed at the Second Tehran International Film Festival

AMERICAN CINEMATOGRAPHER/ 1973

ONE OF THE MOST HONORED guests to attend the Second Tehran International Film Festival was three-time Academy Award–winning American director Frank Capra.

Mr. Capra's presence in Tehran had a twofold significance. Primarily he was there as a member of the distinguished international jury selected to judge the various films in competition for awards. Secondarily, he was present in conjunction with a retrospective of seven of his outstanding films (ten were originally scheduled, but three of these did not arrive in time for screening), and to discuss these films with the crowds of eager film buffs that packed the showings.

Frank Capra, a legend among American (and world) filmmakers, is now retired from active film production. Extremely energetic, however, he remains very active as a kind of "elder statesman" to the film industry, writing, lecturing at universities throughout America and unselfishly passing on the considerable expertise of his long and distinguished career to young filmmakers, in whose growth and development he takes a great interest.

In Tehran, along with the other famed jury members, he was kept hopping from one screening to another during each day, so he was able to manage time for only a very short press conference. What follows is a transcript of that conference.

From *American Cinematographer* 55.2 (February 1974): 168–69, 210–13. Copyright © 1974, 2004. Reprinted by permission of American Cinematographer.

Q U E S T I O N :   *You have recently written a book,* The Name Above the Title, *which indicates that you have now gone into the profession of writing. So you have become a literary man and, being a cinema man essentially, what kind of relationship do you see between this and the cinema, and how have you taken to this bookwriting?*

C A P R A :   Well, I started out as a writer in films. The first job I had was as a gag man—mostly verbal—but I started out as a writer. The reason I wrote this book was because I have a great love affair with film and, since I've retired from making films, I wanted to continue that love affair in some other form. I figured that even though I might not want to make any more films, maybe I could write about them. Writing this book has been a very, very interesting experience. It took me three years to write it, working six or seven hours a day—very disciplined. But I don't think that I've ever enjoyed anything as much as that experience of disciplined writing. Now that I've talked to writers like yourselves, I feel that I've become one of you and I know what your problems are, what your disciplines are. Fortunately, I wrote a book about Hollywood—or about myself, actually—that really captured the imagination. It's become quite a bestseller—almost 200,000 copies in hard cover—and I hope you can read it sometime, because there are a lot of experiences about filmmaking in it. Writing this book confirmed the opinion that I'd had right along—namely, that writing literature and the film are two entirely different media, and I understand better now why many great writers, novelists, and playwrights did not become filmmakers.

Q U E S T I O N :   *What would be your opinion about the relationship between literature and the cinema? We see that literature is getting away from cinema more and more. Do you think that the same thing will happen to music—that there will be a divorce between the two, as time goes by?*

C A P R A :   Music is indispensable to films and I know that we will always have music in films. It may be that there will be two kinds of music—one kind for films and another that is just music as such, but we must have music in films. I hope you understand that film is one of the greatest of art forms, because it uses all of the other classic art forms as tools. That's how pervasive and wonderful an art form it is. It uses music and literature as tools, just as it uses actors and the camera. Actually, we still don't know how to make motion pictures. The great motion pictures have not yet been made. They will be made by the film students who are going to school today—and if they don't make them, their children will. But the great motion pictures are yet to come.

QUESTION: *What was your impression when you saw the new musical version of* Lost Horizon?

CAPRA: I have not seen it. That's because I had heard so much about it that I did not feel that I should go to see it and maybe come out with ulcers or something. I don't like to go to see a film that so many people said was not up to the mark at all. I love films too much for that and I feel sorry for anyone who has that experience. I had a premonition that that's what would happen, because they were tackling a subject that should not have been tackled in a light manner—as a light musical comedy. An opera, perhaps—but not a musical comedy.

QUESTION: *With only a few exceptions, most of the famous films you've made have been comedies. Is there any special reason why you have concentrated so much on comedy?*

CAPRA: Well, I thank God that I have some feeling for humor and some ability at humor, because I think that humor is the saving grace of the theater. Comedy is a very rare thing and a very wonderful way to communicate with people. It disarms people. You cannot laugh at anybody you don't like. You cannot laugh at anything that is brutal or mean or ugly. So laughter is one of the great things that oils the wheels of civilization, and it is one of the marks of civilization. I've been doing a great deal of work with universities in America—spending a week or so at various universities. I've been to about thirty of them and talked to tens of thousands of young people. The one thing they ask me is: "But, what is there to laugh at today?" And I say: "Just look in the mirror and you'll find plenty to laugh at." Until we can do that, until we can look into the mirror and see our own faults and foibles, we are not really civilized. The great mark of civilized people is when they can laugh at themselves. There is just one more point I'd like to make about my films or anybody else's films, and that has to do with the great power of love. Now, you can be cynical and laugh at the word "love," but you'll find that you cannot ignore it. It is the greatest power to move human beings that there is. Every great work of art, every great classic play, every great novel has in it, somewhere, a transcendental love story—preferably, a sacrificial love story. If it hasn't got that one great ingredient of love, it's likely to be passed off as having only a temporary effect. I've noticed among the young students at the universities in the United States that there is a new growing hunger for idealism and for the more humanistic types of stories and for humor and for love, and I can see that especially among the young ladies of the universities. In your writing, ladies and gentlemen, don't be afraid of emotion. It's a wonderful thing, emotion. The human spirit needs uplifting. It always needs uplifting.

QUESTION: *I would like to ask about the rhythm and technique you have achieved in your films, especially in* American Madness. *What is your opinion about this, and what sort of contribution do you make to the art of the cinema at large by achieving this technique and rhythm?*

CAPRA: I'm going to have to talk to you personally. I didn't come down from Mt. Sinai with the tablets. I can only tell you how I feel about it, and that doesn't mean that somebody else doesn't have another system that is just as good as mine or better than mine. One of the things that happened in *American Madness* was that before I made that film I used to see my pictures in a theater and I always felt that the audience was a little bit ahead of the picture. The picture was behind the audience. The audience knew what was coming, and I felt that they kept saying "Come on. Come on. What's next?" I wondered why that was so, because I would see the same picture in a small projection room or on the Moviola and the pace would seem adequate. But the pace seemed to slow down for a large number of people in a large theater. I asked around to see if anyone else had this feeling that their films slowed down in front of an audience, but I didn't get any response. Some people said such a thing was impossible. Yet, I felt that there was some psychological reason why this was happening. Perhaps it was the size of the faces on the screen, projecting vibrations faster than a normal-sized face. Maybe it was the fact that there was a thousand pairs of eyes and ears and these could accept stimuli faster than just one pair of eyes and ears. I tried to research this problem to see if there was any validity to the fact that a crowd could accept stimuli a lot faster than individuals could. Nothing much had been done in the field of human behaviorism at the time, but I tried something for the first time in *American Madness*. I would rehearse a scene and, let's say, it took sixty seconds and it looked just fine at sixty seconds. Then we would speed up the scene so that the actors played it in forty seconds. It was abnormal in the playing, but I noticed that when that scene got on the screen it didn't look abnormal. It had a sense of urgency to it, so that people didn't look away from the screen anymore. For the first time I had the film ahead of the audience, so that they were intensely interested in what was going on. Ever since then I've used that accelerated pace in shooting scenes for every picture I've made—except in the mood scenes, where pace is not a factor at all.

QUESTION: *In your book, you speak of working with the comedian Harry Langdon. Could you tell us a bit more about that?*
CAPRA: I'll try to answer that as briefly as I can, because I have a note here that says we are due at the Ministry of Culture for jury screenings. Harry Langdon was a comedian that Mr. Mack Sennett had hired because he thought he saw something special in that man. There was a strange slowness about him. He was an elfish little creature and he worked at Mack Sennett's for about two years with all the other comedians, but the people who worked with him didn't like him at all because he was so slow. All of the other comedians were moving fast, so they didn't like Langdon. Nevertheless, Mr. Sennett kept telling everybody: "This man has got something and you fellows don't know how to find it." I was a gag writer and there were two of us working together as a team, thinking up routines for the various comics. It came my turn to see this little film they had made of Langdon's vaudeville act, and he certainly was nothing. He had baggy pants and a little hat, but he was doing nothing. My partner said: "I don't know how we can do anything with this man. Only God can help that comedian." Then I said: "Wait a minute . . . Only God can help him . . ." I had just finished reading *Soldier Schweick*. If you all wonder who Soldier Schweick was, let me say that he was a wonderful little soldier who liked everybody. He saw no evil in anybody. The idea was that only God could help him; only goodness could help him—not his luck, not his brains or anything else—just his goodness. We fell in love with that idea and cooked up a story for Langdon built around such a character, and he became a star overnight—fast! Now, the tragedy of this whole thing is that he did not understand this character that we had created for him. He had not created it himself and he did not understand it, but he had one driving ambition: he wanted to do what Chaplin did—write, direct, act and be a big star like Chaplin was. It was so wrong for him to do this, because Chaplin had created his own character and he knew more about himself than anyone else did—but Harry Langdon did not know his own

character. So finally, after we'd made three very successful pictures with him, he decided to make his own pictures from then on—and he went down faster than he'd gone up. It was the great tragedy of a true comedian, a clown. He died very shortly after that. He died because he didn't know what happened to him. And now, I thank you for your excellent questions.

Unfortunately, the pressures of his duties on the Festival jury cut short the duration of Mr. Capra's press conference, but more of his interesting philosophy came out in a private interview with J. V. Cotton, editor-in-chief of the influential French cinema magazine, *Ciné Revue*. Excerpts from that interview are reproduced as follows:

COTTON: *What is the main difference between Hollywood today and the Hollywood you know?*
CAPRA: I would say freedom of expression. Today you can film more or less what you want. We could deal with unsavory subjects too, but because of the Hays Code only with great discretion. We based our films on emotions rather than vices. The trouble is, vices, sexual aberrations, and violence quickly pall. Today there is a tendency to despise great characters. Films deal with anti-heroes, whereas in my day the opposite was true.

COTTON: *Men like violence up to a point, but it seems to put women off. Today's films rarely seem to cater to feminine taste.*
CAPRA: True, but we shouldn't worry too much about this. I see a lot of young people, American students particularly, and I can assure you young people have had enough of violence and sexual freedom. The cinema industry will face a serious danger if it overlooks what the young people are really looking for.

COTTON: *Like it did in renting its old films to television?*
CAPRA: Yes, but remember these old films would not otherwise have ever got shown again. Most of these films are pretty mediocre, and if they are good they're out of style. I believe the public is always ready for a good film. The public hasn't disappeared, it's dozing and waiting.

COTTON: *What do you think has been the effect of the gradual disappearance of the legendary figures of Hollywood?*

C A P R A :   As I said, today we have only anti-heroes. The public likes to identify with film stars but how can you love an anti-hero? Women cinema-goers
can only be attracted to a man who understands, forgives, shows compassion. Gary Cooper and James Stewart were great actors, but also "moral"
heroes. They had a certain something, and they played the parts of characters who were by and large on a higher plane than the ordinary man, whereas
today's stars are mostly far below the level of the audience. How can you
expect the public to be attracted by people who behave like wild animals?

C O T T O N :   *Do you regret the disappearance of the star system?*
C A P R A :   Being an independent, I never liked studio politics much. But that
is a personal view, and I must admit that the star system had its advantages.
A studio might put out seventy-five films a year, of which only ten or so were
made on a really big budget. The others would have a medium budget, and
actors to match. But those films were in a way experimental, for they enabled
the studios to give a chance to new directors, scriptwriters, and actors. Everyone therefore had a chance to show his talents, which is very different from
the case today, when people are afraid to take risks. That is why the indepen-
dents are so conservative today and stick to existing formulas. They've
become freight cars, whereas before they were locomotives. What Hollywood
needs most today is these experimental films. Which are an unthinkable lux-
ury now.

C O T T O N :   *How would you explain Hollywood's present difficulties?*
C A P R A :   There's no imaginative thinking going on there, just the same old
routine. There have been attempts at planning and rationalizing, but this
policy does not fit in with artistic expression. It's a fact all too often forgotten
that a film is above all an art form.

C O T T O N :   *An art form in which stars will always have a role to play?*
C A P R A :   There will always be stars, but today they're being gradually
replaced by directors. Why? Because today audiences have a better idea of
what a film is and how it can affect people. The last great stars in the real
Hollywood sense are undoubtedly Liz Taylor and Richard Burton, but they
too are on the decline. Personally, that doesn't worry me a great deal because
I've always thought it immoral to pay stars astronomical sums which could
be used, often more effectively, on the other aspects of film production. I

think such people are a disservice to their profession. Luckily cinema-goers are beginning to understand this.

COTTON: *So film stars are finished forever?*
CAPRA: Marilyn Monroe was the last. Today nobody goes to see a film just because of a star. Paul Newman and Marlon Brando are among the last survivors of this species, which I think is heading for extinction. But they will never be the equal of a Clark Gable or a Gary Cooper. It's the public who make a star, not the studios. I also believe there are cycles at work. Today we are in an unfavorable cycle for stars, but there's no reason why next year this shouldn't change and we'll have film stars again by the score. But whatever happens, it will be the public that decides, not the studios.

COTTON: *What do you think of the present vogue for violence and pornography in films?*
CAPRA: Everyone's fed up with it, and wants it to end. But the fact is that the producers, especially in Europe, are set on their course. They think it's the only thing. They're crazy, of course. Filming two naked persons thrashing about on a bed, what's that got to do with art? You can make money that way, but I think we're nearly at the end of that road. The same thing with drugs. Young people are much more idealistic than they were ten years ago, and above all they want to have confidence in the future. Also the press has blown the drug thing up tremendously. There are vast numbers of young people who don't even know what LSD is.

COTTON: *Do you have confidence in the future of the cinema?*
CAPRA: More than ever. The development of new techniques such as cassettes, which will enable you to show films in your own home, just like putting on a record—it's an extraordinary breakthrough.

And the Shakespeare of the cinema has not yet been born. Cinema is still young, less than sixty years old, and the best is yet to come. I believe the cinema is the greatest forum of the arts there has ever been. Nobody has ever had the power that a film director has, no saint, sultan or Pope. Nobody has been able to talk to millions of people for two hours. Man is always striving towards ideals, towards something that can inspire him. The most attractive commodity in the world has always been a love story. Every great novel, play or film has always started from transcendental love, the love of a man for a woman, or for a country, or a boy's love for a dog.

COTTON: *And what about yourself? Do you intend to make any more films?*
CAPRA: I worked for forty-five years without a holiday or a real rest. Now, I'm making up for it. I know I could still direct a film perfectly well, but it's time now to look around me. Talent can make you a tyrant or a slave. And I can't help being amazed that in 1973 there are still tyrants and slaves.

A Conversation with Frank Capra

RICHARD GLATZER/1973

GLATZER: *Many of your early Columbia films like* The Younger Generation, That Certain Thing, *and* The Power of the Press *no longer exist. Why didn't you save prints of your early movies?*

CAPRA: Well, nobody thought they were important enough to save. You know, the films we were making in those days were just nickel and dime affairs. They were like today's newspaper—you don't save today's newspaper. And when they were finished, nobody expected to ever see them again. As a matter of fact, many negatives were just thrown out and sold for the silver by smarter men than I. Certainly we didn't think any of these things were masterpieces or anything like that. We were very glad to make them and get paid and go on to something else.

GLATZER: *Yet your attitude changed shortly after you made these films. Your cardinal precept of "one man—one film," which you adopted early in the 1930s, suggests that you thought of yourself as an artist interested in much more than simply getting paid. What made you buck the system and insist on having artistic control over your movies?*

CAPRA: Well, I suppose I'll never be able to answer that question adequately, except that I rebel against control of any kind. I'm a bad organization man; I like to be my own man and I don't like somebody else to tell me what to do. It was just the natural rebel in me that I couldn't take orders.

From *Frank Capra: The Man and His Films,* edited by Richard Glatzer and John Raeburn. Copyright © 1975 by the University of Michigan Press. Reprinted by permission.

Also, I felt that I knew more about films than the people who tried to tell me how to make them.

GLATZER: *More than Harry Cohn?*
CAPRA: More than Harry Cohn, more than any of those executives. I knew what it took to make motion pictures. I knew there was a *way* to do things; like painters know there is a way to paint and sculptors know there is a way to sculpt, I knew there was a way to make films and they shouldn't tell me how to make my films.

GLATZER: *Why didn't other directors feel as you did?*
CAPRA: Well, other directors wanted freedom. Let me tell you, I had a backstop. Down in my heart I wanted to go back to Caltech and get a doctor's degree and teach science. If films didn't work out for me I knew I could make that go. So, I didn't depend on films entirely; if I could make films, fine, I'd make them, but if I couldn't then I would do something else. If I couldn't make films the way I wanted them, I didn't want to make them at all. For many other directors films were their total business, and their income depended entirely on them. When you want your own way in films you stick your neck way out. The chances are only about one in ten that you'll succeed—this is normal in all show business because nobody can predict what is wanted—and on that kind of percentage it's difficult to stick your neck out and say, "Let me do it my way." The chances are you'll fall on your face. And if you do fall on your face, one failure is acceptable, two failures and maybe you get another chance, three failures in a row and you're out. That's a big risk to take. Very few people wanted that total responsibility because they were afraid for their careers. I was not afraid for my career.

GLATZER: *I'd like to hear about your 1928 movie,* The Power of the Press. *Why didn't you mention it in* The Name Above the Title?
CAPRA: An oversight: I'd just forgotten about it. But it was a very good picture.

GLATZER: *What sort of film is it?*
CAPRA: A gangster movie about the power of the press to unearth gangsters when the police can't find them—a prying reporter digs up stuff about a

crime syndicate and brings them to justice. Doug Fairbanks, Jr., was the
reporter.

GLATZER: *I usually don't think of you as a suspense director. Any special scenes
you remember?*
CAPRA: Oh yes, there is a suspense scene in it, a comedy suspense scene
about how Fairbanks escapes from prison. They've put a special guard on
him sitting outside his cell—they realize this reporter is pretty smart and will
try all kinds of things to get out. The guard likes to sleep, so he puts a ring of
keys around his finger and he holds his hand up in the air. He knows that if
he dozes off, his hand will drop and the keys will fall off his finger and hit
the concrete floor and wake him up. That's his alarm system. And it works.
He snoozes, the keys drop, he wakes up and sees that Fairbanks is still there.
But Fairbanks gets an idea. He has his hat with him, and he uses a stick to
poke his hat out through the bars. He manages to get his hat under the
guard's hand, and as the guard dozes off the keys drop off his finger, fall into
the hat, and don't make any noise. The guard doesn't wake up. So Fairbanks
pulls in the keys, opens the door, and lets himself out.

GLATZER: Power of the Press *was your last silent film. How did the transition
to sound affect you. Did you prefer one mode to the other?*
CAPRA: How can you compare them? It's like trying to compare sculpture
with painting; is sculpture better than painting? The art of pantomime had
advanced to a very high degree in the making of silent films. People like
Murnau, Griffith, Ince, and DeMille and others had reached a high degree of
excellence in a language that was universal.

When the film developed a larynx it was an entirely new ball game: a new
element had been added that was a realistic element. You didn't have to
depend so much on photography because people became more real on the
screen. As far as I'm concerned, it was an enormous step forward. I wasn't at
home in silent films; I thought it was very strange to stop and put a title on
the screen and then come back to the action. It was a very contrived and
very mechanical way of doing things. When I got to working with sound, I
thought, my, what a wonderful tool has been added. I don't think I could
have gone very far in silent pictures—at least not as far as I did go with
sound.

GLATZER: *How important is editing to the final film? Some directors—John Ford, for example—didn't edit their films, but I believe you played a major role in the editing of yours. Why?*

CAPRA: No two directors work alike. John Ford didn't have patience enough to do the nitty-gritty of editing. But he shot his films in such a way that they could only be edited one way. He didn't give the editors much film to play with, so they had to edit them practically as he had shot them.

Now I loved film editing—I get a sensuous feeling out of film when I feel it in my fingers. I know what can be done with film: I know what the juxtaposition of scenes can mean for the finished film, how when you have twenty scenes and you put them together there's probably only one or two ways in which that film can come alive and the rest of the ways you can put them together mean dullness. I think that editing is the greatest fun about filmmaking.

GLATZER: *Can we talk about the way you use the camera? In 1932, you wrote an article for the* Cinematographic Annual *asserting the importance of the cameraman in film. Yet you rarely draw attention to a moving camera. . . .*

CAPRA: I move the camera a lot more than you think—all the time. But if you don't see it, that's a great compliment, because audiences are not supposed to see the camera move. You want them to be involved only with the characters on the screen. If you do distract them with camera movements or other gimmicks, then that's bad directing in my estimation.

GLATZER: *Did you have a specific way of blocking out scenes? How far in advance did you visualize how you wanted a scene to be shot? Was it in the scriptwriting stage?*

CAPRA: No, the scripts were all written in master scenes. We never broke them down into individual shots because that was just a waste of time. The set wasn't built yet, you didn't know what kind of cast you would have, so you were just massaging your ego with "Close up . . . long shot . . . cut to this, cut to that. . . ." You didn't need all that detailing. What you need is what the scene is about, who does what to whom, and who cares about whom. The mechanics of shooting have to be left up to the director and crew.

Now that doesn't apply to everybody, of course, because directors all work differently. Some directors want scripts that are blueprinted right down to the last detail; others have to be flexible and let the scenes create themselves. There are different ways of working. All I want is a master scene and I'll take care of the rest—how to shoot it, how to keep the machinery out of the way, and how to focus attention on the actors at all times.

GLATZER: *How improvisational were you while shooting?*
CAPRA: Well, if you work with master scenes, it gives you a chance to open or close them up. If you've got a scene and you get a group of actors who can't play that scene, there is no shoving it down their throats. It'll be a bad scene. So you rewrite the scene, half of it, two-thirds of it, all of it; until you come up with a scene the actors can play—providing, of course, that you're not mutilating a key scene. You can't fool with those key scenes too much. But there are many, many scenes—the expository ones, which are the duds, where you're not dealing with characterization but filling in the plot. It's how you handle these plot scenes that is really important; how you keep the ball up in the air. You don't just set actors up and let them talk; you give them "business" to do while they're yakking. And this is where some directors are much better than others.

GLATZER: *You don't notice expository scenes in* American Madness— *everything moves so fast. I think you give the film short shrift in* The Name Above the Title. *You've seen it again recently—since writing the autobiography—haven't you? What do you think of it now?*
CAPRA: Well, I thought the picture looked as if it were made yesterday. And I was so surprised by it. I gave it short shrift in the autobiography, but I did say that it was a key film of mine because it was the first time I used accelerated tempo. And it worked! The tempo is about forty percent above normal at all times in *American Madness*. Things keep happening so fast that you're afraid to look away from the screen. There's an urgency about it because of the tempo—it just holds you. And of course that's part of what you want to do, hold the audience, hold their interest. You don't want them to reach for that popcorn.

GLATZER: *Even the dialogue seems to be accelerated, with overlapping speakers, people cutting each other off, and so on. It's very cinematic. . . . You anticipate Robert Altman's treatment of dialogue in some respects—and by forty years.*
CAPRA: I didn't know I was doing anything new. It was just the way I felt

about dialogue. We were constantly improvising, there were no rules. Everybody had their own way. We were maturing and we were discovering things. I was amazed at how *American Madness* turned out, how the faster pace perfectly fitted that picture.

I play a number of very important scenes in crowds in that film. I like to fill the screen with people. I love faces, I love to look at people, and I think others do too—all kinds of people, walking in and out. I never try to isolate a scene too much from real life.

GLATZER: *Where did you get your notions of economics that Walter Huston articulates in* American Madness? *They're New Dealish, almost Keynesian.*
CAPRA: Well, yes. But we made the film before Roosevelt was elected. I got the idea for the story from the life of Giannini, a pushcart guy who started the Bank of Italy—the Bank of America today. He started it to finance the vending of Italian fruit and vegetables in California, and he gradually built a little bank. He'd lend money on character.

I remember one time a man came to our house. He'd just arrived from Italy with only the clothes on his back, and a few cans of tomato paste that he'd brought with him in a sack. We passed some around and everybody tasted it. My father said, "Oh, that's wonderful tomato paste. What would you like to do with it?" And he said, "I'd like to make it."

My father took him down to the Bank of Italy, and said, "This man's got tomato paste, and he'd like to make it." So they passed the tomato paste around. And Giannini said, "Can you make this? Do you know how to make it? You've got the recipe?" So he made some at our house, and took it back to the bank and passed it around again. Giannini said he'd build him a plant! So the guy began to make tomato paste. I forget what the hell happened to him. He could be Del Monte.

That's the kind of an egg Giannini was. All the other banks thought he was absolutely nuts, lending money on character. He'd take collateral if you had it, but if you didn't and you had character, he'd lend you money anyhow. So I think he was the inspiration for Walter Huston's character in *American Madness.*

GLATZER: *Could you tell me something about* Soviet? *You started work on it with MGM, never finished it, yet in 1938, in an interview, you said that it was the best thing you had ever worked on.*

CAPRA: Well, it probably was. It was a tremendous melodrama and I had the dream cast of all time—Clark Gable, Wally Beery, Joan Crawford, and the wonderful Marie Dressler. It was about the building of a dam in Russia with an American engineer supervising it. Wally Beery was going to play the role of a commissar who was given the job of building this great dam. He didn't know anything about engineering, but was a man in charge who had made his way up from the bottom of the Bolshevik regime. Marie Dressler was his wife, and a very patient, loving wife she was. Joan Crawford was to play a very, very politically minded gal who was the assistant commissar. Clark Gabel was an American engineer, sent over to help them build this dam.

The conflicts were personal and ideological: The American wants to get things done and the commissar wants to get them done in his own way. Gable falls in love with Joan Crawford, and they have a running battle: she hates anything American and anything that is not Communistic, and he hates anything that *is* Communistic—all this plus the drama of building this dam. Nothing but great battles: they fought nature, they fought each other, they fought the elements, all to get this great dam built.

GLATZER: *Did they get the dam built?*
CAPRA: Yes, they did. I want to tell you about the end of the film. They were celebrating the completion of the dam. The Wally Beery character was particularly complex. One of his hands had been cut off, and on his remaining hand he wore a handcuff—with an empty handcuff dangling—as a symbol of his slavery under the Czarist system that had cut off his hand—he never took this handcuff off. During the celebration the camera pans down the enormous face of the dam and then moves into a close-up and there is this handcuff sticking out of the cement—Beery has been buried inside the dam.

GLATZER: *How did that happen?*
CAPRA: Well, I can't go into the story—it would take all day. But that was the end of the film.

GLATZER: *Clark Gable marries Joan Crawford?*
CAPRA: No, no, he doesn't marry anybody—he goes home.

GLATZER: *How far did you get with the movie?*
CAPRA: We didn't get anywhere, except that we had the script written. It

was a pet project of Irving Thalberg and Thalberg died suddenly. He and Louis Mayer didn't get along, and anything Thalberg had in the works instantly went out when Thalberg died. That story went out, and I went out of MGM with it.

GLATZER: *In some of your films you seem to have a feeling for footloose drifters, especially in* It Happened One Night *and* Meet John Doe. *Would you talk about those years after World War I when you just drifted around . . . ?*

CAPRA: That was a long period, several years. I just bummed around and had an excellent time. I met up with a professional bum named Frank Dwyer, an Irishman who played a ukulele and sang. He taught me how to hop trains, things like that. He also taught me how to make a living selling photographs house to house. If you punched enough doorbells, you could make five or six dollars a day. With six sales a day, you could work two days a week and you'd have enough for the rest of the week. Frank Dwyer . . . what a wonderful character! He lived just as he wanted to, wherever he wanted to. He had this racket, the photographs, that he could make money with whenever he wanted. He had it made!

GLATZER: *Did you get your sense of small towns during this period?*

CAPRA: Got a real sense of small towns, got a real sense of America. I found out a lot about Americans. I loved them. This great country, I saw a good deal of it. I roamed all over the West. I saw the deserts, the mountains, I met the farmers, the people, the people who were working and not complaining. It was a great experience. I met a lot of Gary Coopers.

GLATZER: *Can we talk a little more about the autobiographical dimension in your films? After you bummed around you started to work in the movies; weren't you involved in a small claims suit that was similar to scenes in some of your films later?*

CAPRA: Well, there was a small claims suit. I was working in a film laboratory at the time and I did any odd jobs that came along—editing newsreel footage that came in, and so on. One guy brought in a scenic documentary, a Chamber of Commerce sort of thing, and asked me to write some titles for it. I wrote about thirty titles. Then I didn't get paid, which burned me up. We had settled on fifty dollars for the thirty titles, which was pretty cheap. Still, fifty dollars was a lot of money at that time and he wouldn't pay it. He said he didn't have the money yet. He had thirty-three backers, bankers and real estate people in San Francisco, but they wouldn't give him any more money. So I sued them.

For a sum that small, you can go to a small claims court without a lawyer. So I went to court and they asked me to fill out this huge form. They said, "Who do you want to sue?" and I said, "I have a list of thirty-three people I want to sue." They included the biggest names in San Francisco, men like the president of the Crocker National Bank. I thought if I made enough stink they would pay. The court bailiff said, "Boy, you're going to have writer's cramp doing this thing because you're going to have to fill out thirty-three complaints in triplicate." I said, "I don't care, I've got a lot of time." I took the thirty-three complaints, in triplicate, filled them out in longhand, brought them back, and they were mailed out. It must have cost a fortune for postage.

I didn't expect anybody to show up for the hearing. I just wanted the fifty bucks and I was going to harass somebody. I was sure none of these big people would show up. Well, they did! They all showed up! Thirty-three legal big wigs, representing the San Francisco brass. "Hi Bill!" "Hi there!" "How are you doing?"—you know. They all got together and said, "What's this slop?" They wanted an indignation meeting with the guy who made the film. They thought the film stunk. It cost too much money and it stunk. I was in the middle, so they came down to court to harass me about the film. I said I didn't make the film, I had just written the titles and agreed to get paid fifty dollars. They said, "The titles stink too!" "I don't care whether they stink or not—I want to get paid for my work!" So one guy says, "For God's sakes, so he's not a Shakespeare. These titles aren't very good, but by God he turned them in and they're in the film. Let's pay the guy the fifty bucks."

But who was going to pay the fifty dollars? So one lawyer took off his hat and went around and got contributions from all of them. Then he emptied it on the judge's desk, and the judge counted it to see if it was enough. And the judge put in a dollar of his own. I've loved judges ever since.

GLATZER: *So that's what inspired the judges in* Mr. Deeds *and* You Can't Take It with You. *What about doctors? So many fathers in your movies are doctors— Jean Arthur's in* Mr. Smith, *Gary Cooper's in* Mr. Deeds, *Barbara Stanwyck's in* Meet John Doe. . . .

CAPRA: Well, there was a doctor I met in the Sierras who caught my imagination. He was a very well known surgeon who went there to retire. But the people there needed him, so he organized a little hospital. He'd want to go fishing mornings, but there he was down at the hospital because he was needed. He'd only charge them fifty or sixty cents, but he gave two dollars worth of medicine. He was that kind of a guy. I got to know him very well. I'd try to take him fishing, but they'd catch up with him, blow the horn on the highway, and off he'd go.

When he was dying I went down to see him at the hospital. I couldn't get in because the hallways were so packed with people. When I finally made my way up to his room, I asked his daughter how he was. She said, "He's not very well, but he certainly is glad all these friends came down to see him." I was amazed; none of these people knew one another, but at some point he had touched each of their lives. I never saw such a tribute to a man. There was every kind of person there: conductors, truck drivers, bankers. Where did he meet all those people?

He died a very rich man because he had so many friends. He still seems to me to be a person to be looked up to and to be respected. He worked only for others. So, if you're going to have a father, you ought to have one like that.

GLATZER: *So many of your films have offhand, somewhat improvisatory musical numbers in them—I'm thinking of Gary Cooper and Jean Arthur in Central Park in* Mr. Deeds *or the bus passengers singing "The Man on the Flying Trapeze" in* It Happened One Night *or the "You Can't Carry a Tune" bit between Williams and Harlow in* Platinum Blonde, *and so on. It's almost a trademark. . . .*
CAPRA: Sometimes your story has got to stop and you let the audience just look at your people. You want the audience to like them. The characters have no great worries for the moment—they like each other's company and that's it. The less guarded they are, the more silly it is, the better.

These scenes are quite important to a film. When the audience rests and they look at the people, they begin to smile. They begin to love the characters, and *then* they'll be worried about what happens to them. If the audience doesn't like your people, they won't laugh at them and they won't cry with them.

GLATZER: *How did you work with scriptwriters?*
CAPRA: If you get two people who vibrate to the same tuning fork, then a kinship and a friendship develop and you start bouncing ideas off each

other. You become performer and audience to each other. When that happens, it's a symbiotic relationship; things are better because the two of you are together. The whole is better than the sum of the parts. I've had occasion several times to have that arrangement with writers, where you really were vibrating to the same tuning fork and were audiencing for each other. It's a very, very happy relationship.

There were other times when the relationship was not so happy and I could not get along with the writers; then I had to depend on myself. I just said, "I'll write it myself, to hell with it." Writing is something I liked to do, but if you try to write and direct and produce a show and do it all yourself, you have a great many headaches to take care of. Whereas if you get a writer who understands you and you understand him, he takes on the bulk of the work of writing the script. Now that's a very fine arrangement. So you ask how do we write scripts? Well, you get together with a writer you like and who likes you.

GLATZER: *Could you talk a bit about your relationship with Robert Riskin?*
CAPRA: Robert Riskin was a very talented man with a fine ear for dialogue. That ear for dialogue was what really intrigued me about Riskin. People always sounded real when he wrote their dialogue, and I worshipped that.

We were good friends. We saw each other a great deal—went out together. It was a very wonderful relationship, and a very profitable relationship for both of us, in the sense I spoke of before—the sum of our work was greater than the individual efforts we both put in.

GLATZER: *You admit in your autobiography that you and Riskin had difficulty creating an ending for* Meet John Doe. *Did Doe commit suicide in any of the alternate endings you considered?*
CAPRA: Yes. In one version, the movie was to end in a short scene, played on the steps of City Hall. Walter Brennan is waiting for Cooper to show up, still waiting for him, not knowing he's upstairs on the roof. Barbara Stanwyck is running upstairs. We see Cooper on the roof about to jump. And we cut down to Brennan. Suddenly Brennan hears something, turns around, and my God he sees—we don't show it—he sees the body on the steps. He rushes onto the steps, cradles Cooper in his arms, and says, "Long John, Long John, you poor sucker, you poor sucker." That's the end.

GLATZER: *Did you distribute that ending to any theaters?*

CAPRA: No. You just don't kill Gary Cooper. It's a hell of a powerful ending, but you just can't kill Gary Cooper.

GLATZER: *You obviously liked working with Gary Cooper and Jimmy Stewart: between them, they appeared in five of your movies. Could you talk about the differences between them?*

CAPRA: Cooper is the more mature person, at least he gives you that impression. He also gives you the impression of being a more solid, earthy person. He's simple, but he's strong and honest, and there's integrity written all over him. When you're dealing in the world of ideas and you want your character to be on a higher intellectual plane than just a simple man, you turn to persons like Jimmy Stewart because he has a look of the intellectual about him. And he can be an idealist. So when you have a combination of an intellectual who is also an idealist, you have a pretty fine combination.

GLATZER: *What about actresses? You used Jean Arthur and Barbara Stanwyck a good deal, and got an Academy Award–winning performance from Claudette Colbert. What were the differences among them?*

CAPRA: First of all, I think all three of them are just great. Jean Arthur is a warm, able, lovable kind of a woman who has a very feminine drive. I think of her as a woman who is always looking for someone to marry, looking for that man she could give her whole life to, but who can't seem to find him. A tough gal with a heart of gold.

Claudette Colbert is another type of woman, much more intellectual. She knows what's going on, and she's a bit of a rebel. She doesn't want to be told what to do. She was perfect for *It Happened One Night,* because she was a shrew and she had to be tamed by someone we like. She wasn't looking for any man, she wasn't looking for any romance. She was much more intellectual than the women Jean Arthur played.

Barbara Stanwyck started out with a pretty hard life. She was a chorus girl at a time when the gangsters ran the nightclubs, and that was pretty tough on the girls. Life was pretty seamy. So she can give you that burst of emotion better than the other two can. She is probably the most interesting of the three. She's also the hardest to define: she's sullen, she's somber, she acts like she's not listening but she hears every word. She's the easiest to direct. She played parts that were a little tougher, yet at the same time you could sense that this girl could suffer from her toughness, and really suffer from the penance she would have to pay.

GLATZER: *I like the sense of complete characterization your bit players often provide, even in extremely minor parts. How did you accomplish this?*
CAPRA: Well, I didn't treat them like bit players. I treated them all as stars. Whether they were in that picture for ten minutes, or ten seconds, that time they were on the screen had to be perfect. If the so-called bit people are believable and can involve the audience in a sense of reality, the audience forgets they're looking at a film. They think they're looking at something in real life. The bit people have a great chore because they're helping to make that background real. If the audience believes in the small people, they'll believe in the stars.

I'd take a great deal of time casting those parts, and a great deal of time playing them. I don't mean I shot many takes or had many rehearsals, because I did not. But I spent a lot of time talking with the actors.

GLATZER: *Did you often act out the parts for them?*
CAPRA: No, I didn't want them to ape me. That's another way of directing, and men like Lubitsch did that very well. I wanted to stay out of the picture entirely. I wanted audiences to think it was all happening for the first time. I gave each of the actors a personality, a sense of being, a sense of existence—no matter how small their part, even if it was a walk-on. I'd say, "You're a little bit worried because your father is in the hospital." Give bit actors an identity, and boy, they come to life! They look real.

GLATZER: *Of your contemporaries, which directors did you admire most, and why?*
CAPRA: That's a difficult question to answer because no two directors work alike—each one has his own style, and his style may not suit someone else. So it's difficult to compare them, and I can only tell you about some of them whose pictures I've liked.

John Ford I liked very much; I think he probably knew more about picture-making than all the rest of us put together, and I think he made some of our best films. I know his stock is going down at the moment, but I think his films will live. John Ford was an artist: he was an Irishman, he was pig-headed, he was all kinds of things—but he loved films with a passion, and the films he made show this passion. I think when a hundred years roll by, Mr. Ford will be right up there with his films.

Another man whose films I liked very much was Leo McCarey. I liked his comedies—when he started to do dramas, he was just lost. But his comedy films were about as funny as anyone has ever made. Delightful, delightful comedies they were.

Howard Hawks is another guy I admire very much, because he's a real craftsman. He knows his tools, and he knows their limitations. He uses his tools expertly, like a surgeon. He makes films that only he could make. You're never bored by a Hawks film.

William Wellman's films are never boring either, because Wellman himself is not a boring man. He's a man who talks like he wants you to think he knows nothing, but he knows a great deal about a lot of things.

These men all have one thing in common: a passionate love of film. And they each have a style. You see their films, and their personal stamp is on them. It doesn't make any difference where the story came from, or what actors are in it, the style is there. Only when people achieve that distinction of putting their own mark on something—their style—can you really call them filmmakers.

GLATZER: *What about Orson Welles? Do you admire him as a director?*
CAPRA: No, not particularly. I wouldn't put him with the people I've mentioned at all. First of all, he hasn't made enough films to stamp anything. As a director, he's made very little beyond *Citizen Kane* and *The Magnificent Ambersons*. I know that *Citizen Kane* is supposed to be the nearest thing to the second coming of Christ, but I don't think so.

GLATZER: *Making the* Why We Fight *series must have been very different from making a dramatic film. . . .*
CAPRA: But not so different. You see, the fact that I had never made a documentary before was a great help; I didn't have a documentary mind, I had a dramatic mind. Here was the world stage, here were actors, here were plots, here were stories, and I told them dramatically. You had the world's greatest heroes and the world's greatest villains competing. You had a chance to dramatize it with film. I think what was different about those documentaries was that history was dramatized, and I think that was their main attraction.

GLATZER: *Did your wartime experiences have any effect on* It's a Wonderful Life?
CAPRA: Yes, the war did affect me. I didn't want to see another cannon go off; I didn't want to see another bomb blow up. War lost its glamour for me. Just to see those trembling people in London during the Blitz, poor sick old ladies crying, crying in terror . . . children. There's got to be something better than bombing old ladies and children. I lost . . . there's nothing glamorous about war. I didn't want to be a war hero, nothing. That's why I made a movie about an ordinary guy.

GLATZER: *Is that why you moved away from politics? I feel that* It's a Wonderful Life *is your least political major film.*
CAPRA: Yes, it is. But then I made *State of the Union.*

GLATZER: *But did your coming back from the war influence you to make this movie about an anonymous man in a small town?*
CAPRA: I wouldn't be a bit surprised. I couldn't be interested in anything else. I certainly wasn't interested in things like *The Best Years of Our Lives* or anything like that. I didn't want to see anything more of war—the brutality of it so upset me and so filled me with a feeling of the incompetence of the human race. If the best way they can think of settling an argument is dropping bombs. . . . There's nothing accomplished by that. Nobody's licked, because you can't lick the people. They'll just hold on and sit it out.

   I never lost faith in people; I just lost faith in leadership. I couldn't cheer when I would see the films of the destruction of Germany—I couldn't cheer at that. I wanted us to get Hitler, but what was happening to us in London was happening to people in Germany, and I thought, "God, how stupid." The inadequacy of thought, of feeling, and of leadership. . . . What the hell good were the leaders? Right then and there I felt that war—which had been pretty glamorous to me before—seemed pretty unglamorous, and rotten.

GLATZER: *It seems strange that* It's a Wonderful Life, *the movie you had the largest number of scriptwriters for, is the film that seems to me to be your most personal work. Didn't Clifford Odets write some scenes for it?*
CAPRA: Yes, Odets had written a script before I saw Philip Van Doren's story. The story itself is very slight: it came from a Christmas card. It's slight in the sense it's short, but not slight in content. I bought it from RKO. They

had already had three scripts written—Connelly and Odets and Trumbo had each done one. I read all three scripts, and kept a couple of scenes from Odets's version.

GLATZER: *Which ones?*
CAPRA: Well, the relationship between the boy and the drugstore man. And that was all from the three scripts; we wrote entirely new scripts. I had some awfully good writers working with me, but somehow they couldn't see what I could see in the thing. I finally just sat down and wrote the script the way I wanted it to be. So that's why it is a very personal statement.

GLATZER: *One of my favorite scenes in that movie is when Jimmy Stewart and Donna Reed are talking long-distance on the telephone to Sam, and Stewart realizes for the first time how much he is in love with her.*
CAPRA: I think that's one of the best scenes I've ever put on the screen. I love that scene. It's an offhand and offbeat way of playing a love scene. Scenes like that are just great when you can find them, because love scenes are so difficult to stage. It's very difficult to get a real emotion out of them, you can't play them straight. So you have to find some way to play a love scene that is a little bit offbeat so people don't laugh at it. Love scenes are funny, the audience is right on the edge of tittering. All you have to do is to put in a reactive character—somebody looking on at the love scene—and you get a laugh immediately.

GLATZER: *The post-war criticism of* It's a Wonderful Life *underrated it considerably, I think. The realism of* The Best Years of Our Lives *seemed to be more what critics wanted in 1946. When people see the two films today, they seem to prefer* It's a Wonderful Life.
CAPRA: I think that people understand films better now than they did then. They were labelled "corny" then because people didn't know what to call them. The critics particularly wanted the more obscure things, the more negative things. This positive attitude toward life, this optimism, this great reverence for the individual that is dramatized in all of my films was a little bit too sticky for them at the time. Yet, are the people today any cornier than they were in those days? No, people today seem to be much more aware of something that is real, good, and true than even people of my day. So to me that's a big plus. There is no generation gap between my films and the present generation at all.

Why We (Should Not) Fight: Colonel Frank Capra Interviewed

GEORGE BAILEY/1975

FRANK CAPRA BROKE into the movies by writing gags for Mack Sennett. He went on to direct the screwball comedy *It Happened One Night* and then *Mr. Deeds Goes to Town* and *Lost Horizon.* He became one of the few Hollywood directors with creative independence from the studios and continued to make films into the 1960s. In the view of history, however, Capra's most important work may turn out to be his *Why We Fight* series, seven propaganda films made to be shown to American soldiers during World War II. The films compiled newsreels, enemy documentaries, foreign features, combat footage and Dimitri Tiomkin's music into dramatic contemporary histories. The purpose was to persuade Americans to go to war.

Thirty years later Frank Capra was seventy-seven years old. He was touring the colleges and answering questions like "What was Jean Arthur really like?" But in this post-Vietnam interview Capra paused to consider the moral questions of film as warfare:

CAPRA: I'll tell you what we had to do. We had to convince the soldiers, the young punks. Now nobody is tougher to convince than young punks. Everything they see, they smell a sense of "Well, they're trying to sell us a bill of goods." This we knew at the very beginning. And we knew what we

From *Take One* 4.11 (September 1975): 10–12. Reprinted by permission of the Estate of Irving Greenberg, publisher of *Take One.* In the original contributor's note, George Bailey is represented as wishing "to acknowledge Professor Tom Bohn, whose dissertation on *Why We Fight* was of help in preparing for the above interview."

were up against if we didn't do a good job. If the soldiers didn't accept the *Why We Fight* films, then we were lost.

BAILEY: *It seems to me that if you were merely making a film to change the ideas of a particular group of men, then the films would not last. But they obviously have. In fact I think that some of them are getting better.* The Battle of Russia *is an epic.*
CAPRA: We were dealing with the greatest heroes and the greatest villains. We were dealing with the greatest novel material that ever was. Across this world stage there were these great out-sized characters. A battle of the giants. When you say "epic," yes, we are dealing with epic-sized people and epic-sized events.

BAILEY: *The epic in* The Battle of Russia *seems to be the enemy, Hitler, against the heroes, the Russian people. You did not set up Stalin as a hero. You emphasized the Russian peasants, even their religion.*
CAPRA: We had a political problem with Russia on that film. The problem was that a hell of a lot of people on our side were not about to be sold a bill of goods by the Communists. We were their allies, but that was all. Communism was not something we desired. So we stayed away from politics and made it a people's battle. As a result *The Battle of Russia* was one of the best episodes of the series and a true one.

BAILEY: *That's a technique of propaganda, isn't it? It is easier to hate an individual than, say, all Japanese people.*
CAPRA: In every case we never said to hate the people or blame the people. We blamed Hitler and his maniacal sense of Herrenvolk. We showed that Hitler had to lick the Germans first. The same way with the Japanese. The warlords shot all the liberal-minded people. The Germans had to do away with everything liberal in their country before they could venture off.

BAILEY: *You mention in your book,* The Name Above the Title, *that the first scripts you got for the series were from some unnamed Hollywood writers and that you could not use them because they were [avowing] the Communist line. What was so different about them?*
CAPRA: There is a party line that you can smell.

BAILEY: *The party line changes from time to time.*
CAPRA: We smelled these guys. For instance, before Hitler and the Russians

got together—the division of Poland—Hitler was a bum and Roosevelt was God. But as soon as they signed that agreement, then Roosevelt became the bum and Hitler was a pretty good guy, overnight.

BAILEY: *So in those rejected scripts there was something about Roosevelt?*
CAPRA: The same jargon. You can pick up any kind of jargon and instantly recognize what it is. "The ruling circles." They were against us as much as anybody else.

BAILEY: *China was the hardest problem, wasn't it?*
CAPRA: That was the toughest. We handled it *generally.* Generally Sun Yat Sen was their Lincoln. Generally their fight was liberalization against the dynasties. Generally we didn't go into the fight between the Communists and the warlords. As a matter of fact, when we made *The Battle of China* the Chinese were still all fighting the Japanese.

BAILEY: *Earlier we were talking about honesty in films. You said that these were "the most objective films ever made." But oversimplification can be a form of dishonesty. For example you set up a lot of dichotomies in the films. You have the free world against the slave, the religious world against the atheists, and civilization versus barbarism.*
CAPRA: I think it was barbarism.

BAILEY: *An oversimplification, though. Was Russia a free, religious country?*
CAPRA: Well you understand these were our allies. We were fighting a common enemy at the time, not each other. Unless you get into that, you won't understand the simplifications. We weren't telling the political history of each country. We were all in battle fighting this combination of Hitler, Tojo, and Mussolini.

BAILEY: *So because of the war you had to simplify things.*
CAPRA: Not simplify things; we had to *eliminate* things. It didn't matter to us whether the priests were having trouble in Russia. The immediate thing was the destruction of the war machine.

BAILEY: *The average GI at that time was probably not very informed at all. He did not know what was going on in Russia.*

CAPRA: The average GI of eighteen years old, when they took him and put a uniform on him, was so uninformed. He had this free world/slave world as the only way you could reach that guy at that moment. You give him a lot of "but-on-the-other-hand's" and you confuse him completely. This is it. The chips are down. It is us or them. It was that way. It was not a football game; it was *survival.* Unless you get the idea of survival, you won't understand the war.

BAILEY: *Some critics said that when your films are bad, they are bad because they are merely an illustrated lecture. The narration is too heavy.*
CAPRA: They are wordy because first of all you are dealing with several nations. But also you are dealing with the fact that *Triumph of the Will* is a goddam wonderful show. It's very easy for young people to say, "I like that!" "Here's the power and strength, and what's wrong with that?"

BAILEY: *The way you cut* Triumph of the Will *footage to make it just the opposite really proves once and for all that film is editing, that in the end that's where the strongest part of film is.*
CAPRA: Yes, yes. We took their own footage and tried to make it backfire on them. I knew that if we manufactured something, shot some scenes, got some horrible looking guys to play the Nazis and got some good guys in white hats to play the Americans, then we would fail. That's why we stayed with *reality* as far as we could.

BAILEY: *What I don't really understand is why Hollywood filmmakers were asked to make the series of documentaries when people like Pare Lorentz, Joris Ivens and Robert Flaherty were already working on government films.*
CAPRA: It was General Marshall himself. He knew the Signal Corps operation. He had seen their films, and he didn't like them. He didn't think they were professional enough. They didn't carry the kind of sock he wanted.

BAILEY: *He thought that documentaries in general were dry.*
CAPRA: Dry stuff. And so he said, "If I'm sick I go to a doctor. If I want a film made why don't I go to the guys who make films?"

BAILEY: *Once you got the job it was natural for you to bring the people you knew personally from Hollywood, people you could trust. But there is almost a total absence of documentary filmmakers in your crew. You told that anecdote about John Grierson.*[1] *Is that really true?*

CAPRA: Sure it's true. I couldn't make that up. He was such a big shot, and he had contempt for Hollywood people entirely. And the fact that they were going to make such *holy* stuff as documentaries!

BAILEY: *So what happened after you made the films. Grierson must have seen them. What did he think?*

CAPRA: I never saw him again.

BAILEY: *In your book you mention Flaherty once.*

CAPRA: I had a great respect for Flaherty. I like his films. I liked him. He was getting to be an old man. I called him in one day and said, "Don't you want to do something about the war?" It was quite late, maybe 1943. And Flaherty said, "Yes, Frank, I would very much."

"Well pick your subject. I'll help you, give you crews, everything. What would you like to do?"

"I want to do something about how the war affects the people in the little villages."

"Okay," I said. "I'll give you carte blanche. Where are you going to go?"

"I'd like to go to Louisiana."

BAILEY: *So he already had the idea for* Louisiana Story.

CAPRA: He didn't want any part of war; he was a softer man. I knew what he wanted. He wanted to film some people.

BAILEY: *The same film he always did.*

CAPRA: The same damn film. And I gave him the full opportunity. Well,

---

1. Frank Capra, interviewed by Dominique Noth for WMVS-TV, Milwaukee: "At the time I had to make the documentaries I had never seen one. And I didn't know anybody who had ever made one. We in Hollywood had heard about documentaries. We thought they were a lot of kooks with long hair making these things. . . . And suddenly I was faced with the making of a series of documentaries for the soldiers. . . . I had heard that the god of documentary filmmakers was in Washington. His name was Grierson. . . . So I made a point of trying to meet him. . . . And I said, 'Mr. Grierson, everybody tells me you know everything about documentaries. I've been given a job here. How the hell do you make documentaries?' And Grierson looked at me and said, 'Ha, Ha, Ha.' And he walked off."

what happened was there were uniforms all around him, people asking him in the morning what to do and all that. And I finally got calls from the crew down there. "Mr. Capra, we are not doing anything. We're just sitting here."

BAILEY: *Which is apparently the way he made all his films.*
CAPRA: Yes. I remember calling him on the telephone. "How are you doing?"

"Well, Frank, I don't know."

Actually he hadn't found a new subject he wanted to do yet. He was just fooling around and had a big crew waiting.

BAILEY: *He was just not suited to working under any pressure or organization.*
CAPRA: No he wasn't. Wrong era for him. A gentle man. So we called it off.[2]

BAILEY: *What about Joris Ivens?*
CAPRA: I did not know Ivens except by name.

BAILEY: *Pare Lorentz?*
CAPRA: I saw Pare Lorentz in New York, and I said, "Why aren't you part of this thing (the war effort)?" I gave him the opportunity to join us. He didn't want any part of working with anybody from Hollywood. I wasn't going to apologize for my gang from Hollywood. I thought they were pretty good. See, I don't like the position of these long-haired kooks who say, "Hollywood, you smell."

BAILEY: *Well Lorentz had been burned a couple of times.*
CAPRA: Yes. Lorentz is a peculiar guy. He's always hurt. He made that one movie and I guess they didn't put his picture on money for that.

---

2. Both Arthur Calder-Marshall in *The Innocent Eye* (Penguin, 1970) and Richard Griffith in *The World of Robert Flaherty* (Greenwood, 1970) report that Flaherty shot "newsreels" for Capra. They make no mention of Flaherty going to Louisiana during the war. Both imply that the idea for *Louisiana Story* came after Flaherty was commissioned by Standard Oil. Frances Flaherty in her book *Odyssey of a Filmmaker* (Arno, 1972) reports that Flaherty, after being commissioned, insisted on a three-month survey of the company's locations to find a topic. But, she reports, they headed first for Baton Rouge. After a tour of the Southwest they returned to Louisiana and then submitted his outline script to the sponsor.

BAILEY: *You recently made it clear that if you had to do a film about Vietnam, you would make a film called* Why We Should Not Fight.[3] *Why didn't you make that film?*

CAPRA: I had no opportunity, really. And I wasn't about to sabotage the government.

BAILEY: *Even though you thought the government was doing the wrong thing in this case?*

CAPRA: Not that they were all wrong. I just remember General Marshall coming back and saying, "If we ever land one soldier in Asia, we'll regret it forever and ever." And it is proving right. We sent a few and then a few more and a few more, right down into the quicksand.

I have a feeling that nothing happens except it has some meaning. Events have their own meaning. I think Somebody's really looking out for us. But I think Vietnam has made war much tougher to put across.

BAILEY: *Do you mean harder to get someone to believe in, to participate in?*

CAPRA: Yes.

BAILEY: *How do you explain Hollywood? The only real Hollywood film about the Vietnam war, the combat at least, was* The Green Berets. *But in World War II there were films even before the war. There were films about Korea.*

CAPRA: They didn't know what to say about it. Everybody was confused.

BAILEY: *Even in the early days? In 1964 there was little confusion.*

CAPRA: You have to understand that everybody's hero, Jack Kennedy, started this thing. And Kennedy things can't be all bad. We didn't think we

---

3. Frank Capra, interviewed by Dominique Noth for WMVS-TV, Milwaukee: "I made the *Why We Fight* series because I was perfectly agreed that we had to stop Hitler from overrunning the world . . . and doing away with the democratic form of government. But when I got finished with World War II, I was so tired of war that I thought it was the silliest, most stupid, most archaic form of human endeavor that was ever invented. . . . And I thought there must be better ways to settle things than to bomb women and children. . . . So I came out a pacifist against all war, not just Vietnam. . . . So I could not possibly make another program like *Why We Fight*. I probably would make something like *Why We Should Not Fight*."

knew everything about it. We heard four presidents saying the same thing, four different kinds of president, all saying that we had a mission over there.

BAILEY: *If they were all saying the same thing, then why couldn't you make a pro-war film in Hollywood?*
CAPRA: Because *nobody was believing them.* We would say, "Okay, I guess you are right. You know more than we do." But there was nobody so involved that he would say, "We have to go over there and knock off these Vietnamese." I didn't know a Vietnamese if he came up and bit me. There was no such thing as the Herrenvolk idea. Poor little bastards there. Everybody was confused. They still are.

BAILEY: *Did you see* The Green Berets?
CAPRA: No.

BAILEY: *It was really a lousy movie.*
CAPRA: I am quite sure it would be a lousy movie.

Frank Capra

JOHN F. MARIANI/1975

THE ISSUE OF FRANK CAPRA'S admitted sentimentality
("Capra-corn") is not quite so obvious as it seemed even five years ago. Anyone now re-examining his most important films—*It Happened One Night, Mr.
Deeds Goes to Town, Mr. Smith Goes to Washington, Meet John Doe, It's a Wonderful Life,* and *State of the Union*—must realize that a Frank Capra picture is
not a gushing paean to an idealized America but a satiric critique of the insid-
ious evils implicit in a free enterprise system where control of the media is
the first step toward demagoguery. More important, Capra's films have held
up as films, for as one of the original advocates of the "one man, one film"
idea, he was able to fashion a body of work perhaps more personal than any
other Hollywood director of his era.

His technique—unobtrusive camerawork, colloquial and picturesque
composition, head-long pacing—was part of an individual style others so
often copied that it became the model of "screwball comedy" in the thirties,
even though Capra's films were darker and more troublesome than their
happy endings at first indicated. Capra was not so sophisticated as Sturges,
nor as sardonic as Wilder, but as a stylist he even now has more power to
move audiences than both those satirists put together. *Sullivan's Travels* and
Stalag 17 have dated badly, but *Mr. Smith* has not. And *It's a Wonderful Life*
now looks to be one of the masterpieces of the American cinema—a small-
town American dream turned into a nightmare of suppressed paranoia. It is

From *Focus on Film* 27 (1977): 41–47. Reprinted, with additions from the original manu-
scripts, by permission of John F. Mariani.

the other side of the coin Raoul Walsh depicted three years later (1949) in *White Heat*—a post-war America suddenly severed from its traditions and hell-bent on achieving unfamiliar fantasies of greatness.

Capra is a slippery filmmaker and, merely because he is so comedic and so alert to his audience's expectations, we have failed to notice the impeccable orchestration of his comic tragedies in which a lovable hero is brought to ruin by the very forces that utilize that lovableness for sinister purposes. In *Meet John Doe* Capra suggested that folk heroes are manufactured, not born, and that they too should be suspect. But the ideas behind such heroes are a constant inspiration nevertheless.

The following interview was held when Capra gave a lecture at Sarah Lawrence College in Bronxville, New York, following a screening of his film *It Happened One Night*. Dressed in a hot pink jacket and maroon slacks, Capra was tanned and freckled, looking more like a successful Sicilian wine dealer than a film director. When one young student asked him what the "pattern of comedy" was in the film, Capra looked puzzled. "You got me," he replied. "That's a little deep." When another student suggested Capra had confronted the issue of women's liberation head-on back in 1934, Capra laughed. "My dear lady, I wouldn't think of trying to reform anybody—ever. I'm not a sadist!"

MARIANI: *How does it feel to have a class of college students today respond to a movie you made in 1934 as uproariously as they did?*
CAPRA: It surprises me. It's just really a phenomenon that they would be so moved and respond the way they did to that thing. I can't understand it, except in some way perhaps they've got some kind of hungers we don't know about. I feel this very strongly in the way they gather round me, ask me questions. I'm not a great performer. Maybe it's because it's what I stand for rather than what I am.

M: *Well, just a few years ago colleges probably would have been showing foreign or political films rather than a Frank Capra comedy or a John Ford western. Why have things changed?*
C: Well, I think it's only normal, because the myopic eye of the eastern seaboard doesn't rate Hollywood very high. They're not oriented to what happens west of the Hudson, and it's been going on for a long time. Film in the rest of the world is either a pillar or the central core of the national culture. Here film is still a dirty word and Hollywood is a dirty, stinkpot place

three thousand miles away—what good could come out of Nazareth? Now it's changing. For a long time the administrators and presidents of these universities feared film as something that was trying to pollute the purity of the other academic disciplines, and, you know, maybe they're right. Kids can't use English anymore and perhaps they don't read English anymore. They're smart as hell; I don't know where they get all their smartness. So this is worrying academia, because this is a powerful Dead End Kid that's being turned loose behind their ivied walls, and the pressure for film studies comes not from [those] above, who always try to kill it, won't give it any money. The pressure comes from the kids, because it's a film revolution and it's their medium. And an amazing thing is happening in Hollywood. These kids from film schools, many of them not thirty, are knocking out great big blockbusters the first, second, third time out. Who ever heard of this before? My God, I had to learn and learn before I had a big hit. Today they study it as an art form, with reverence. We had no reverence for this stuff. We'd make a picture and throw it out.

M : *Well, wasn't Griffith held in high esteem as an artist? And what about the foreign directors like Ophuls, Murnau, Lang . . .*
C : The word "artistic" really didn't exist. We didn't worry about something artistic. We didn't think of David Griffith as something artistic. We thought of him as a guy who made goddamned big pictures—and made money. You see, I backed into films, and for the first few years I was working I was only in it for the money. I didn't give a damn for any other director. I was my own teacher and my own student. I wasn't worshipping at anybody else's feet because I didn't know what to worship, didn't know what things were important. And this worked out pretty well for me. I didn't bother anyone else and they didn't bother me.

Now as far as Mr. Griffith was concerned, *every* director owes everything he has to D. W. Griffith, because he made the so-called "flickers" a great art form. We may have discovered color and sound and wide screens, but as far as the technical construction of films—close-ups, cross-cutting, parallel stories, flashbacks—all those things Griffith gave us, a great, great legacy of technique, and every director in the world [owes him] gratitude.

M : *Why do you think someone like Griffith could not survive into the sound era, yet someone like yourself, who was basically just a gag man, came to full flower after sound?*

c : Well, Griffith when he was making *The Birth of a Nation* would borrow money to make his films, like that Frenchman, Palissy, who used to burn his furniture to make his ceramics. Anyway, Griffith had to scrounge to finish it, and it took back about eighteen million. It couldn't play in these flea-bitten nickelodeons, so they had to build big theaters to play a thing like this. He used dolly shots, tracking, oh Christ, he used everything! Then *Intolerance* was even bigger. Well, Griffith could probably make one a year and the theaters couldn't exist on that, so machine production came along to supply enough product. The only way they could make enough product was the American system of the assembly line. The tail was wagging the dog. Well, Mr. Griffith was not an assembly line man, and he simply died from a lack of people to finance him. Plus the fact that he was getting a little senile, hitting the bottle too much, and that was his demise. The studios were glad to get rid of him. The corporations he started to make his big pictures . . . well, it was really a cruel business.

Now I didn't have much difficulty crossing the sound barrier because I was graduated from Caltech, and I knew what sound was. As a matter of fact, I had an advantage over most.

M : *In your autobiography,* The Name Above the Title, *you say that Colbert and Gable really had no interest in* It Happened One Night *at first. Were they difficult to work with?*
c : No, after we got going Gable was very easy to work with, especially in this film because for the only time in his life he played himself. This was Clark Gable as he was, and he never got another chance. He went back to playing those rotten love stories they always put him in. He was really a very happy-go-lucky guy.

Claudette Colbert was great, too. There was one scene, when they're hitchhiking, when she said she didn't want to show her legs, she wouldn't dress and undress, bad for her image—although she really had a pretty lush figure and great-looking legs. When it came to that scene she said, "I don't want to lift my skirt, I don't want to do that sort of thing." So I said, "O.K., you don't want to do it, we'll get a double." So we got some chorus girl and started to shoot the shot, and Claudette Colbert was looking on, and then says, "Get her the hell out of there, those are not my legs!"

M : *Was the film considered risqué when it was released?*
c : Risqué? Yea. But there were no four-letter words. They never even held

hands. It was all in the mind, and that's where it belonged, and that's where it would stay.

M :   *Was this the first of these films of the reporter and the escaping rich girl?*
C :   Well, in those days the reporter was always getting the girl. Reporters were the hotshot people of that era. *The Front Page* was made at that time about a reporter. They were tough guys, those reporters, and attractive figures.

M :   *Did the audience laugh as heartily at the film in the 1930s as the audience did here last night?*
C :   Not really, not as hard as you did here. The editors used to put space in for the audience to laugh, but tonight you laughed *over* laughs.

M :   *How many cameras did you use to shoot* It Happened One Night?
C :   We used two cameras.

M :   *Did you diverge from the original script much?*
C :   Oh, that's very difficult to say. You tend to find things to use as you're shooting, and you adlib a lot. For instance, remember that piggyback scene where they're crossing the river? Well, we were shooting down by the side of that river, [the scene] was late at night, and the sun shone down there and made this beautiful reflection. And I said, Jeez, we gotta use this. So we made up the crossing of the river. That was completely adlib. You see what happens when you shoot without too much attention to script; that's when it seems to turn out the best.

We always had a great deal of improvisation. Because, you see, I came from the improvisation school. We never wrote anything, our gags were all visuals. We didn't have jokes. We had scenes that could develop into a routine. We'd tell a director, "How about if a cat drinks some beer and gets drunk?" The director would say, "Yeah, he'll jump in the milk." And from there on cat chases dogs, cat sings "Three O'Clock in the Morning," and so on. We didn't have a word gag. And these sight gags carried over into my sound films.

M :   *I've always loved the sight gag in* It's a Wonderful Life *that revolves around the ball on the rickety bannister in George Bailey's (James Stewart's) house. At first it's just an annoyance, then it becomes the symbol of his desperation, then he kisses it at the end after he is saved.*

C : That's right. And you see how we used it: you can explain the inner feelings of the man through an inanimate object. It's a very difficult thing to know how to use a sight gag.

M : *What about the scene in* Mr. Smith *where Jimmy Stewart's nervousness is shown at meeting Senator Paine's daughter by dropping his hat?*

C : Ah, the hat! We shot that scene straight and he was fooling with his hat and, when we saw it, we thought we'd cut it into the scene and then, after we saw the rushes, we decided to play the whole scene on the hat. Those kinds of things are difficult to write in. You can't think of them beforehand.

M : *What about the high school dance sequence in* It's a Wonderful Life *where Stewart and Donna Reed fall into the swimming pool? How did that come about?*

C : Well, I'm glad you asked that. It's cute. That was on the first day of shooting. We had all these people out there and we shot this scene. I didn't know there was any pool there. We were out at Beverly Hills High. So we knew we were going to do this Charleston contest, the sequence was all laid out. And someone said, did you know there's a swimming pool under here? I said, a swimming pool? Let's see it. So somebody went and opened it, and I said, Jesus, we've gotta use this, that's all. We just ran into it and I just took advantage of it. See, that's the importance of making your own films, you can make those decisions. Otherwise you'd have to call the studio and ask to use it, and they'd say, no, f'Christ's sake, leave the goddamned thing closed!

M : *Ann Miller, who appeared in your film* You Can't Take It with You, *once told me that you never told actors what to do on a set, or how to act, but that there was a kind of Sicilian law-and-order that ruled.*

C : It's true. I never told any actor or actress how to act. I was only involved in whether they were thinking right; then they could do no wrong. Let them do their own thing. I could talk to them about what the scene involved, what the relationships were, the emotions, and particularly how to think right. Because, if you think right, your hands, your feet, they follow.

M : *My favorite scene in all your films is the one in which James Gleason talks about patriotism with Gary Cooper in a bar room in* Meet John Doe. *How did you direct that?*

C: That's one of my favorites. I wrote that scene. I wanted to get a patriotic thing in this part but, you know, you can't shout patriotism, you can't have a guy spout it. If I start to tell you about it sober, you won't listen. But if I'm drunk, well, that's a different story. I can say, "You know, I *love* this country—" and I pester you and you say, O.K. you love this country. And I gagged it up with that cigarette. When you get into that hairy stuff, you've got to do it a certain way, you laugh at it—but you listen. It's touching that way. Being drunk, having trouble with that cigarette, that's the only way this hardboiled guy would talk that way and expose himself.

M: *What about Gary Cooper? Was he easy to work with?*
C: Oh, I had enormous respect for that guy. He's a very underestimated actor. In *Mr. Deeds* he played that courtroom scene for almost ten minutes and he played it very well. It takes a real actor to do that. His great power is in his presence. He's been in many lousy movies but he never looks bad; he just rises above all his movies. You can't make him look bad. That's why the audience wouldn't accept him jumping off the building in *John Doe.* You can't kill Gary Cooper. He had too much "clout." Tell your story to somebody else but don't kill Cooper. That guy just represents America to me. He's strong, he's able, he's kind, he wouldn't steal a penny from you, but if you cross his path, he'll kill you. Or at least give you a punch in the mouth. This is what America is, I think.

M: *As it's said about John Ford, did Frank Capra have a stock company? You seem to use people like Ward Bond, Thomas Mitchell, Edward Arnold again and again . . .*
C: Oh yea, about eight or nine people—Bond, Mitchell, Barbara Stanwyck— surefire people we liked. And for the lesser parts we said, gee, maybe we can keep some of these actors going. If one director made a picture a year and I made a picture a year, that's two pictures they could count on. We just kept them in business.

M: *I've always wondered why, after using the great American faces like Stewart, Gable, and Cooper, you never used Henry Fonda.*
C: Henry Fonda, good as he is, is not my cup of tea. I didn't think he *was* America. He represented to me some kind of stylized, eclectic—is that the

word I want?—elite intellectual and he was very much of the stage. He just never appealed to me.

M : *Who were some of your favorite cinematographers?*
C : Well, I had one of the best, Joe Walker, the guy who invented the zoom lens. And Bill Daniels and George Barnes. I've used others, but those three were my standouts. They were so wonderful because they knew what the hell you wanted to put in and there's nothing they wouldn't do.[1]

M : *Did you do your own montage sequences?*
C : You ever hear of the name Vorkapich?[2] Well, he had a very fine way of doing those things. We did some of them but, if we wanted something special, we'd get this guy Vorkapich. Now what you'd do is to lay out a storyboard with long shot, close-up, some newspaper headlines or whatever, and you'd print it and he'd execute it, shoot the footage himself. He was excellent at doing this sort of thing.

M : *You're very sparing in using noticeable camera effects, although the camera moves a lot more than most people believe in your films.*
C : Oh boy, the camera moves all over, but you don't see it. It only moves when the actors move. It moves like—well, when you want to see close, the camera takes you up there. So, that being the case, I play important scenes in crowds. I like to use people as a backdrop instead of scenery. And I think people's faces are scenery.

The reason I use crowds is that for me movies are a people-to-people thing, not a director-to-people, not a cameraman-to-people, not a writer-to-people thing. The great illusion of the movie theater is that you go in there and there's just shadows—Jesus Christ! No people, no life, no blood and flesh up there. The illusion takes place in watching people's faces, and [viewers] get

---

1. Joseph Walker photographed most of Capra's films during the thirties, including *The Miracle Woman, American Madness, Lady for a Day, It Happened One Night, Broadway Bill, Mr. Deeds Goes to Town, Lost Horizon, You Can't Take It with You, Mr. Smith Goes to Washington,* and, later, *It's a Wonderful Life.* George Barnes shot *Meet John Doe* and *Riding High;* William Daniels shot *A Hole in the Head.*

2. Slavko Vorkapich was born in Yugoslavia in 1898, made some early expressionistic films in the U.S. in the twenties and thirties, and then worked for RKO where "Montage effects by Slavko Vorkapich" became his hallmark on numerous films. He later freelanced.

involved. And when they get involved they laugh, they cheer, they care. You can't involve them with a sunset, you can't involve them with a hand-held camera. The only thing you can involve them with is people, they are interested in other people. Now the trick is to keep the machinery out of the way. Use it, but never let it protrude.

M : *There's always a great deal of rain and snow in your big scenes. Why?*
C : Rain, of course, I can tell you, is for me an aphrodisiac. I go out in the rain and I get icicles. I love the rain! And I love the mood rain brings. Now, what do you do in these damn films? You can make them bare, you can take the scenery out, you can make them on a stage where people just stand still and talk to each other. One thing that I always thought was that the weather should be part of the world stage. The winds, the rain, the snow, the cold, the heat. So it's a part of the stage as far as I'm concerned.

M : *The rain always seems to come at climactic moments, such as in the rally scene in* John Doe.
C : You know, that rain cost a helluva lot of money. But there's something about the rain and that sea of umbrellas—there's a mood established that's very arresting. I think that scene's improved immensely by the rain.
    It takes a little doing to handle that kind of thing. You have to act like a field marshal, got to keep track of things. But for someone like me, who was an engineer, that comes a little easier, you know? I'm used to planning the shots.

M : *Was that scene in the rain planned out on paper first?*
C : Oh, that would have been absolute chaos if you didn't have it. You had to tell everybody exactly what they were going to do. So I went out to Wrigley Field with the crew and shot at night. We had about 1,500 people, but by morning we had only about 500 left. They just went off. But the cameramen, the lighting men, special effects crew, sound crew, rain crew, all the other crews went off to Wrigley Field and we selected one set. And we had a storyboard—it was a book about two inches thick—every shot, every angle, planned and drawn.

M : *Do you use storyboards for every scene?*
C : No, only for those special ones. I still have the board for the rain scene.

It's really a very interesting board. Anyway, I'd have as many as seven cameras set up. Certainly five or six. Then the more cameras I had in one set up, the more I could do in one move. I think we made the whole thing in twelve or fifteen moves in six days. We took along these brass plates which would have a scratch on them, 1A, 1B, Camera A, Camera B, 2B, C, D, E, and so on. Then we'd plant these where the cameras would be. Then we'd plant plates for the sound: SA, SB, and special effects, rain—"R." So all I had to do was call out "R1, SA," and so on. Everybody would take their places. Scene one. We never even rehearsed where they went. We'd put a stake down and the metal plate on top so you could find them in the night. So when one sequence was over—and those rain machines were big—needed a lot of people to move them—we'd call scene two. The people who were wet would try to warm up in the stands. We had a lot of heaters to keep them warm. And the crew jackassed these enormous pieces of equipment around. But they knew where they were going. And so you bring order out of chaos from that. It was like a military action.

M : *There is a great deal of criticism of the press in your films, often as the force of evil, the villain.*
C : Well, the press, of course, in those days was the power. They didn't have television, and radio wasn't yet in competition, so people like Hearst were very big. And also, reporters were very, very wonderful characters. They were the glamorous characters. A foreign correspondent used to act like the Count of Monte Cristo. They were glamour pusses, they had excitement about them—crime, cops, busts, sex, booze . . .

M : *But they didn't want to be characterized that way, did they?*
C : Oh, no! They didn't like the Tommy Mitchell character in *Mr. Smith* because he was a drinker. But reporters made very good leading men because they weren't pantywaists, they were tough guys. You could get a little sentimental with these guys when you got them drunk or in a tough spot. You gotta understand that at the time, when we had real economic censorship, if we made a villain out of a Frenchman, we couldn't play in Paris—they'd ban all of Columbia's pictures there. So all our villains were Americans; had to be if we wanted to sell our pictures abroad. If we made a labor leader a villain, boy, the labor unions would descend on us; if we made one out of a nurse, the same thing. So finally, to get some kind of conflict into the story, you

had to get some bastard. Finally we had to resort to some guy who was white, rich, never worked, never had a job, stateless, mindless, just a cardboard character. Ridiculous! That's how it kind of grew that we tried to make *ideas* the villains, like war, hunger, amnesia, the Freudian subjects. Now we had some real villains. If we used sex or violence we had something to blame it on—blame it on something else, blame it on mother.

You had to get an Edward Arnold type. Now the bankers didn't seem too organized. *Everybody* disliked them. You know, the banker has one sympathetic and one glass eye.

Another thing that I did was to change the classic four of the stage—hero, heroine, villain, comic. In *Platinum Blonde* I combined the hero with the comic and also made him a reporter. And it made it very much richer. Like in *It Happened One Night* Gable is the leading man but he's also the comedian.

And I always loved journalism, always reading the editorial pages to find out what the hell they thought.

M : *Did you suffer through the Red Scare of the late forties because of the social content of your films?*
C : Yes! We had a helluva time with *Mr. Smith* when it came out in '39. And *State of the Union* had trouble. Writers in the papers started reading communist propaganda into it—y'know, watch this guy. As a result, I was thrown out of the Vista project at Caltech. Took me quite a while to get over that. It was very much a traumatic experience. But I could see the accusations coming from way, way back. When I did *The Battle of Russia,* I had gotten material from the Soviet Union. I thought, Jesus Christ, I'd always heard about "security risks." Now I know.

M : *There is certainly the view in your films that nothing in the democratic or judicial system will save your heroes. In Mr. Smith it is only the remorse of Senator Paine that saves Smith's hide. Is that a criticism of the American system of government?*
C : Sure, but it's a criticism of the American misuse of government. Not with the American way. In America the orphan of freedom can be a bastard, but you have other ways to cure that.

M : *Is a concept like the John Doe Clubs closer to what America should be like?*
C : No, that was an outcome of times of stress, times of depression, when

people help each other out. They have to in order to survive. And you know, I think that when times are tough the people that survive are these ordinary people who are not afraid to show their feelings.

M : *That sounds like the last scene of Ford's* The Grapes of Wrath.
C : They will survive. All the intellectuals will be knocked off or starve. The strength of America is in the kind of people who can plant a seed, sow the grass.

M : *Did things happen in the Depression as they happened in your film?*
C : During the Depression, people helped each other out, and they are today. There are more people around today helping each other than there are people kicking each other in the teeth. All I'm saying is, O.K., maybe good doesn't exist all over but neither does evil. Maybe good isn't going to take over but neither will evil.

M : *Well, during the Depression did you feel that it was possible that a demagogue could take over?*
C : We felt it very strongly. There were a lot of people who had these paramilitary things like in *John Doe,* you know. They were preparing to defend themselves come the revolution. There were motorcycle troops. There are today. The Minutemen is an old organization and they still meet. The John Birch Society and even worse. This was not a thing I thought out. It was being talked about.

M : *Well, do you think it's true for the present generation what John Cassavetes said about you: that it's not America we've been believing in all these years, it's Frank Capra? How much does Frank Capra's America have to do with the real America? Is yours an ideal?*
C : I wanted to glorify the average man, not the guy at the top, not the politician, not the banker, just the ordinary guy whose strength I admire, whose survivability I admire. The guys like Gary Cooper.

M : *Preston Sturges seems to share some of the same satirical sense about America that you do. Do you think he might owe anything to your films?*
C : Yea, he might, but I doubt it. He made some of the funniest films ever made, like *The Miracle of Morgan's Creek.* If he ever heard your question,

though, he'd flip! Jesus, he was a strange guy. Carried his own hill with him, I tell you. He had a wonderful success on the stage, a very risqué thing, yet very humorous.[3]

M: *This is a very skeptical question, but William Wellman's* Magic Town *looks like it should have been a Frank Capra picture, but it just doesn't work as well. Why do you think that is so?*

C: Don't blame it on Wellman. That was Bob Riskin, who I thought was just wonderful and who wrote a lot of scripts with me. We worked together on this script. He had a brother who was egging him on to make his own pictures, and I did too. "Bob," I told him, "I'm not going to share credit for collaborating with you on this thing. This is a director's medium. You want credit on these films, go write your own and make them." So he did. And they were both just stinkers. One with Grace Moore, never saw it again.[4] And this *Magic Town* that he did after the war. He got his brother and financed the thing, and he thought we had a model way of doing things. So he tried to repeat a trend and you must *never* follow a trend. So here was Jimmy Stewart and Jane Wyman, and I said, let me read your script, for God's sake. No, goddamn it, he wanted to make a picture without me, prove himself. And he was down shooting this thing, and I couldn't help him in any way. And his brother said, Jesus, it's not going very well. So I got my good friend Bill Wellman and said, you want to finish it? The thing's in trouble.

M: *So much of the picture was already shot?*

C: Yeah, Bill stepped in at the last week or so.[5]

M: *Many movies today are just following trends, trying to copy the success of some other picture for purely commercial reasons.*

C: The easiest way to go broke is to follow a trend. You're bound to go broke

---

3. *Strictly Dishonorable* (1929).

4. *When You're in Love* (1937).

5. I asked William Wellman about this and his story differs: "Frank's just being kind about it. I was in on that thing from the beginning, and I wish I never started it. It stunk! Frank and Bob had a big argument about the picture and Riskin asked me to do it. I told him this is the kind of picture only Capra could do. It's not my kind of film. In my book Capra's the greatest, and if you think *Magic Town* has anything good about it at all, there's something wrong with you."

and you should go broke. You're taking someone else's material and trying to top it. But this is what the businessmen are looking for; they're trying to find a way to capitalize on a hit, so if *The Godfather* is a tremendous hit, a lot of little *Godfathers* are made that lose their shirts. *The Godfather* started a trend. Now if you want to make a success, you start anew, you go against the grain. And be irreverent, be an individual. If everybody's making tragedies, you make a who-done-it.

If I knew how to make a purely commercial film, I'd be the richest man in the world. There is no such thing as making "commercial" films, for commercial purposes. You wish you could always make a thing that audiences will like. If you make documentaries, it's another thing. But if you make theatrical films, and they're not successful in theaters—well, let's not equate success with mediocrity. Because great success can also involve great artistry. All the great artists were successful. You'd be surprised how successful Michelangelo was in his time. And Shakespeare was very successful in his time. And he's the granddaddy of all the writers. You must not equate failure with art.

M : *Who are some of the new young filmmakers you admire?*
C : Bogdanovich, Friedkin, Lucas, Aldrich, Scorsese. I thought *Mean Streets* was a helluva beautiful picture.

M : *I guess as an Italian-American, I loved that film for its detail in relation to my own cultural background. In Coppola's* The Godfather, *there is a montage sequence during the war between the families, with newspaper headlines intercut with a gang member sitting playing the piano. And I noticed he was playing just the way my father, who taught himself, did—on the black notes. And it just sounded so much like the music I heard as a child of an Italian-American family.*
C : I don't think that's an Italian-American thing, really. I play on the black notes too. Irving Berlin played on the black notes. He had a moving keyboard. If he wanted to play something in the key of C transposed from G or something, he'd just move the keyboard, and played the black notes.

M : *Any chance Frank Capra might ever tackle another film?*
C : Sure, I'd like to. You know, I still know how to make a movie. But I'm not as young as I was, and in movies you have to be able to make decisions fast enough. At my age you spend time thinking about the decisions you make, you slow down a little. And I *know* that I can't make the films the way I want to make them, the way I think they should be made.

Interview with Frank Capra

HARRY A. HARGRAVE/1976

BORN IN 1897 NEAR PALERMO, Sicily, Frank Capra emi- grated to America at the age of six. While his father labored in a small vineyard near Sierra Madre, Frank worked his way through school. Graduating in 1918 with a degree in chemical engineering from California Institute of Technology, he joined the Army and taught math in San Francisco until the Armistice was signed. In San Francisco he "backed" into a movie career. Knowing nothing about movies, he talked his way into directing a one-reel picture, *Fulta Fisher's Boarding House*. In Hollywood he wrote gags, first for Hal Roach, then for Mack Sennett. Sennett assigned Capra to create a character for Harry Langdon. The collaboration was successful, and Langdon hired Capra. *The Strong Man* and *Long Pants* followed. The two parted, and in 1928 Capra joined Harry Cohn at Columbia Pictures in a partnership which was to be one of the most profitable in the history of the movie business. After a good start with *That Certain Thing,* the new Columbia director made eight silents in two years before graduating to sound with three Jack Holt "talkies."

In 1930, he directed his first big hit, *Ladies of Leisure,* which made a star out of Barbara Stanwyck. Other early successes with Columbia included *Dirigible; Platinum Blonde* with Loretta Young, Robert Williams, and Jean Harlow; and *American Madness,* with Walter Huston. In 1932, Frank Capra directed one of his favorites, *The Bitter Tea of General Yen,* with Barbara Stanwyck and Nils Asther. Capra followed with a box office smash hit, *Lady for a Day,* which

From *Literature/Film Quarterly* 9.3 (1981): 189–204. Reprinted with permission of *Literature/ Film Quarterly*. Copyright © Salisbury University, Salisbury, MD, 21801.

netted Academy Award nominations for Best Actress (May Robson), Best Director, Best Picture, and Best Script. But it was to be the next film for which Capra would receive the first of his four Oscars. The year was 1934, and the picture, *It Happened One Night.* No other movie had then ever won Oscars for Best Picture, Best Director, Best Actor (Clark Gable), Best Actress (Claudette Colbert), and Best Screen Play (Robert Riskin). This was one of many successful collaborations between Riskin and Capra.

Broadway Bill came next. In 1936 he won a second Oscar for *Mr. Deeds Goes to Town,* with Gary Cooper, and one of Capra's favorite actresses, Jean Arthur. In 1937, Capra created Shangri-La for *Lost Horizon,* with Ronald Colman, Jane Wyatt, and Sam Jaffe. A third Oscar was awarded Mr. Capra in 1938 for *You Can't Take It with You,* pairing Jimmy Stewart and Jean Arthur as young lovers, with Lionel Barrymore and Edward Arnold as their fathers. *Mr. Smith Goes to Washington* brought Jimmy Stewart and Claude Raines face-to-face in a Senate battle. It is a film that affirmed Capra's faith in democracy and the innate dignity of man.

In 1941 *Meet John Doe,* starring Gary Cooper, proved to be one of the hardest-hitting films of Capra and screen writer Robert Riskin. Before entering World War II, Mr. Capra finished *Arsenic and Old Lace,* released in 1944, starring Cary Grant. He joined the Army shortly after Pearl Harbor and began the seven films of the *Why We Fight* series. Those are considered classics in the documentary field. For them he won another Oscar and received medals from General Marshall.

In late 1945, Capra formed his own production company, Liberty Films. For the new company he made what has come to be his favorite film, *It's a Wonderful Life,* again with Jimmy Stewart. It ran nip and tuck with William Wyler's *The Best Years of Our Lives* for Best Picture of 1946. Katharine Hepburn and Spencer Tracy were the stars of Capra's screen version of *State of the Union* in 1948. After selling Liberty Films to Paramount, Mr. Capra made two films with Bing Crosby for Paramount, *Riding High* in 1950, and *Here Comes the Groom* the following year. Between pictures Capra made a series of four hour-long television shows on science for the Bell Telephone Company, before teaming with Frank Sinatra in 1958 for *A Hole in the Head.*

Capra's most recent feature is *Pocketful of Miracles,* made in 1961 with Glenn Ford, Peter Falk, and Bette Davis. In 1964, he directed a documentary film on space travel for the New York World's Fair. And in 1971 he wrote his autobiography, *The Name Above the Title.* During the last few years Mr. Capra has lectured and held film seminars in over fifty American and Canadian schools, sharing his film experience with thousands of students and faculty members. The following interview between Mr. Capra and three interested students was taped on March 24, 1976, on the campus of North Carolina State University. Frank Capra's visit to North Carolina State University was made possible by grants from the National Endowment for the Arts and the Film Institute of the University. During his stay, March 15–24, 1976, he met with film classes, talked with individuals interested in the movies or in film careers, and lectured nightly to students and the general public after screenings of his major works.

Q: *Could you tell us about the silent era in films? What was it like directing in the silent era?*

CAPRA: Well, the principal difference between the silents and, let's say, sound, was that we didn't use scripts. We had a thing called a scenario—at least some of the very expensive films did have a scenario of some sort—very thin. Just with titles as to the kind of story. But Mack Sennett in the comedy department never wrote anything; nothing was written in Mack Sennett's studio. He didn't like books; and if you brought in a book, he'd throw you out. "No gags in books," he'd say. He had been a water boy to an Irish section hand, and this Irish foreman became his idol. He wished he could be just like him: strong and positive. There were never books around there, and he just thought that visual humor couldn't be found in books; and he was right. There were no word jokes; there were visual jokes. They were visual things; and these you had to think up without any paper. And we just discussed the sequences and what would come next in a two-reel comedy. The plot was quite simple, and what we'd try to do was to get comedy routines to fill in the plot. The gag men were separated and cut into two gag-men teams. And they would work on that. Now you would tell the routines that you thought up to Mr. Sennett. If he liked them—and of course he was a great audience—if he liked something you could hear him laugh for two blocks; he'd just open his mouth and guffaw. I guess his great strength was what he liked and what he laughed at was pretty surely what the audience would laugh at. So he was sort of an audience barometer. If he liked the routine he'd work on it too, but he was not an inventive man himself. He'd try to tell a joke and even forget the punch line; he was not funny in himself. But he was a great audience. And if he liked your routine, you were allowed to go and tell the director the routine; and if the director liked it, he'd shoot it; if he didn't like it, he wouldn't shoot it.

Q: *Wasn't there an occasion when you thought of an idea, and he didn't like it? What happened then?*

CAPRA: Yes, there was an occasion. There were occasions when he didn't like the idea. I had an occasion once about a wheel with Ben Turpin, the guy with the crossed eyes. He was making love to a girl. He had taken her out in the moonlight in his buggy, and he tried to get amorous, and she didn't want any part of it. Every time he'd get amorous, the wheel would almost slip off because his rival had unscrewed the wheel from the axle, so this wheel would almost go off. But when she pushed him back, she'd be saved for the wheel would move back over, too. But finally, of course, the wheel came off, and he fell down. Well, that's a running gag. You can use it and get a routine out of it. And he said, "No, that isn't funny." Well, I thought it was very funny; and so I told it to an actor who was working on the Ben Turpin show, and he thought it was funny; and I said, "Why don't you tell it to the director?" So he went around and told the director. The director loved it, and he shot it. Then Mr. Sennett went into the projection room to see the rushes, and here was this gag.

Q: *Why didn't Mack Sennett like it?*

CAPRA: He didn't think it was funny. That was his right. He always said, "Whose name is over the gate?" "Your's Mr. Sennett." He raised heck about that gag, and he said, "All right, we'll leave it in. I want to teach you a lesson. But I'm taking you to the preview. I'm going to prove to you that it's not funny." Well, we did go to the thing, and it was very funny. And boy, I came out to raves and everything else. I came out rubbing my hands, and he says, "You're fired."

Q: *What did you do then?*

CAPRA: Being fired by Sennett was not all that serious because if you came back and walked in front of the gate and looked penitent, with your old clothes on, and he saw you walking in front of that gate when he came [in] in his big car and when he went out in his big car (you had to be there all the time), he'd see you doing penance in front of that gate with his name on it. Well, in about three days he'd let you in. You'd get your job, and that was Sennett.

Q: *How did he compare with Hal Roach? Did they work along the same lines?*
CAPRA: No. Hal Roach was more of a structured person. He was not quite as slap happy as Sennett. He was more structured [about] the thing. It was more of an assembly-line proposition. At Sennett it was a happy-go-lucky, free-for-all thing—anything went.

Q: *How long did you wait before you started working with Harry Langdon?*
CAPRA: I was there about a year before I started working with Harry Langdon.

Q: *Did he hire you? I mean did he see your work and say, "Hey, I want that man to direct?"*
CAPRA: I just was a gag man for Harry Langdon for about another year. I just wrote his material. I didn't direct Harry Langdon until he left Sennett and went on to make feature pictures, and I became his director on the film we saw the other day, *The Strong Man.*

Q: *Did Harry Langdon do his own stunt work?*
CAPRA: No, you can't let the star of your show do stuntwork. If he breaks a leg, then the whole thing goes to pieces. No, you use doubles all the time.

Q: *A lot of people didn't make the transition to sound. They didn't survive. How did you survive?*
CAPRA: It was just a period of transition. You were still in the business of telling a story. That's the business of entertainment; that's really not such a new business. Except that we were dealing in words now as well as in pictures. The transition was not that difficult. Almost anybody who knew anything about films, silent films, survived into sound. It was not a great change for people to make. It was a great change physically for the studios. They had to soundproof the stages, spend a lot of money, build new stages in many cases. They had to get a tremendous amount of new equipment they didn't have before. The recording equipment was very, very expensive. But oddly enough very little production was stopped because of the change. They just

kept on making silents and sound, and then gradually changed over to sound without losing stride.

Q : *Mr. Capra, what film do you think first fulfilled your aims or purpose as a director?*
CAPRA : My purpose as a director was to make money. So I was very happy when the audience liked the very first one I made because that was my aim. At that time we got very little money; at Mack Sennett's I got $35 a week. When I starting directing for Harry Langdon, I got $600 a week, which was quite a jump. That was our main thrust—money.

Q : *Did you not have your own film company—was it Liberty Films?*
CAPRA : That was almost thirty years later.

Q : *Whom did you form it with?*
CAPRA : I had been in the army; and when we got out of the army, I formed it with people who had been in the army: William Wyler, George Stevens, and a businessman named Sam Briskin. There were three directors and a businessman.

Q : *Did this company have any purpose as such?*
CAPRA : Yes, we wanted to make independent films, not make films for a studio, just make them for ourselves.

Q : *Did you use any star, or did you . . .*
CAPRA : We used whatever people we could get. We hired for each film. We'd expand for making a film, and contract. Expand and contract; that way we didn't have any great overhead to carry.

Q : *You went from gag writer to director. Did you ever think about going any further than director into some other . . .*
CAPRA : There is no higher calling in the world than being a director. What more can you want than to be a filmmaker?

Q : *All your life you believed in the motto: "One Man, One Film."*
CAPRA : Yes, I knew nothing about the stage, and I knew nothing about anything else really when I started in this business. I graduated from Caltech

as a chemical engineer, and that was what I was going to be. I couldn't get a job. I sold apples on the street until I got into filmmaking. That's all there was to it. I had an opportunity to get a job with a film company, and that was what started me. The first film I made was a little one-reeler. I did the whole thing because nobody else knew anything about it, and everybody knew less than I did, and I knew nothing. So, you can see how we were the blind leading the blind. Anyhow, there's when I started with this, "One Man, One Film" idea. I could not understand how anybody else could write the material for you and then you'd shoot it; and then you'd give it to an editor, and the editor would put it together the way he wanted it; and then the producer would do it up. I just didn't understand how all of this could happen and yet produce an art form. This was a committee. Everybody would give their own interpretation to that film. And naturally, when a committee dabbles in art, they don't come up with much. You've heard that a camel is a horse made by a committee. I thought that if this is an art form at all, it's the guy that makes the show. The so-called artist should have control, not the actors, not the wardrobe people, or the song people, or the photography people. I was able to put that idea into execution at Columbia Studios, a very small studio down on Poverty Row where I became the big fish in a very small pond; therefore I could ask for things that I couldn't get any other place. And the first thing I asked for was to have complete control of what I was doing. Since they needed me and the films I made for them made money, that was very fine with them. And they could fire me at any time. That's the way I did inaugurate this "One Man, One Film" idea. I was the first hired director to be able to do that. Of course, if you owned your own company, you [could] do anything you wanted to. But I didn't own my own company. A man like DeMille owned his own company; therefore he could put his name where he wanted to, and he could really control his material. And today it is practically "One Man, One Film" all over the world.

Q: *Could you choose your own technical people then?*
CAPRA: Right, you have to choose as much as you can. I mean, you just can't choose at will. People who are working some other place won't stop there to come to work for you.

Q: *How did you begin working with Robert Riskin? Was that by accident?*
CAPRA: No, Robert Riskin came out when Columbia hired a lot of young

playwrights. He came with the bunch. There were about six or seven. He came out with that bunch. And we worked together on our first film, which was *Platinum Blonde;* and we became very good friends, and we started vibrating to the same tuning fork, and then we worked together on about twelve films.

Q: *Also Dimitri Tiomkin did a lot of your musical scores.*
CAPRA: Yes, Tiomkin scored a lot of films. He was a Russian. He emigrated to Paris, and began to speak French with a Russian accent, and knew German with a Russian accent. He began to speak English with a Russian accent, and finally he began to speak Russian with no accent or with an odd accent. So he's a man who can't speak any language anymore without an accent. But he's a wonderful musician. I gave him the first opportunity he had to score a film, which was *Lost Horizon,* and that was the most expensive thing Columbia had ever made, and to give it to an outside man who had never had any experience in scoring a film was really something that the studio thought was absolutely crazy. But I wanted something new and different, and I thought that this man could give that Russian-Asian quality to the music that I thought the picture ought to have.

Q: *When did you decide to put music behind them?*
CAPRA: Music is another tool which you are able to use in telling a story, as you use sound, as you use color. These are all tools. Your principal tools, of course, are the actors. The others are all accessories to your storytelling. So you use them as you think the story should be colored by music, or by sound, or by color, or by photography, to advance the mood or the style of the scene that you're shooting.

Q: *Could you tell us what happened at the Academy Award dinner for* Lady for a Day?
CAPRA: Well, I thought I'd made films that merited at least the attention of the Academy—of course everybody thinks that. But I thought it very strongly. *American Madness, Platinum Blonde, Dirigible,* films like that [had] been mentioned at least. But since we were a very small studio, we didn't have many votes, probably not more than two votes in the whole studio. When *Lady for a Day* came along, it was a very big hit in theaters, with the public as well as with the press and the critics. And it also was a big hit with

the Academy voters because it was nominated for four categories: Best Picture, Best Actress, Best Writing, Best Directing. It was a tremendous thing for
me. I looked up the records and no film had ever won four major Oscars, and
I thought here's a chance to make a sweep; this is probably the best picture
for the whole year; and anybody who votes for anything else is out of his
mind. So I was really sure that we'd get at least four awards. I became impossible to live with. We moved in from the beach; I rented a big house in Beverly Hills to be seen around; I gave parties; I went to restaurants and stood
around so they'd see me; and I got a tuxedo made by a tailor, expecting
surely to be seen; and I rehearsed speeches, I wrote lots of acceptance
speeches; and I practiced them before a mirror so my voice would break in
just the right place. My wife was in her ninth month of pregnancy, and she
just locked the door and thought I'd lost my mind. And I had! So I went to
the Academy dinner at the Biltmore, and Will Rogers was the master of cere-
monies. He was giving out the awards. The first celebrity I ever knew was
Will Rogers. I thought this was a good omen. I had invited about ten friends.
The first was the writing award, and I thought Bob Riskin's going to win this,
and I'm going to win the next one. It was not *Lady for a Day;* it was for *Little
Women.* Victor Herman and Sarah Mason were called up to the stand, and I
thought Oh, my goodness. Well, I said, okay, I'll settle for three. The next
one was mine, and Will Rogers began talking. It was dark, and I had this
crumbled up little speech in my hand, and I unrolled it and tried to look at
it, and I couldn't, and he said: "The envelope," and he looked at it and he
said, "It couldn't happen to a nicer kid than this, and I've known him for
such a long time, and he came from nothing"; and every word spelled me,
of course, and finally he said, "come up and get it, Frank." Well, everybody
at my table leaped in the air, and it was a long walk to the dance floor. I went
around people's tables saying, "Excuse me, excuse me," etc. And I got to the
dance floor, and the spotlight was going around, and I was saying, "Here I
am! Over here!" And finally the spotlight goes over and stops and picks up
another guy on the other side of the dance floor, and it's Frank Lloyd, the
director of *Cavalcade.* I was actually aghast and astonished standing there in
the dark, and Will Rogers embraces him and everything else, and finally
somebody said "Down in front!" right behind me, and I moved. And that
long walk back with everybody yelling "down in front" was the most misera-
ble thing I've ever had happen to me. And I was so mad at the Academy I

said that if they ever, ever, ever give me one, I won't accept it. Well, the next film was *It Happened One Night* . . .

Q: *Where you won everything?*
CAPRA: I was there.

Q: *And you accepted?*
CAPRA: I accepted.

Q: *While you were at Columbia, Joseph Walker was the director of photography for most of your films. Could you tell us about this collaboration. How did his style affect your style in motion picture?*
CAPRA: Well, he had no particular style. What he was interested in was trying to figure out what you wanted. But he was innovative. He wouldn't be stopped by anything; you couldn't really stop him. If you had something difficult you wanted to get, some kind of a mood, he'd do it. He knew how to get it. We did a lot of experimenting together with the use of lenses and with the use of masks and with the use of gauze, and things like that.

Q: *Although you feel that the camera in its relation to the movie should be as unobtrusive as possible, how do you feel about unique camera angles and expressionistic lighting in respect to creating or in helping to emphasize a mood? Would you think it's all right as long as it's used in that . . .*
CAPRA: If it's trying to emphasize a mood, yes. But if you see the machinery, the story's going out the window. It is not a machinery-to-the-people medium. It's a people-to-people medium. The actors are telling the story. You can only involve the audience in the lives of the actors and characters that the actors are playing. You can't involve them in machinery. They don't give a darn about a sunset, or a fast moving camera, or a hand-held camera, or anything like that. These are ego-massaging, little, egocentric things that directors indulge in, and we indulge in for ourselves and for each other. But audiences are bored with that.

Q: *Maybe I've just seen old prints, but I'm wondering do you use a soft focus effect to create a romantic or nostalgic mood. I noticed in* It Happened One Night *in some of the shots of Claudette Colbert it seemed that she was in soft focus to suggest her romantic interest in Clark Gable.*

CAPRA: Well, it's not just to suggest her interest in Clark Gable. You want her to look very nice at that moment, and that's done with long focus lenses where the focus will become very narrow; and if you focus on the person's eyes and nose, everything back of their head gets soft because it goes out of focus. So you get a feeling of a kind of a softness about the whole scene which transmits itself into the mood of the girl if she's in a soft mood. We did a lot of that kind of stuff—a lot of work with four inch lenses, even six inch lenses.

Q: *How about deep focus? Do you use that in* American Madness *to dehumanize a mob, or did you use it in other aspects?*
CAPRA: We used that mostly to widen the focus so that more people would be in focus, and that's when you use a wide angle lens, and you get great depth of focus with that. And you get a very short depth of focus with the larger lenses, the three and four inch and the six inch lenses. So we'd use, let's say, a 35mm or a 25mm lens on the wide shots where everybody would be in focus, even those close and those in the back.

Q: *Normally it seems that when I'm watching your pictures that the camera is usually objective, letting you see the whole thing; but then occasionally it will switch, like in* Mr. Smith Goes to Washington, *and become subjective; in other words the camera will actually become one of your characters, and let the audience see what that person sees. Can you elaborate on that?*
CAPRA: That's point of view. It really depends. If I'm photographing some-body, and he is looking up here, and I know what he is looking at, then you have to photograph what he is looking at from that point of view just to follow the continuity. You don't disorient the audience. There's nothing that makes an audience more unhappy than to be disoriented. They don't know where you are. If you make a sharp reverse cut for no reason at all, they don't know what happened. So their mood of being with the film and being part of it is broken, you see, that's just bad direction. Whenever you break an audience's mood, you're just asking for trouble. So you use machinery, but it must never be seen. The interest must always be on the actors. That's what the audience is interested in, in the people who are to make these decisions, the actors. But how you get there, that's your business, not theirs. They don't want to know about that.

Q: *Leland Poague in his book* The Cinema of Frank Capra *says that in your editing style you cut a lot between shots. Is this because of your emphasis on dialogue and the story or do you only use this frequent cutting in scenes where you're trying to build suspense?*

CAPRA: Well, you follow the interest. That is the guideline there. Where's the interest? Who does the audience want to see? Whose face do they want to see react to somebody else coming in the door? What effect is that going to have on them? You follow the interest of what is happening; and if you just use that as the guideline, you'll find that you will do the right kind of cutting. Who do you want to see next? Who do you want to see in that moment? Now these are cuts with closeups. A closeup is an emphasis. You want to get up close so you can see that person's face, the person's eyes. What are her thoughts at this moment? Closeups are for dramatic purposes— not just to speed up or not just for glamour. They must have a purpose. Every cut must have a purpose. One of the principal things about it is to get the smooth flow, the filmic flow, the dynamic of film. You can edit a film so that it flows very smoothly from one cut to another. You don't know where you have a cut; you just don't know. Your interest flows back and forth, back here this way and that way, and it's just wonderful the effect you get when you do it right. The audience doesn't know it or have to know anything else. They remain fascinated by what is going on. That's what you should try to accomplish. There are many ways to put scenes together. Many, many ways. But only one or two are worth a darn.

Q: *How many cameras did you use?*
CAPRA: Mostly three.

Q: *Three at once?*
CAPRA: Yes, but there are a lot of problems. You can light one camera; and if you light two cameras, the problem is doubled; and if you light three cameras, your problem goes up geometrically. The problems with three cameras are eight times what they are with one. But it's worth the effort because then you've got that scene photographed from three different angles, and you just intercut those angles at will. You can go from one to another without fear of stopping the pace or the effects of the scene or anything else, because it is one scene being photographed from several angles. And if you have to stop in between and photograph all those angles separately, you're liable not to

get the same intensity, the same character of the scene, the same kind of mood of the scene, the same feeling of the scene as when it's photographed all at the same time. And then you pick up closeups from one of the other cameras at the same time that the master scene was being photographed.

Q: *What sort of techniques did you use in editing to help bridge a time gap in a story?*

CAPRA: All kinds of gimmicks have been used: going from a tree with flowers to a tree with snow on it. A lot of these things you think are necessary, but the audience is so far ahead of you that all these things bore them. So if somebody is going into the elevator on the eighth floor, you can bring him right out of the building on the next cut, and the audience will thank you. They know he went down. It just accelerates telling your story. You just don't have to follow him down, and follow him getting out, and all his long walks. That's unnecessary. They do it in television because they've got to fill up time.

Q: *Do you use headlines for bridging a time gap or just going forward?*

CAPRA: Information. In a play that used to be done by the butler and the cook talking in the kitchen. They gave you everything that happened the night before: who was what, who was with whom, who slept with whom. They give you a lot of this exposition part. Exposition is dreary stuff, and it has to be made kind of interesting. That is why you have to use your ingenuity to make exposition interesting. I used newspaper headlines and that kind of thing that would have a kind of flow to it. Other people do it other kinds of ways. But the whole thing is how do you tell exposition, what happened. You're in this interval between this sequence and that one, it may be a week or a year. What happened during that time? Tell it short, quick, exciting; make it interesting.

Q: *I was amazed at some of the technical solutions you came up with, like how to show cold.*

CAPRA: Well, I have a passion for credibility, and I tried to make a film believable, and that starts, of course, with getting very good actors for all the small parts; because if you believe the small people, you're more liable to believe the derring-do of the stars. And, of course, such things as snow that looks like snow, and cold that looks like cold are made more credible when we see breath of people that are working in the scene. If you get in the 20°s, your breath shows. If you're supposed to be in the 20°s, and there's no breath, the audience knows something is phony about that scene. And in a word they just don't believe the scene, and then they won't believe the story. But if you make all those things credible, and they believe that you're out in the cold or that you're in the Arctic, then you believe everything.

Q: *How did you solve that problem in* Lost Horizon?
CAPRA: I took everybody to an ice house. We hired an ice house and made a studio of it, and threw out the swordfish that were piled up in it, and brought in the actors.

Q: *Did you go on location when you made your movies?*
CAPRA: Location wherever it was possible. It was too costly then. The equipment was not as fine and miniaturized as it is today, and it was rather cumbersome. If you went out to take a closeup of two people away from the studio, you had a retinue of over fifteen trucks following you. It was a very expensive thing. Now that is all over with. You can make a picture any place in the world with the equipment that you can put in a station wagon. And many pictures are shot that way. Interior and exterior, all are shot right on location.

Q: *In most of your films, you focus on the average man, your John Doe, your little man, the individual who is typical of everyday life. I guess it's the little man versus the big man, and in many of your films you were against politics or political bosses. Would you go into detail and say why?*
CAPRA: Well, about the little man. I like people, I think people are just wonderful. I also think that people are all equal in the sense of their dignity, their divinity; there's no such thing as common man or an uncommon man. To me they're all—each one has something unique. Each one is actually unique. Never before has there been anyone like you. Never again will there be anyone like you. One mold, one young lady. So you're a very unique person, so is he, so is he. You are something that never existed before and will never exist again. Isn't that wonderful? Isn't that something pretty exciting? So I look at you as something that plays part of a great whole, an equal part of everything, or else you wouldn't be here. That being the case, I just always liked to get down to people that are supposed to be the mob, and I

find very interesting people there. I like people, and I get right into them. I use people a great deal for background. I shoot many scenes in crowds because I think people are more interested in other people than they are in anything else. They love the faces; they don't know who the devil they are, but they like them because they are people. You could put a camera inside of a window, let's say a grocery store or a restaurant or a jewelry store, and just photograph the people from the inside window-shopping. And you watch the various faces that come in and look; they're just fascinating. You are an audience by looking at them in the projection room; you can't take your eyes off them. They are interesting per se to other people. That's why I direct my attention to the people or to the actors that are representing people, and they become credible, and they know who they are and then the audiences care for them. The biggest thing is that I want them to care about these people.

Q: *Your characters seem to represent certain ideals, like all of mankind should stick together and love and . . .*
CAPRA: Well, the advent of the human race has been because of idealists and not because of masochists, or cynics. That's all pretty dry. It gets you nowhere. It's the idealists who walk alone and live alone and swim up the stream.

Q: *They're non-conformers?*
CAPRA: They're non-conformers. And it's the idealists that are non-conformers. And they're the ones that finally become the folk heroes. I don't know where we're going, but we came up from some kind of a jungle, and we're better off now than we were in the jungles. Some of us have little more compassion within us and forgiveness within us, and make a kind of an evolution. I don't know where we're evolving to, but the idealists will have a great deal to do with where we're going.

Q: *You "discovered" a lot of new talent, like Barbara Stanwyck. What kind of talents did you look for in a prospective actor or actress?*
CAPRA: I don't know what I looked for.

Q: *Were you just told to go look at Harry Langdon and make something out of him?*

CAPRA: Yes! That's right. And we managed to do something with Harry Langdon. But I don't look for anything in people. I look for interest; if they attract me, they're interesting. That's a point in their favor.

Q: *I've heard that with Barbara Stanwyck, you would rehearse all the other actors before she came on the set; and when she came on, she just went through it and did it in one take.*

CAPRA: She was very difficult to work with because she was unskilled in that she started as a chorus girl and she worked her way to be a kind of ingenue, and she was very, very stage-minded. She had only one performance to give to the audience and that was the performance she gave when she gave it. She'd give the best performance in a rehearsal. And every time she did it again, well, that was new to her, and it would not be as good as the first time she did it, and each succeeding time she did it she would go downhill. Now this was a great problem because you have to rehearse these scenes with other people; you have to see that everybody else knows what they're doing. And then you get an actor that leaves the best performance in the rehearsal. That really creates a problem because then you will not get her best performance on the film. So with her, I realized that she was new and young and fresh and dewy-eyed, and that she would not be able to master this technique that other film actors had mastered: to keep their emotions down in rehearsals and save them for the time when they needed them during the takes. So I just had to invent ways not to rehearse her. And that's where the three camera thing started with me so I'd have more cameras on at one time so really I didn't have to do as many takes with her. We were trying to get all the different kinds of angles; we tried to get all the angles we possibly needed, the important ones in a scene, the first time. This created problems in lighting, it created problems with the other actors. They hadn't heard of her; they didn't know—I didn't give a damn whether they'd heard of her or not, I knew she'd be marvelous. Everybody'd stop just to look at her. She really had power—a lot of young, fresh power. She'd make you believe anything she did. So in that way we had to shoot Barbara Stanwyck on her first film, *Ladies of Leisure,* and on a couple of other films; but not too long after that, of course, she learned to control herself, because other directors might not go to these lengths just to baby her and protect that first scene she would do.

Q : *You liked characters or actors who played themselves, didn't you? Is that what you were looking for? Gary Cooper on the screen as well as off screen has struck me as almost the character he played.*

CAPRA : Well, he'll play that character better than he will any other charac-ter. And in a sense every actor puts himself into that part. No two actors would play the same role alike because they are different people. Each one is a unique individual. They have no likenesses at all. And they'd play the same part, but not the same. That's why when I'm casting a part I try to get the actor that I think will do that part as I see that part.

Q : *What messages should filmmakers be conveying to the audience?*

CAPRA : The message is that we should forget messages. You have Western Union for that.

Q : *What ideals?*

CAPRA : Entertainment. Just entertainment. It's show business, it's theatri-cal, it's theatrics. What message have you got for the world? At your age? You're still learning. You're still absorbing stimuli from the outside. You still don't know. You've got opinions, but your opinions will change. You'll go back and forth as you make your way through life. You'll realize that your opinions were probably in a sense prejudiced. And you will find that they will change. So what gives you the right to give the world a message? See? You wait for that message. Don't worry about that message. You worry about entertainment. You worry about making things interesting and tell a story in an interesting way. Never mind the message. That message will come out. If you have anything, it will come out. But it will come out when you can give that message with entertainment; and if you're going to make tracts instead of dramas, people are not going to come to see them. They won't pay money to come and hear tracts, religious, political, or any kind of tracts that you have in mind. But the audience is the main thing you must think about, not the critics. That's the reason we make films; that's the theater. A theater is not a theater without an audience.

Q : *I was reading some critiques on your major films by Leland Poague in his book. Do you think that he overemphasizes the sexuality in your films?*

CAPRA : I'm not too familiar with that part of Poague's book. You just can't forget sexuality. It is a part of everyday living. It is part of what we live with, and it is part of the great joy of living. I don't think we could eliminate it. I don't think we can downgrade it, nor do I think that we should defile it. And when you see explicit sex scenes on the screen, they are defiling one of the most wondrous things any human being can experience.

Dialogue on Film: Frank Capra

AMERICAN FILM/1978

FRANK CAPRA CALLED his engaging autobiography *The Name Above the Title,* a reminder that his movies are very much his own. It's a reminder few moviegoers need. Films like *It Happened One Night, Mr. Deeds Goes to Town, Mr. Smith Goes to Washington,* and *It's a Wonderful Life* bear his unmistakable stamp.

Capra's films are marked by zestful pacing and unfailing optimism. They unabashedly celebrate the simple virtues and strengths at the heart of American life—most often small-town life. Capra's characters virtually personify the qualities we like to see in ourselves: an easy friendliness, a basic honesty, a strong sense of justice. The characters form a gamut of American types, and through Capra's movies, stars like James Stewart, Gary Cooper, and Clark Gable took on much of what became their screen personas.

The man who has had so much to say about small-town America in his films was himself an immigrant. He was born in 1897 outside Palermo, the capital of Sicily, and he was brought to America—providentially to Los Angeles—six years later. In a period when few immigrant young people went on to higher education, Capra entered the California Institute of Technology. He emerged a chemical engineer, just in time to join the army.

When Capra returned, unable to find the right position, he took a number of jobs, even one as a gag writer. It was that stint that introduced the young chemical engineer to entirely different possibilities. Soon he was writing for

From *American Film* 4.1 (October 1978): 39–51. Reprinted by permission of the American Film Institute.

the "Our Gang" comedies and also for Will Rogers. Then came Mack Sennett and Harry Langdon, and Capra found himself a film director.

Hollywood's greatest period—the thirties—happened to coincide with Capra's greatest period. Much of his best work was done, in fact, in the latter part of the decade. But Hollywood film directing was only one of the careers Capra undertook. During World War II, Capra directed the documentary film unit of the War Department and made the *Why We Fight* series. In the fifties, he turned to science documentaries for television.

In the Dialogue, Capra discusses some of the directions his life has taken, recalls the heady early days, and, most important, sheds some light on what makes his films so entertaining. For one thing, as he demonstrates at the age of eighty-one, he himself has always been entertaining.

QUESTION: *In your early days in the movies, you were a gag writer. How did you work?*

FRANK CAPRA: It was more talking than writing, even in silent films. There was paper around, but nobody ever used it. Mack Sennett was the great school. He'd put you to work in twos. One writer could talk to the other, try something out on the other, find out what's a good idea. If you got together on something, he'd call you in. "Now, what you got?" You'd tell him what you had. If he laughed, great, the audience would laugh. But he himself was not funny at all. If he tried to tell a joke, he'd screw it up and give you the last line first. But, boy, when he laughed, the audience was going to laugh. It was a real litmus test.

If he liked something, he'd say, "Go tell it to the director." Then the two of you would go to the director, tell it to him, and you hoped *he* would like it. The directors in those days were miraculous. You just gave them a hint, and they'd take it from there. You would say, "A cat drinks some beer." That's all. They'd have five minutes of scenes out of that. That's the way things were done. But never a written word. Sennett would not allow a book to come into the studio. He'd say, "No gags in books. No gags in books." He was afraid of intellectuals. He wanted you to be down to his level, where you made him laugh and he made you laugh, but with funny stuff that wasn't witty or wordy, but clownish, visual.

QUESTION: *When you worked with Harry Langdon in* Tramp, Tramp, Tramp *and* The Strong Man, *what effects were you after?*

CAPRA: Well, first of all, we invented a character for Langdon. It was an elfin character, a child-man. He had to think like a child-man. Chaplin depended upon wit to get himself out of trouble, and Harold Lloyd on speed, and Keaton on pure stoicism. But Langdon's character had the mind of a child, a very slow child at that. You could just see the wheels were going very slowly. He could do a beautiful triple take. He'd see something, a lion or a beautiful dame or whatever. He'd look at it and then come back and look at it again and come back again and then suddenly see it on his triple take.

So the character we had must not be smart. He must not outsmart anybody. Only God was on his side. If a brick was going to fall on him, why, he'd just pick up something at the right time, and the brick would miss him. But he had nothing to do with it. God was his ally and took him through life because he was so innocent. He represented innocence. Wit, speed, stoicism, innocence—one word each for those four great comedians.

QUESTION: *God is on the side of many of your characters—some critics think too much so. What's your view?*
CAPRA: In *It's a Wonderful Life,* I showed a little angel who hadn't won his wings because he was such a lousy angel. But the characters themselves had an idealism within them that eventually won out. They reached for something they had inside, and they came up with a handful of courage and wit, and they beat their adversaries with it. Not with prayer. The only prayer you'll find is when Jimmy Stewart goes into that saloon and he says, "Show me the way, God. I'm at the end of my rope." He just barely says it when he gets punched in the nose. Then he says, "That's what I get for praying." I'm wise enough to know that you can't make a religious tract or a political tract out of a film. People go into a theater to be entertained, titillated, inspired. But they don't go in to hear a tract.

You've got to dramatize whatever idea you have. You have to dramatize it with people, not through sermons. Audiences will not buy it. But they will buy a human being who's trying to do the right thing for his fellow man, and they'll cheer like hell for him if he's got odds to win out. They will buy that. They'll cheer for the good guy, for the guy who's got compassion, forgiveness in his heart, for that good samaritan. Those kinds of people counteract all the meanness there is in the world. They're idealists. They will go down fighting for a lost cause, and you cheer for them. That's the closest I can get to heaven.

QUESTION: *The Harry Langdon films launched your directing career. What followed?*

CAPRA: I became a director at Columbia, then a small studio in Gower Gulch on Poverty Row. I made pictures for $20,000 each, one every six weeks—two weeks to prepare it, two weeks to shoot it, and two weeks to finish it. Films then were not as well developed as they are today in style or technique, so practically every time you made a picture you learned something new. I was my own student and my own teacher because I was a complete stranger to this business. All I had was cockiness, and, let me tell you, that gets you a long way. You've got to believe in yourself, and you've got to make the other fellow believe that you believe in yourself.

This, of course, was the schooling I picked up from Harry Cohn at Columbia. He was a terrific man to work for, because he challenged you every day. But you couldn't let him win an argument, because if he won an argument, he'd fire you. He didn't want people he could win arguments with. He wanted people who were so confident that he could trust them to spend his money. He didn't want people around who asked him what he wanted. He knew he didn't know anything about directing. He said, "I know by the seat of my pants. If my ass squirms, the picture stinks. If it doesn't, it's great." Which produced that wonderful crack from Herman Mankiewicz, "Harry, what makes you think the whole world is wired to your ass?"

QUESTION: *What was your own view of filmmaking?*

CAPRA: I thought the camera was something that should see life as it was, and I thought the microphone was something that should hear life as it was. That didn't mean you couldn't invent here and there. But I thought what you should see were people as they would be under the circumstances. Beyond that, I didn't go in for fancy shooting. I stylized only one film, *The Bitter Tea of General Yen.* You should see it. It's different from anything else I ever made. It's a good film, some fine acting, but there's a kind of sheen over the whole thing. Camera tricks. We used silk stockings over the lens at different places to give a different effect. Where we wanted to see something clearly, we just put a hole in the stockings with a cigarette. We did all kinds of little things like that.

But that's the only film in which I ever tried to become arty, because I was trying to win an Academy Award. I had complained once to Harry Cohn that I was making better pictures than the other guys were making. Why shouldn't I win? He said, "They'll never vote for that comedy crap you make. They only vote for that arty crap." So I thought maybe I'd have to try one of these arty things. *The Bitter Tea of General Yen* is a love story between a Chinese warlord and an American missionary. Beautiful show.

QUESTION: *You mentioned what audiences will buy. How have you found out what they will buy?*
CAPRA: By previews. I show the film. That's the only way you'll ever know. There's no way you can predict what the picture's going to be, even when you put the last little bit of paint on it, until a thousand people see it.

QUESTION: *Did you try films out on your crew or your friends?*
CAPRA: No, no, no. They don't pay. A paying audience in the theater is the only way you get the truth about your film.

QUESTION: *Can you think of a film for which you got the truth the hard way?*
CAPRA: The only terribly catastrophic thing that happened was the Shangri-La picture, *Lost Horizon*. We saw that picture in a room with about fifteen people. Boy, we thought we had the greatest thing. We began thinking in terms of millions, billions. Harry Cohn called his people in New York and said, "Come here, you bastards, I got a big one. I got a seller." But wise he was, because he said to me, "Let's take this out before we shoot our heads off here and show it to an audience." I said, "It's a little long, it needs cutting." It was three hours. He said, "Oh, let's go show it. Let's take it to Santa Barbara, and if we can knock off those snobs up there, we've got it."

Well, we took it to Santa Barbara, and they laughed all the way through the picture. Worst thing that ever happened, unreleasable, a tragedy. One half of the budget for the year was in that picture, two million dollars, and at that time that was a hell of a lot of money. I thought the picture was wonderful, but the audience said no. I didn't know what to do.

I went walking around the mountains and the hills thinking, going through it scene by scene. What could possibly have made him laugh? I went over every inch of that film, and I couldn't find the answer. I finally came back to the studio, and I said, "Let's take it out again, and let's put the main title on the beginning of the third reel. Let's not play the first two reels." That's all we did, and it was an entirely different picture. It was a releasable picture by not showing those first two reels.

QUESTION: *What was in those first two reels?*

CAPRA: I've forgotten. I hated them so much. I got those two reels, both the cut negative and the cut print, and I went out to the incinerator. It was nitrate film, and one at a time I threw them in there. Bang! Whew! Fireworks in Hollywood. Everybody was calling the police department, saying, "What the hell?" I can't tell you what was in those two reels. The audience told me. The audience said, "It's funny. It stinks."

I finally quit sending people to previews in my place, because they never came back with the same story. So I used a tape recorder. I hung a microphone over the balcony and recorded the sound and the audience. Where laughs were too long and the audience laughed over another line, we lengthened that out so we could get another laugh. We'd cut where it seemed to be too long and where the audience started cracking peanuts. We could do all this the next day in the quiet of the cutting room, after listening to the tape. So we'd tailor like a tailor, who tries on something and, if it doesn't fit, rips it apart and sews it up again.

We'd preview a picture with many different audiences, and anybody who has enough ego to say, "I won't do that. They've got to like my picture the way it is or else. The hell with them"—well, he can have it. Many think that way: I don't give a damn about the audience. The trouble is that the audience is the third dimension of a film. The audience is part of a film. If you want to love the theater, you must first fill it.

QUESTION: *When you were at Columbia in the early days and the stars were at the larger studios, how did you get your performers?*

CAPRA: We had to steal stars in some way or another. We had no young stars of our own. How in the hell could I get Gary Cooper to play a part? Ronald Colman? Jimmy Stewart? Spencer Tracy? These people were under contract to different studios, and Columbia had nothing to trade. The big studios could trade a star for a star, but we had nothing. So the usual way to do it was to get the actor crazy about the script and the part. Then he would make so much trouble at his studio to be allowed to go and play it that the studio would let him to keep him quiet.

That was the way we cast our leading parts. Our secondary parts were easier, because we had a big pool of day players. John Ford and I practically had a stock of them together. We'd use the same people: Beulah Bondi, Frank Faylen, Tommy Mitchell, and maybe five or six others. We almost guaranteed these people two pictures a year—one of mine and one of his. I'd do about one picture a year, and whenever possible I'd use a known quantity of acting, people I could count on.

QUESTION: *For* It Happened One Night, *you managed to get Clark Gable, who was a big star at a big studio, MGM. How did you talk him into coming over to Columbia?*

CAPRA: Just by being honest with the man. He fell in love with the picture right off the bat. Really, that's the only picture in which Gable ever played himself. He was that character. He loved doing those scenes. I think that he was actor enough and smart enough to realize that he was having a hell of a lot of fun.

QUESTION: *Did Robert Riskin write the script with Gable in mind?*

CAPRA: He wrote it for Robert Montgomery, and Robert Montgomery turned it down. Then we were ready to abandon the script. Nobody would play it. Comedies do not read very well in script form, especially light comedies. They're too fluffy. We were going to do away with the whole picture when we got a phone call from Louis Mayer at MGM. Mayer said to Harry Cohn: "Herschel, I got a man for you to play that bus megillah that you can't get off the ground." And Harry Cohn said, "Oh, the hell with it. We're calling it off." Louis Mayer said, "Oh, no, I've got the man here who's been a bad boy, and I'd like to punish him." He wanted to punish him for asking for more money by sending him to Siberia, which was Poverty Row, where we were. We wouldn't have made the picture, you see, without Mr. Mayer wanting to send Gable to Siberia.

QUESTION: *Riskin wrote a number of films for you. How did you two work together, say, on* It Happened One Night?

CAPRA: I read *It Happened One Night* in a barbershop in Palm Springs. I said, "This would make a pretty good show." It's got outside—I wanted to be outside with the camera—it's got this new thing called autocamps, which were motels. So I asked the studio to buy it for me. When we got to working on it, Bob Riskin and I went down to Palm Springs, rented a bungalow for three or four weeks, and just worked all day long to get our first draft of the story. It's difficult to tell who would and who would not write it. Generally, I would be a little ahead of him on material; then we'd talk it over, and he'd put it together in words. So we'd have a rough draft. We'd go back, and I'd do the casting and all the rest, and he'd do the polishing up. Now scripts to me have never been a gospel of any kind. If it's good, you should stick with it. But you also have to tell a story visually, and a script is not visual. The visual sometimes just takes over. Don't forget you're making a film, not photographing a script. It's difficult for writers to understand that—unless they become directors.

QUESTION: *Your films have aged well. What do you think keeps them fresh?*
CAPRA: That they're probably as humorous now as they were then is due to the fact that they stay away from the temporal, from the one-liners of the day. You stick with things that are humorous at all times, under all occasions—generally visual humor, not so much word humor, not so much jokes, not so much one-liners. You stay away from funny lines, because a funny line may stick out so much it will date your film a year later. So you use humor more than comedy, if that makes any sense to you. You watch out for a gag that's about a man living today who won't be alive tomorrow. You've got to try to make something that is more or less eternal, that more or less happens to everybody at all times.

QUESTION: *What led to the rapid pacing in some of your work?*
CAPRA: A picture called *American Madness* was the first time I had the idea. I would go to theaters with large audiences, and I felt they were always a little ahead of a film, a little impatient to see what's next. In the projection room, the film would look fine; in the theater, it would look slow. Something was wrong. Maybe a thousand pairs of eyes and ears accept the stimuli from the screen faster, or maybe the large faces on the screen project the stimuli faster. I thought I would speed up a film and see what happened. So I sped up *American Madness*. What might be shot in one minute's time, I'd shoot in forty seconds. It looked sped up when I saw it in a projection room; the dialogue was faster than normal. But when I got the thing on the screen, the audience was afraid to look away. So I had technically acquired another way to interest an audience. They couldn't look away, because something was happening up there. For once I thought I was ahead of the audience. That meant I was holding the audience more with the same material. From that time on my pace increased.

QUESTION: *The actors didn't fight the faster pacing?*
CAPRA: You'd be surprised how smart actors are. When they are interested in doing something new, they take your lead. Actors are wonderful. I once said, "There are no bad actors, only bad directors." It's almost true, it really is. If the stars don't have confidence in a director, then they begin to lose confidence, and you have spotty performances. But if they think you know what you're doing, they're with you. I treat every actor as a star, even though the part is small. Ellen Corby, who plays the grandmother in *The Waltons*, had one line in *It's a Wonderful Life*. Jimmy Stewart is passing out money. "How much?" he says. "Twenty bucks," she says. I went up to her, and I said, "You're asking too much. Ask for $17.50." So when he came to her, she said, "Can I have $17.50?" Jimmy Stewart didn't know she was going to ask that. He looked at her, and automatically he just did the right thing. He kissed her. But Ellen Corby, with just that one line, grabbed you.

QUESTION: *Were rehearsals important to you?*
CAPRA: I didn't rehearse a scene very much. I talked it. Say there were five actors in a scene. I'd put the actors around a table, ask them to read what's in the script, and I'd walk around and listen. I'd hear clunkers. I'd hear lines that didn't fit that particular actor because the lines were written when we didn't know we were going to cast him. No two actors could play the same part the same way. Each actor brings his own clout. The lines have got to fit him. The actor is your tool. It isn't the director to the audience or the camera- man to the audience. It's actors to audience, people to people. People are interested in other people more than they're interested in any other thing. Individuals are important. Those are my key words. The importance of the individual and the freedom of the individual are the two things that kind of make me go, politically and artistically. Those are two things I believe in and two things that are basic philosophies behind my films.

So as I heard the scene, I tried to fit the lines to the actors as best I could. I had a typewriter right there. I rewrote. Then I tried to tell the actors exactly what the scene meant. Where does that scene fit in the story? When the actors know where they are, their lines are easy. I did not want them to learn their lines before they sat down, because then they created their own charac- ters, and their own characters might not be the characters I really wanted. When I shot the scene for the first time, it was the first time they actually rehearsed the scene as a full scene. Seventy-five percent of the scenes I used were that scene. There is a quality about that first scene, a nowness, a jum-bledness. The actors usually listen when somebody's talking, because they don't quite know yet what he's going to say. At the edges it's rough, but it's life.

I would try to photograph the scene as fast and as furiously as possible. I'd use two, three cameras. I would not let the actors leave the set. I'd keep all the makeup and hair people out entirely, because they take up so much time. My principal aim was to shoot as fast as I could, to maintain the quality of that scene from setup to setup until it was over. The speed part of it was just so they would not lose the intensity, the heat, the understanding. I wouldn't let them go out and tell each other jokes. I wouldn't let them phone their agents. Nothing. I kept them right there and got them on film while they were hot.

QUESTION: *You said you've often altered lines to fit the actor. How have the writers reacted?*
CAPRA: I don't give a damn how the writer feels. When I'm making a film I use more than a writer. Actors, photographers, editors, all kinds of people are involved in making a film.

QUESTION: *What did your experience as a screenwriter teach you about the way a scene should go?*
CAPRA: Well, I just had this basic, simplistic idea that a scene should look natural, that a scene should look as if it was happening just now. The dia-logue would have to fit that proposition. You'd leave danglers, you'd leave interruptions. The words were just another way of helping people believe the scene. The trick is to involve the audience.

But you mustn't disinvolve them with mechanical tricks. They must not see the machinery. They must not see the camerawork. They must only see the people.

QUESTION: *The* Why We Fight *series you made for the government helped galvanize America during World War II. How did it develop?*
CAPRA: The job was given to me by the army chief of staff. He selected me because he thought I was an individual who could work in the army mess. If I could make my own way through Hollywood, I could hack it through the army. Here we were, going to put ten million kids in uniform—hot-rodders

they were called then, indifferent, apathetic, undisciplined, as the young always are and always will be in America. But what kind of soldiers would these kids make—with their long zoot suits and their long chains and all that paraphernalia they had?

General George C. Marshall, the chief of staff, said, "The Germans and Japanese are counting very heavily on these kids not even making it. They think they'll run like hell when the first shot is fired. I don't think so. I don't think free people will run when fired at. But can they take homesickness? Can they take discipline? Can they stand doing nothing for months upon months? That takes more discipline than the actual shooting." Then he gave it to me straight: "I've got in mind a series of films that will tell these boys why they are fighting. And if we tell them why and they believe the answers, we may be all right. If they don't believe the answers, we're in for it, we've had it." So that's how the army films got started.

QUESTION: *How did the screenplay for* It's a Wonderful Life *come about?*
CAPRA: It was my first picture after having been in uniform and out of theatrical films for five years. I was scared to death. There had been an enormous turnover in Hollywood. I came back and met people, and they'd say, "Frank who?" But William Wyler, George Stevens, and I put together Liberty Films, and we started to make pictures on an independent basis. I was to make the first film. I didn't know what to select. It certainly wasn't going to be about war. I had had my bellyful of war, and I came out of it a confirmed pacifist.

We were at RKO, and Charles Koerner, the studio head, came in and said, "Have you got your first project?" I said, "No, not yet." "I've got just the story for you." I said, "Don't worry about it, Mr. Koerner, I'll find it." "No," he said, "my wife said there's only one guy, Frank Capra, who can make this film. You've got to read it. We've got three scripts on it—one by Marc Connelly, one by Dalton Trumbo, and one by Clifford Odets." I said, "Well, what about the scripts?" He said, "Oh, they missed the idea." "What idea?" "The idea I got when I bought this Christmas card. I paid $50,000 for it. All you have to do is pay me for the Christmas card, and I'll give you the scripts." I said, "You paid $50,000 for a Christmas card? Boy, I've got to see *that* Christmas card."

And there it was, three small pages, about nine paragraphs, knitted together with holly and stuff, that a man had written to send to his friends.

It was a little Christmas story about a man who thought he was a failure and who was given the opportunity to come back and see the world as it would have been had he not been born. He finds out that *no* man is a failure. Well, my goodness, this thing hit me like a ton of bricks. I finally read the scripts. But they didn't go any place with the theme. I didn't like any of the ways they treated it. So I wrote my *own* script.

QUESTION: It's a Wonderful Life—*and much of your work—centers on the importance of the individual. Did you have a sense of your own freedom as a moviemaker in Hollywood's heyday?*

CAPRA: I was the enemy of the major studios. I believed in one man, one film. I believed that one man should make the film, and I believed the director should be that man. I just couldn't accept art as a committee. I could only accept art as an extension of an individual. One man's ideas should prevail. Well, this was not taken very seriously to begin with, believe me. But Harry Cohn found out it worked. I said to John Ford, "John, come over to Columbia. You can make any film you want. Cohn? Hell, he's a mouse." Leo McCarey, George Stevens—I brought all those people to Columbia, and they made their best films there. Everyone loved it, because it was one man making a film. MGM had wonderful directors, but you didn't know who they were. You never heard their names. But you heard me. I made my own films, and everybody knew it.

I was fortunate all around because I worked in a small place, and I became successful in a small place, and I became much more important in a small place than I would have in a great big place where there were a lot of important people. But I also worked. I worked like hell. I was at that studio twenty-four hours a day. Film just absolutely amazed me. I loved to be at the Moviola. I loved to feel the film. To me it was sensual. Once in a while I'd stop and look at a frame, and it finally hit me that in the molecules of that frame is the whole life story of man, right there in that funny little piece of plastic.

QUESTION: *When did you decide you had something to say that had to be said in film?*

CAPRA: I suppose I should first tell you that I graduated from Caltech as a chemical engineer. I couldn't get a job after I came back from World War I. I backed into films. If someone wanted to pay me for these silly little things I was thinking of, fine. I was saving money very fast, because I had in mind going back to Caltech and getting my doctorate in physics. It was one of the reasons I got what I wanted—because I could be arrogant. This wasn't to be my career. I didn't care. It was only after *It Happened One Night* shook the Oscar tree that I began to think: Wait a minute. Maybe I'm pretty good at this. Maybe this should be my life. Boy, they're opposites, science and art, and I chose films.

But at the time I made that choice I said, "God-damn it, I'm going to make films the way I want to make them. I want to say what's inside me, and I'm going to say it in films, and I'll bet people are going to like it." I decided that every film I made had to say something, besides being entertaining. That was number one, because I knew I had to hold an audience. If you get your audience laughing, then they are vulnerable, they like you, and they listen. Humor is a great force to bring the audience together and to bring them to a place where they listen. If there is any great secret, it is that.

QUESTION: *Why don't you make another film?*
CAPRA: Because I've made them. Well, the real reason is that I had those damn cluster headaches for ten years. They stopped me cold. I ceased having them in 1971. But by that time I was getting a little old and a little tired. You've got to be young to answer questions fast, not caring and not really knowing if the answers are right or wrong. It doesn't make too much difference, because if you just flip a coin to answer the questions, you'll be fifty percent right, and fifty percent right is a hell of an average in show business. When you lose the ability to answer questions fast—and that's what you've got to do when you're a director, answer a million questions with bedlam all around you—well, you've had it in the major leagues. Worst of all, when you wonder if you've made the right decision, you're on the other side of the hill, and you're going down. Going downhill never interested me. Going up the hill did. I was a cocky little bastard—I still am—and for me coming in second is like coming in last. When I felt I couldn't make a picture exactly as I thought I should make it, then I said, "Well, I'll try something else."

QUESTION: *Are there movies you always wanted to make that you never got around to making?*
CAPRA: Oh, God, yes. I always wanted to make *Cyrano de Bergerac*. That guy with the long nose fascinated me. I could never get to the damn thing. I wanted to do the story of Luke, *Dear and Glorious Physician*. There is a story

there that is great. He was a scientist who got mixed up with this religious stuff, and it took a hell of a time to convert him. It was really very dramatic. Also, I always wanted to make a Western. I finally wrote a Western that I thought would make a hell of a story. It was called *Westward the Women,* about the women coming into the West and what their effect was. But I worked at a studio that didn't have any horses. So I sold the story to William Wellman. He made it at MGM. It's been a regret to me that I've never been able to make a Western. A man riding a horse across a prairie is poetry in motion.

QUESTION: *Optimism is in short supply these days. Do you still believe there are Mr. Smiths and Mr. Deeds in the world?*
CAPRA: Certainly they exist today. The Deeds and the Smiths and the Baileys are to be found in all nations and classes and all through the ages. You may find one in every block. They represent an aristocracy. Not an aristocracy based on power or influence, but an aristocracy of the compassionate, the plucky, and the sensitive. Sensitive for others as well as for themselves. They carry on the human tradition, the one permanent victory of our queer race over cruelty and chaos. And their pluck is not swankiness, but the courage to endure, to stand up and say, "No. I won't go along to get along." Thousands and thousands of them die in obscurity. No headlines, no television. I'd say that we need films that remind us that if good does not have the world to itself, then neither does evil, as many filmmakers would have us believe.

History is not made by the high priests of sadism and savagery. History is made by the idealistic rebels, men and women who walk alone and think alone in defiance of the pressures of ignorance, greed, and fads. The need today is for courageous artists with ideals, because they are gifted with the freedom to lobby for all mankind, to become the paladins who with art alone can knock off the dragons of deceit, wherever and whoever they are.

A Lighthouse in a Foggy World

WILLIAM M. DREW/1978

IT WAS A WARM fall afternoon in the Sierras, a perfect setting for a meeting with a man who had always championed the natural over the artificial. It is here that Frank Capra has made his summer home for over forty years. It is here that he once fished with friends like Wallace Beery and the editor of the *New Yorker* magazine, Harold Ross. Greeted at the door of his home by his charming wife, I was conducted by Mr. Capra into a room where he has been working on a book which he was hoping to complete in a few weeks. It was difficult to believe that this vigorous, intellectually dynamic man was eighty-one. Like the High Lama in his classic 1937 film, *Lost Horizon*, he seems to have defied the aging process. Yet, in our conversation, he was able to reflect upon a career that had begun over fifty years ago in the golden age of silent films—a career that reached its apogee during another golden era, the 1930s. During those years, Frank Capra was one of the few men in film history who consistently attained great commercial success while remaining true to his own artistic vision. In the Depression years—years that were shadowed by growing war-clouds—the Sicilian immigrant became the perfect spokesman for the traditions of American democracy and the foe of materialism and tyrannical regimentation. Today, Frank Capra's films enjoy renewed popularity and the great director himself remains, as one of his characters in *Meet John Doe* describes Lincoln and Jefferson, "a lighthouse in a foggy world"—an eloquent spokesman for the freedom and dignity of the individual.

From *American Classic Screen* 3.6 (July–August 1979): 14–16. Reprinted by permission.

QUESTION: *You have often stated that you entered motion pictures almost by accident after graduating from the California Institute of Technology and travelling around the West for three years. Was there anything in your personal experiences or background that led you to make the switch from science to art?*
CAPRA: Hunger was the driving force.

QUESTION: *Did you have an interest in theater or literature at the time you were a student?*
CAPRA: I had no amateur interest in theater. I had a better than average interest in literature, especially poetry. I discovered Shakespeare, which was quite a discovery. I loved Shakespeare, Dickens, Emerson, Browning, Tolstoy, and De Maupassant. The first book I ever read was given to me by a lady when I was delivering newspapers at the age of ten. She asked me, "Have you ever read a book?" "No," I said, because at that time I had only read newspapers. She then asked me, "Would you like to read a book?" She gave me a copy of *The Three Musketeers*. That was the one book I had for some time.

QUESTION: *Do you think your interest in literature in your student years had any influence on your ultimate choice of a film career?*
CAPRA: I'm sure everything you do influences you. It made me very interested in tales, but not in any theatrical sense. My career at that time was science.

QUESTION: *In the 1910s when you were attending Caltech, did the excitement of the early film industry in California make any particular impression on you?*
CAPRA: No, as a matter of fact, people at Caltech were snobbish about films and looked down on them. They were the elite and I shared their views at that time. I hoped to become a professor.

QUESTION: *You have said that from the time you made your first film,* Fulta Fisher's Boarding House, *in 1921 you were fascinated by films. Did you decide then that this would be your career?*
CAPRA: I was still not thinking of films in terms of a career. Being a logical man, a scientist, it seemed a waste of time. I was trying to make money all that time. I still thought it idiotic for a scientist to be making films. I was fascinated with the technical aspects of film, but I didn't then think of them in terms of expressing ideas.

QUESTION: *Who do you feel had the greatest influence on your early directorial career?*
CAPRA: Nobody. I don't think I saw another major director working until after *It Happened One Night.* It was very fortunate that I was working for a small company, Columbia, since it gave me the freedom to be my own teacher and my own student. It was a great plus for me.

QUESTION: *Your films with Harry Langdon,* The Strong Man *and* Long Pants, *have long been acclaimed for their artistic merit. Do you think at this time you were a conscious artist?*
CAPRA: We didn't think in terms of art in those days. We were just trying to make good, entertaining films.

QUESTION: *When do you think the artist in you emerged?*
CAPRA: After *It Happened One Night.* I had to marry one or the other—science or film—and I married the harlot. Then I began to concentrate on using films to express ideas.

QUESTION: *During the twelve years you were associated with Harry Cohn at Columbia, did he ever require you to make a film you didn't want to make or didn't believe in?*
CAPRA: No. My pictures kept making money for him and, having agreed on a budget, I could make any picture I wanted to make. I had great respect for Cohn. I never went over budget. That was my bow to the people who trusted me.

QUESTION: *Of the fifteen features you made at Columbia from 1928 to 1932, which are your favorites?*
CAPRA: *American Madness, Rain or Shine*—that was a very funny film, *Dirigible.*

QUESTION: *Recently I saw* The Younger Generation, *the part-silent, part-sound film you made in 1929, which was based upon the Fannie Hurst play,* It Is to Laugh. *I was very impressed with it. Were you consciously making an idea film?*
CAPRA: Yes, I was. I selected the story of a Jewish man who disavows his family. It was close to home because of my similar immigrant background.

QUESTION: *How did the FBO Company, the ancestor of RKO, become involved in this Columbia production? They're listed in the credits.*
CAPRA: We rented their studio to shoot the sound sequences.

QUESTION: *Like most of your contemporaries, you had many opportunities to experiment and develop your style by directing a number of low budget films, before making the masterpieces of your maturity. Do you feel that the industry today provides beginning directors with those same advantages?*
CAPRA: I think it's easier for a director today to keep his mind on the story. We had to know everything about a film—lighting, lenses—we'd experiment with extreme close-ups. I'd often work from 6:30 in the morning to 8:30 at night, and I'd come home and have dinner in bed. We were pioneers. Today a director comes out of a film school and everything is done for him so he doesn't make mistakes.

QUESTION: *I've heard that many directors in Hollywood sought but were not allowed to edit their own films. It's been said that John Ford shot scenes in such a way that they would have to be edited as he envisioned them.*
CAPRA: Well, John Ford had claustrophobia, and didn't like to spend time in the projection room.

QUESTION: *You've said that you established with Cohn full control over your work. Did you supervise the editing of your films?*
CAPRA: Yes, I did.

QUESTION: *Did you supervise set design, costuming, and music?*
CAPRA: Not so much. I would not butt in where efficiency was already there. I had the best in the business, people like Edith Head, and I wanted them only to understand what the mood of the scene was.

QUESTION: *You are unique among American directors in that all but two of your films (*The Bitter Tea of General Yen *and* Lost Horizon*) are set in twentieth century America. Why did you favor the contemporary American setting?*
CAPRA: I only made films about Americans. I knew Americans. I didn't know foreigners in the sense that I didn't have enough knowledge about how to get comedy out of a foreigner. I worked with material I knew.

QUESTION: *You often contrast the naturalness and warmth of the small town with the affectation and impersonality of the big city.*
CAPRA: This is purely subjective. I saw the very seamy side of the city—the alleys—so I wasn't particularly impressed with the city. I thought people in the country were more honest, and had more love for each other than people in the city.

QUESTION: *Another unique aspect of your work is that more than any other director you seemed to be fascinated by the newspaper world. Why do newspapers so often play a pivotal role in your films?*
CAPRA: When I was growing up, the newspaper men were the interesting men of the time. They were the glamour boys. Newspaper men were highly respected because they had the power to communicate.

QUESTION: *But you did portray D. B. Norton, the powerful newspaper publisher, unfavorably in* Meet John Doe?
CAPRA: Yes, during the Depression there were people who built up paramilitary forces in case there was a revolution so they bought up newspapers as a weapon.

QUESTION: *One recurring theme in your work is the emptiness of materialism.*
CAPRA: You can't buy happiness. I was never after riches. If you have full control over your films, your "self" gets in the films. Films are autobiographical when the director is allowed full control over them. It was this control—one man, one film—that made Columbia.

QUESTION: *Were you allowed that kind of control throughout your career?*
CAPRA: No. At Paramount (1949–1951) I worked for a studio which had control over me.

QUESTION: *Is that why you became relatively inactive in theatrical films in the fifties?*
CAPRA: Yes, I found it difficult to work under those conditions. At Liberty I had made two of my finest films, *It's a Wonderful Life* and *State of the Union.* I think that *State of the Union* was my most perfect film in handling people and ideas.

QUESTION: *I know you worked with a number of writers in your career—Robert Riskin, Sidney Buchman, and Myles Connolly—to mention a few. But no matter who is credited as the author of the script, your major films all seem as though they were written by the same man. How did you make the script reflect your personal point of view?*

CAPRA: I wrote a great many scenes, but I never took credit. After we had our script conferences, it was often difficult to tell who was responsible for specific scenes or dialogue. I would absorb somebody's writing. In telling my story, I would try to involve people with people. The actors were my principal tools.

QUESTION: *Many writers in Hollywood in the '30s and '40s were unhappy with their work and were writing for the money . . .*

CAPRA: They still are.

QUESTION: *How did your writers feel about the cinema?*

CAPRA: I tried to use the best writers. My writers could work only for me. I worked with a writer every day. It was different than someone writing a script away from you.

QUESTION: *Did your writers share your political and social beliefs?*

CAPRA: I worked with rights and lefts, greens and blacks. I was trying to get across the fundamental idea, the importance of the individual, and they shared this belief. I don't believe in writers being polarized. I think that people should be able to do whatever they goddman please, but I have the feeling that people who become polarized are hypocrites. It's all right if my side does it, but it's wrong if your side does it.

QUESTION: *Do you think that great literary figures that were actively involved in social and political causes were polarized?*

CAPRA: Writers like Tolstoy and Hugo were not polarized. They were spokesmen for all humanity in their causes.

QUESTION: *You, like your contemporaries, Griffith, Ford, and Vidor, have been called liberal, even radical, by some critics, and conservative, even reactionary, by others. How do you explain this?*

CAPRA: These critics are polarized. We're not polarized enough for them. I think it's evil if a communist kills someone and evil if a fascist kills someone. I think it's immoral for a government to kill anyone. The importance of the individual is essential. My films dealt with the society versus the individual. I'm against regimentation. Any government which puts people in a herd is not for me, and when you can't speak, write, and think what you want, you're in a herd.

QUESTION: *Would you amplify on your statement in your autobiography that "Scientists broadly hint they should be the new 'Herrenvolk' to regiment the human race into conformity?"*
CAPRA: There are a lot of scientists who think that science has to eventually take over the world. Their science is their religion.

QUESTION: *Attempts to organize society on an allegedly scientific basis have led to genocide.*
CAPRA: Yes, genocide is possible if you believe in survival of the fittest. Compassion, honesty, nobility go by the board. The human spirit cannot be put in a pigeonhole. You can't predict, for example, how an audience will react. Human beings cannot be homogeneous. I think that's the reason for many of the revolts in the world today. People are rebelling against massiveness. There is a showdown every day between a Brave New World of controlled living and controlled thinking and an age of greater freedom for the individual. And I'm betting on the individual.

Capra: The Voice Behind the Name Above the Title

NEIL HURLEY, S.J./1980

FRANK CAPRA WAS BORN in Sicily in 1897 and migrated with his family six years later to the United States. After three weeks in steerage, the Statue of Liberty was sighted. Capra's father carried the boy up on deck and pointed out the towering emblem of freedom with the torch of hope, saying, "There's the greatest light since the Star of Bethlehem." The family then took another three weeks to reach Los Angeles, where they settled in a predominantly immigrant ghetto. Capra educated himself at the California Institute of Technology and served as an army lieutenant in WWI. He travelled the West after his discharge and saw a diversity of resourceful, independent, and high-spirited frontier types. These experiences would later mark the plots and characters of his major films.

Having chanced onto movie making in San Francisco in 1922, he directed the one-reeler *Fulta Fisher's Boarding House*. It was a success and he went on to Hollywood where he worked as prop man, film cutter, and comedy gag writer. After working with Hal Roach and Mack Sennett, Capra began to write material for Harry Langdon. He worked on the comic's first full-length film, *Tramp, Tramp, Tramp* (in which Joan Crawford appeared), and then directed two of Langdon's silent comedy classics: *The Strong Man* (1926) and *Long Pants* (1927).

After directing the unsuccessful *For the Love of Mike* in New York in 1927, Capra returned to Hollywood where he worked for Harry Cohn, who was struggling with a small Poverty Row studio called Columbia Pictures. With

From the *New Orleans Review* (Winter 1981): 64–75. Reprinted by permission.

the advent of sound, Cohn, probably thinking of Capra's scientific back-ground, asked him to think about sound films. After directing six silent films in 1928, Capra experimented with sound effects in *Submarine* and with talk-ing sequences in *The Younger Generation* (1929).

Capra's early sound films were action and adventure romances made on low budgets: *The Donovan Affair* and *Flight,* both made in 1929 and both star-ring Jack Holt; *Ladies of Leisure* in 1930, which made Barbara Stanwyck a star. *Platinum Blonde* in 1931 starred both Loretta Young and Jean Harlow, while *American Madness* featured Walter Huston and Pat O'Brien. This last film, reflecting as it did the economic concerns of an America riven by the Depres-sion, began Capra's career as an auteur-director whose skills and indepen-dence enabled him to make the profound social statements which the world would applaud.

In 1933, Capra directed *The Bitter Tea of General Yen* with Barbara Stanwyck as a Christian missionary attracted to an austere Chinese warlord played by Nils Asther. The suicide at the end touched a theme Capra would repeat in *Mr. Smith Goes to Washington* in 1939, *Meet John Doe* in 1941, and *It's a Wonder-ful Life* in 1947. In these vintage political parables there would always be a self-sacrificing populist hero. Capra also had a box office hit in 1933 with *Lady for a Day,* which he would later remake with Bette Davis in 1961 as *Pocketful of Miracles.*

In his autobiography, *The Name Above the Title* (1974), Capra said that he shook the Oscar tree with *It Happened One Night* (1934), which starred Clau-dette Colbert and Clark Gable. The film won the five major Academy Awards, for Best Picture, Best Actress, Best Actor, Best Writer, and Best Director—a record not matched until *One Flew Over the Cuckoo's Nest* in 1976. *It Happened One Night* set a style for Hollywood's screwball comedies, and was the first "love on the run" film of any note. Capra and writer Risken continued to collaborate on a series of hits: *Mr. Deeds Goes to Town,* made in 1936, featured Gary Cooper and Jean Arthur, had a marvelous supporting cast, and illus-trated the Capra romance with verbal and sight gags, "larger than life" char-acters, and the "pixilated" sisters Margaret McWade and Margaret Seddon. But the film, despite the comic touches, would end with a public admission of guilt by the woman to save the hero from being declared insane. In Capra's best work there is generally such an obligatory scene of public humiliation by which private guilt is atoned for through a shameful confession which then leads to a happy ending.

In 1937, Capra attempted his most ambitious film with *Lost Horizon,* a fantasy of a Tibetan utopian community named Shangri-La. Ronald Colman played the lead in a film which ranks as one of Hollywood's most distinguished. *You Can't Take It with You* in 1938 was another comic tour de force with a forced happy ending quite untypical of Capra's endings where in general evil is neutralized but never extirpated definitively—it can and probably will strike back. From 1942 through 1945, Capra served as a colonel in the army supervising the *Why We Fight* series, a compilation of documentary footage edited to serve the Allied cause in the war against fascism. He earned the Distinguished Service Medal for his work.

In 1946, Capra completed *It's a Wonderful Life* starring James Stewart, Donna Reed, Lionel Barrymore, and an excellent supporting cast. The film remains a favorite of Capra's, as it does for Jimmy Stewart. The film is a supernatural fantasy in which an angel comes to rescue a man who has given up hope and attempts suicide by drowning. As in *Meet John Doe,* the film ends on the note of Christmas. In 1948, Capra—always more successful with stage adaptations than with scripts from novels—adapted another play, *State of the Union.* The film was a Liberty Films Production, the product of an independent firm Capra had set up with directors George Stevens and William Wyler. Shortly afterwards Capra admits that his "nerve to failure" gave out. Headaches, financial concerns, new audience expectations, television, foreign competition, and creeping old age all contributed to his decline, although he remained active. In 1950 and 1951, he directed two light musical comedies: *Riding High* and *Here Comes the Groom,* both with Bing Crosby.

Capra remained popular through revivals, retrospectives, and television reruns, survived some savage attacks by film scholars, and has now become firmly enshrined in the pantheon: his films effectively capture the spirit of the New Deal, and have an intense nostalgic effect even on youngsters. His screen characters shine from within—rarely does the screen radiate with such improvised sincerity. His philosophy was that of Griffith—"one man, one film"—and he brought to moviemaking an independence and an audience perspective in his conviction that the common man is really quite uncommon.

This interview was conducted by Neil Hurley, S.J., in La Quinta, California, in January, 1980.

NOR: *You had a lot of freedom working for a marginal studio, Columbia, in Gower Gulch, referred to in the industry as "Poverty Row." Was that independence important?*

CAPRA: Well, yes, it was. We made pictures very cheaply. *That Certain Thing* cost $20,000. So, we made money, but I wanted to make movies the audience liked and would remember. I was trained at Caltech as a chemical engineer and "backed" into movies. You know, I never meant to stay in the business. That helped my arrogance—made me independent.

NOR: *You mean that you intended to go on in science?*

CAPRA: Yes, I figured that, if they wanted to pay me money for thinking up gags, then that was fine. But the first good job that came along would have finished it for me. I really wanted to go back to Caltech and get a Ph.D. in physics.

NOR: *You worked for Harry Cohn, a legendary tycoon in Hollywood. How did you relate to Cohn?*

CAPRA: Well, he hired me although I had never met him. I was called in one day by an aide of his to talk about a directing job. He asked me how much money I wanted. I told him I wanted to work and that the money didn't matter. I asked him how they chose my name. Did Mr. Cohn want me? The man replied: "He doesn't even know who you are." "Well," I said, "how did I get picked?" Cohn's man answered: "Your name was at the top of the list—Capra, C—and Cohn always picks the top name in any list. What was good enough for God when he picked Abraham is good enough for Harry Cohn." So I got the job. Well, when I met him and told him I wanted the right to write, direct, and edit my own picture, he was a little surprised that I dictated all the terms. He said: "Well, what rights do I have?" I told him: "You have only one right. The big one. You can fire me, but that's the only right you have." Surprisingly, he gave me everything I wanted—cast, money, and every support. So we got along fine and I made money for him.

NOR: *That was in accord with your philosophy: "One man, one film"?*

CAPRA: Absolutely. There has to be one person, one artist, who brings it all together. You can't make a good film, either commercially or artistically, through a committee. They say a camel is a horse which was made by a committee.

N O R : *Frank, I know that* Lady for a Day *in 1933 was your first big success, but tell us about* The Bitter Tea of General Yen, *made in 1934, and years ahead of its time.*

C A P R A : Yes, *The Bitter Tea of General Yen.* That film was banned throughout the British Empire because of the theme of miscegenation. You see, Nils Asther played a Chinese warlord who falls in love with a Christian missionary, played by Barbara Stanwyck. It's a clash of cultures, of East and West. The plot was controversial for Hollywood, but for a long while I wanted a nomination for an Oscar by the Motion Picture Academy. Cohn didn't care. He said that they only give Oscars for that artistic crap. Well, I wanted at least a nomination, so I looked for some "artistic crap." I read a book and decided to do it. It was *Bitter Tea.* We shot it with a woman's silk stocking over the camera lens and gave the film a style, a certain silky texture. We burnt holes in the stocking with a cigarette if we wanted a brighter focus on something, or someone to appear more clearly. The film didn't cost much, but it had a class look. Well, it's strange but Radio City Music Hall wanted to book it as the first film to open the Music Hall, the world's largest and most beautiful theater. The Rockefellers built the Music Hall and I was surprised when their board director, a businessman, Mr. Van Schmus, called me to say that, of all the films they could pick from, they wanted *The Bitter Tea of General Yen.* Now, remember, the British Empire had banned this film which the Rockefellers wanted—you know, the people considered so . . . well . . .

N O R : *Elitist and exclusive?*

C A P R A : Yes, you know, "bedrock rightists." Well, *Bitter Tea* was so popular at the Music Hall that it was held over for a second week. Mr. Van Schmus later came to me and said that I was so lucky for them that he guaranteed to run any picture of mine at the Music Hall sight unseen. And he did. All my films premiered at Radio City—a tremendous boost to Columbia Studios.

N O R : *Frank, you speak in your autobiography,* The Name Above the Title, *about* It Happened One Night. *I understand that it was a punishment assignment for Clark Gable, that Cohn insisted the film be made since Louis Mayer wanted to "spank" him for being naughty.*

CAPRA: Yes, I went to Cohn when we had troubles with the film. I felt we should drop it, but Cohn said that Mayer would be mad at him if Gable weren't punished. Well, we had to make the film so that Mayer could send an actor to Siberia.

NOR: *That made Gable's career, didn't it? He was "spanked" into an Oscar, so to speak.*

CAPRA: Well, Mayer sent us over a good actor and we sent him back a star. MGM had to triple Gable's salary after that.

NOR: *In your book, you say that with* It Happened One Night *you shook the Oscar tree. Did such sudden success create problems?*

CAPRA: Yes, it did. You see, I always felt I could "walk away" from movie-making and go back to science. Leave the harlot—that's how many people and I viewed Hollywood. With *It Happened One Night,* I was not able to think that anymore. I was under contract with Columbia to do two pictures a year. What could I do now? The world was waiting for me to top *It Happened One Night.* I got sick. I mean, I wished myself "SICK" as an escape. After all, I knew people died young. That might be a way out. Sounds crazy, but it's true.

NOR: *Is that when you had that mysterious encounter with the "small faceless man" who influenced your career by that brief visit you describe in your book?*

CAPRA: Yes, I was down, very down. A friend with religious connections came to see me. I told him bluntly I didn't want to hear any of that "religious crap." He merely asked that I see a friend of his—so I obliged.

NOR: *In the book you say your friend put the radio on in the next room and Hitler's voice came booming out. Meanwhile, the "small faceless man" berated you for wasting a talent which reached tens of millions in a dark theater for two hours or so, while that Nazi Führer only reached a couple of million at most for fifteen minutes.*

CAPRA: Yes, I was shattered. I never saw the man again, but he jolted me. Also, at the time, I went to talk with a priest. When he heard that I was in the doldrums and couldn't move forward in my career, he told me to stop feeling sorry for myself and to get my ass back to Hollywood and start making pictures.

NOR: *Then you made* Mr. Deeds Goes to Town. *Working with Gary Cooper in such a film—does your conception of a prepared script change when such a photogenic person walks on the set?*
CAPRA: You can't imagine how much. The chemistry of a good actor changes everything. The script takes on life, it becomes three-dimensional when those actors walk across the set. It's magic—there's nothing like it. And, you know, it's different with each actor.

NOR: *Who's the most electrifying actor you ever watched?*
CAPRA: James Cagney. The technicians and crew made every effort to watch him perform. He radiated a special quality which no one else had before or since.

NOR: *Did you ever try to obtain his services from Warner Bros.?*
CAPRA: Yes, several times, but I couldn't.

NOR: *It wasn't easy, then, to borrow stars from the major studios.*
CAPRA: No, it wasn't, but I had a way of doing it. Irving Thalberg at MGM loved movies and he particularly liked what I did. So, I had a habit of going down to his office without an appointment and sitting there. I'd read magazines. Visitors would go in and out of Thalberg's office. He'd lead them out and see me sitting there. Finally, he'd ask me what I was doing there. I'd say that I just needed a few minutes to talk to him about something urgent. After he led me into the office and sat me down, I'd tell him I had this great part for, say, Wally Beery. Could he lend him to me? Thalberg would say that it was impossible but that Warner's had someone who was just as good. I'd answer that they would never give him to me. With that, he'd call Jack Warner or some key person under him and say: "Listen, Capra has a helluva part for one of your stars. He'll be calling you." It would often work but, with regard to Cagney, I never was that lucky.

NOR: *You discovered Jean Arthur, didn't you?*
CAPRA: Well, not really. She was around for a while and had made films for Columbia. I saw her in some rushes by accident and liked her. I thought

she'd be ideal opposite Cooper in *Mr. Deeds*. But Cohn didn't agree. She was under contract to Columbia but Cohn said she had a face—half angel, half horse. He even called a Paramount executive to have him tell me how disappointed they were with Jean. But she was wonderful—on the screen, that is. On the set, she was nervous, unsure, and at times would vomit after a scene.

NOR: *How did you overcome her insecurity?*
CAPRA: Well, it wasn't easy. I'd change her lines deliberately. Like most actors, she'd memorize the lines and set the character. I wanted spontaneity, so I'd take lines out of the middle of the script. She'd be furious but the results were marvelous. You know, she saw *Deeds* for the first time with me at Southern Methodist University about two or three years ago. She cried and thought it a lovely picture. Yes, she couldn't even stand to see herself on the screen. That's what a nervous condition can do.

NOR: *Frank, you had a reputation for having a relaxed set. Actors enjoyed making films with you. What is your philosophy of directing?*
CAPRA: Well, I came into pictures as an audience. I had no training as a student or a technician or a theater person. I had the viewpoint of the audience. Movies are essentially "people to people" communication. It's the actors who communicate so I felt we had to make it possible for them to be as real, as believable as possible. Movies are different from live theater. When you look through the proscenium arch you want to suspend disbelief. Your attitude is "tell me a story." But in movies, the audience wants to see reality and people who represent ones they might meet.

NOR: *In theater, the live audience reflects back the energy of the stage actors and, if it works, the experience "takes off." The problem in film seems to be that the energy of the actors is focused on the camera lens, but not on a real audience. Is that the case?*
CAPRA: Yes, that's true. That's why I tried as a director to create an invisible audience. One of my tricks was the hidden camera.

NOR: *Like the scene in* Mr. Smith Goes to Washington *when a concealed camera shoots Jimmy Stewart getting off a bus.*
CAPRA: Something like that, yes. But we did it in the studio. I'd have the cameras rolling when the players didn't expect us to be shooting a scene.

They would be more natural, less inhibited. For example, in the scene in *It's a Wonderful Life* when Donna Reed and Jimmy Stewart are coming home from the school prom.

N O R :   *They just fell into a pool and have changed clothes. She's in a bathrobe and he's in football togs. Is that the scene?*
C A P R A :   Yes, they're just discovering each other. The moon is out and they're singing "Buffalo Gal, won't you come out tonight?" Well, Donna Reed was never sure when Stewart was acting or not, whether he was just talking to her or whether we were shooting the scene.

N O R :   *That gets close to theater—to an unscripted spontaneous performance—but preserved on celluloid for all time.*
C A P R A :   I guess you could say that. Now, I never wanted to photograph a play as it was on the stage—like, say, *Arsenic and Old Lace,* or *State of the Union.* I remember I wanted to do *Life with Father,* but the playwrights, Howard Lindsay and Russel Crouse, wanted it done exactly as it was produced on the stage. William Dieterle, a good director, got the assignment. I saw Lindsay after the preview and he was disappointed. The film was a flop. The audience won't accept a photo-"play." They want to believe in the characters in a way that's different from the stage where you expect and allow for illusion. Casting is one way. I picked Jimmy Stewart for the role of senator in *Mr. Smith Goes to Washington* rather than Gary Cooper because the political ideals expressed by the senator would not be convincing on the lips of Cooper. He was a down-to-earth man, a man of the people. I needed a college type, an Ivy League college type, to speak those great lines of admiration for Washington, Lincoln, and other national heroes.

N O R :   *Jimmy Stewart graduated from Princeton, I believe.*
C A P R A :   That's right. He was perfect for the part.

N O R :   *Did you ever consider Henry Fonda for the part?*
C A P R A :   Yes, often, but I decided against it because I thought he was a bit studied. He *seems* an actor whereas Stewart and Cooper are less "actorish," more like people we might meet in everyday experience.

N O R :   *What other techniques besides casting did you use for creating "believability," enhancing the sense of real life?*

CAPRA: Well, I always wanted the audience to have identification with the principal actors—especially the man and the woman. So I used "non-story scenes," that is, intimate dialogue and romance to show the couple getting to know each other. It really had nothing to do with furthering the plot or moving the story along but through these scenes the audience would take a greater interest in what was going to happen to the couple.

NOR: *I recall two fine such scenes in* It Happened One Night. *The "walls of Jericho" scene in which Gable puts up a blanket for modesty's sake so that Claudette Colbert would feel secure. They had registered at the auto court motel as man and wife but weren't. The other scene is the romantic moonlit scene outdoors when they leave the bus. Neither scene is essential to plot movement but does convince us of their love so we are really concerned about what happens to them later. You mentioned to me once another non-story scene in* You Can't Take It with You. *Could you recall that please?*

CAPRA: Yes, the scene between two people who lived in different worlds. Jean Arthur belonged to a zany family and worked as a secretary for a financial tycoon played by Edward Arnold. Well, his son—that's Jimmy Stewart—was to be a banker also because he came from seven generations of bankers. Now, he's in love with a girl, Jean Arthur, who is below his social station. That's the plot—how they are to come together—but, if the audience is going to care, I have to let them share a moment of intimacy with them. So, I have Stewart tell about how he wanted to explore with a friend the mystery of how the sun's energy makes the grass green through chlorophyll. At that moment, he's a human being with a dream and not a rich man's son.

NOR: *Your players radiate on the screen. Obviously you lavished special care on them.*

CAPRA: Well, I like people, especially faces. Even in a crowd I always study faces. I think the audience is the same way. They want to see faces. That's the "people-to-people" communication. Now, if the actors memorize their lines and recite them by rote, they set the characters. It becomes "actorish"—less than believable.

NOR: *John Ford did not hire James Barton for* Tobacco Road *because he could not be directed after so many stage performances. Is that the same way you feel about theatrical memorizaion of parts?*

CAPRA: Yes, actors are supposed to commit their lines to memory. I deliberately discouraged it. It's heresy, but I want the human person to emerge out of a believable situation and not to be preset. I used a lot of first "takes" for that reason; about 75 percent of my scenes were first "takes." They weren't polished, they had slight hesitations, they were imperfect. But they had freshness and were believable. And the audience liked those scenes.

NOR: *One of my favorite scenes is from* Meet John Doe—*you remember—the scene in the tavern between Gary Cooper and Jimmy Gleason, who plays Henry Connell, the editor. We've seen him as a hard-boiled newspaper man but in this scene he's in his cups, trying to smoke a bent cigarette, which he can never light. The scene is humorous and yet profoundly moving. Was that a first "take," Frank?*
CAPRA: Well, yes, it was. You see we had to show this man as patriotic, as completely opposed to the manipulation of the John Doe Clubs by Edward Arnold.

NOR: *Yes, Arnold played D. B. Norton, a man bent on using John Doe to start a third party so he could become president. Though Connell worked for Norton, he wanted to warn Doe that he was being used by Norton and Barbara Stanwyck's Ann Mitchell, whom he loved.*
CAPRA: Well, if you're going to have a guy like Gleason's Connell give a patriotic speech, it's more believable if he's been drinking. He's vulnerable—more apt to show his "insides." So, that's why we did the scene that way.

NOR: *You use drinking scenes and drunks a great deal in your films, Frank. I can recall Gable quits his job in* It Happened One Night *under the influence of drink. Then there are crucial scenes in taverns or of drinking in* Mr. Deeds Goes to Town, Mr. Smith Goes to Washington, It's a Wonderful Life, *and* State of the Union. *Is this another way of loosening up the characters?*
CAPRA: Yes, you see you have to prepare the audience for serious swings in mood, for deep emotions. They're tricky parts of a film for they can backfire. Take *It's a Wonderful Life.* Jimmy Stewart has his back to the wall.

NOR: *Wasn't there $8,000 from his family bank mislaid by Thomas Mitchell, a drunk?*
CAPRA: Yes, that was the straw. He felt defeated. After the angry scene with the family, [Stewart] goes to a bar and orders a drink.

NOR: *He's a lonely drinker, though he's surrounded by happy people.*
CAPRA: That's right. Well, he says a prayer: "Oh God, I'm at the end of my rope. Show me the way!" It's a short prayer but we believe it. He's desperate and has nowhere to turn. If we showed him on his knees in church or in a private corner, the audience wouldn't take to it. But in a bar, right after gulping down a shot of whiskey, we are inclined to believe it. Then, a man recognizes him as the one who told his schoolteacher wife "off" on the phone—and socks him. That's what he gets for praying. That's natural. Someone expects immediate help and look what happens. A man is "blue" so he drinks—but it opens him up. You see inside the man. That deepens the story and helps the interest.

NOR: *You also use music to loosen up your characters and to bridge plot scenes.*
CAPRA: Yes. Well, I love music and so do audiences. My music is not philharmonic, not heavy. It's music "by the people, for the people, and of the people." The little people make the music—they play, they sing, they dance. The songs are not difficult—parade music or popular standards.

NOR: *Have you ever thought of doing a musical?*
CAPRA: Well, Irving Berlin wanted to do one with me but I refused. It's not my thing. I did give him an idea, though. A group of people come together each year for vacation and holidays and sing songs they like. Berlin met me in London some years after and said: "Hey, let's do that picture we talked about." I said I couldn't. (I was in the army.) He said it was a great story and he would write a song for every holiday. I told him he could use the idea if he liked. That was the film with "White Christmas" and other hits.

NOR: *What about humor? What role does that play in your work?*
CAPRA: Well, humor is perhaps the most disarming element anyone can use to create both "believability" and a receptive mood for your message. Drinking for fun is humorous. Musical scenes of people enjoying themselves can lead to humor. But whenever you have humor, you have the audience on your side. They will follow you.

NOR: *In other words, you create goodwill. You dispose them to accept the serious moments. In* Lost Horizon, *for example, you have two excellent supporting actors, Edward Everett Horton and Thomas Mitchell, give comic relief to, undoubtedly,*

*your most solemn film. We smile when we see them in the opening scene for we feel
at home with them.*
CAPRA: Yes, that's so—but then they are realists, slightly skeptical of any
idea of Shangri-La. If they accept the utopia in the Himalayas, then the audience will. What I tried to do with *Lost Horizon* was make the early scenes so
believable that the discovery of Shangri-La would not seem unreal, that the
mood of realism would carry the audience over into the fantasy. You know,
fantasy is so hard to do on film.

NOR: *Because movies are intrinsically a "reality-oriented medium," I suppose.
But there are strains of humor in* Lost Horizon *and especially in your political
films. I notice at the end of* Meet John Doe, *where the scenes have been rather
heavy, you show a black janitor smoking while he's cleaning the tile floor of the
building from which Gary Cooper's Doe is going to jump on Christmas Eve. When
he hears footsteps, he puts the cigar under his porter's cap.*
CAPRA: That breaks the tension and prepares the audience for the drama
which will follow on the tower.

NOR: *Just as the drunken porter scene provides comic relief in Shakespeare's* Mac-
beth. *There's another important scene in* Meet John Doe—*Walter Brennan's
explanation to Warren Hymer and Irving Bacon, two fine comics, of what he means
by a "healot," that is, people who run after other people with money. It's very
humorous and yet contains a point of view. It's instructive. Did you write that?*
CAPRA: Yes, I did. It was comic but it had a social point worth making.

NOR: *Walter Brennan's The Colonel uses a pun—"healot" and "lots of
heels"—to bring out the change that comes over people when they rise too fast.*
CAPRA: Yes, there are "healots"—people become "healots" without even
knowing it.

NOR: *To go over to something more serious—suicide. This theme recurs in your
films. If not suicide, at least attempted suicide. It's in* The Miracle Woman, The
Bitter Tea of General Yen, Mr. Smith Goes to Washington, Meet John Doe,
and It's a Wonderful Life. *I have the suspicion this is personal with you, that you
were pushed to the edge of hope and even near-despair.*
CAPRA: Well, I was a college graduate—the only one in my family who
really wanted an education. After my year in the army in World War I, I

couldn't get a job. I sold apples on the street. I saw people without arms or legs selling apples. I didn't belong there doing that. I was well and able. At home my brothers teased me because I couldn't find work. They tossed money to me and said: "Go out and get a pack of cigarettes." One day my mother called me aside and said: "Frank, you must go. I can't stand to see what your brothers are doing to you." She gave me ten dollars, some bread and cheese, and I left. She was a woman who believed you had to draw your end of the plow or else you were better dead. She never called a doctor. She believed you either could make it or weren't fit to live.

NOR: *So you knew what it was to touch bottom, to feel like a failure, to be rejected by those close to you?*
CAPRA: Well, I never resented it. I understood it, but it hurt at the time.

NOR: *In two of your best films,* Meet John Doe *and* It's a Wonderful Life, *the heroes contemplate suicide but don't. Is this a false "happy ending"—a concession to Hollywood formula as critics such as Parker Tyler believe?*
CAPRA: I can see why people think that but I trust the audience. They don't want to see Gary Cooper or Jimmy Stewart die. In each film both men suffer. John Doe is pilloried with fruit as he stands in the downpour in the stadium; he's broken. Stewart's George Bailey sees no meaning in life when, through no fault of his, he loses the $8,000. The audience knows they've suffered and are willing to die.

NOR: *In a sense we have a Biblical parable—a Gethsemane, then a resurrection of sorts.*
CAPRA: The suffering is there as in life. We experience ups and downs—that's life.

NOR: *Christmas is crucial in both films also.*
CAPRA: Yes, Christmas makes people vulnerable, brings out deep feelings. No one is neutral. People either feel more joyous or sadder. It's a time when some people feel lonelier, more abandoned. There are many suicides that time of year.

NOR: *A Christmas setting in* Meet John Doe *and* It's a Wonderful Life *heightens the suicide mood for John Doe and George Bailey.*

CAPRA: Yes, it does, but it also makes the audience expect a "happy ending."

NOR: *So you are trusting the audience, its aspirations, its unconscious needs.*
CAPRA: I would say so. As I said, I brought to films the perspective of the audience.

NOR: *Any last comments, Frank, before we close?*
CAPRA: Yes. I cannot explain my career or my life. I was ambitious growing up in the ghetto. I knew as a child that I would be a front-runner, a success. I always wanted to abolish evil—the injustice and ugliness I saw all around me. Why I came into film, I'll never fully understand. Remember, I was a chemical engineer, then a wandering bum. Why I met Lucille [indicating his wife seated nearby]? Why *It Happened One Night* was ever made? I wanted to drop it. Why so many things?

NOR: *Like the mysterious "little faceless man" who came and went but influenced you greatly.*
CAPRA: Yes, like that too. My life is . . . well, I'm getting a heck of a lot of help from somewhere! You know, no one will believe it, but before every scene I shot, I said a silent prayer. Hard to believe, I suppose.

INDEX

CONVERSATIONS WITH FILMMAKERS SERIES

PETER BRUNETTE, GENERAL EDITOR

The collected interviews with notable modern directors, including

Robert Aldrich • Pedro Almodóvar • Robert Altman • Theo Angelopolous •
Bernardo Bertolucci • Jane Campion • George Cukor • Brian De Palma •
Clint Eastwood • John Ford • Terry Gilliam • Jean-Luc Godard • Peter
Greenaway • Alfred Hitchcock • John Huston • Jim Jarmusch • Elia Kazan •
Stanley Kubrick • Fritz Lang • Spike Lee • Mike Leigh • George Lucas •
Michael Powell • Martin Ritt • Carlos Saura • John Sayles • Martin Scorsese •
Steven Soderbergh • Steven Spielberg • Oliver Stone • Quentin Tarantino •
Lars von Trier • Orson Welles • Billy Wilder • Zhang Yimou